Orality and Translation

In the current context of globalization, relocation of cultures, and rampant technologizing of communication, orality has gained renewed interest across disciplines in the humanities and the social sciences. Orality has shed its once negative image as primitive, non-literate, and exotic, and has grown into a major area of scientific interest and the focus of interdisciplinary research, including translation studies. As an important feature of human speech and communication, orality has featured prominently in studies related to pre-modernist traditions, modernist representations of human history, and postmodernist expressions of artistry such as in music, film, and other audiovisual media. Its wide appeal can be seen in the variety of this volume, in which contributors draw from a range of disciplines with orality as the point of intersection with translation studies. This book is unique in its exploration of orality and translation from an interdisciplinary perspective, and sets the groundwork for collaborative research among scholars across disciplines with an interest in the aesthetics and materiality of orality.

This book was originally published as a special issue of *Translation Studies*.

Paul F. Bandia is Professor of French and Translation Studies at Concordia University, Montreal, Canada, and Associate Fellow at the W.E.B. Du Bois Institute, Hutchins Center for African and African American Research at Harvard University, MA, USA. With interests in translation theory and history, postcolonial studies, and cultural theory, he has published widely in the fields of translation studies and postcolonial literatures and cultures.

Orality and Translation

Edited by
Paul F. Bandia

LONDON AND NEW YORK

First published 2017
by Routledge
2 Park Square, Milton Park, Abingdon, Oxon, OX14 4RN, UK

and by Routledge
711 Third Avenue, New York, NY 10017, USA

Routledge is an imprint of the Taylor & Francis Group, an informa business

© 2017 Taylor & Francis

All rights reserved. No part of this book may be reprinted or reproduced
or utilised in any form or by any electronic, mechanical, or other means,
now known or hereafter invented, including photocopying and recording,
or in any information storage or retrieval system, without permission in
writing from the publishers.

Trademark notice: Product or corporate names may be trademarks or
registered trademarks, and are used only for identification and
explanation without intent to infringe.

British Library Cataloguing in Publication Data
A catalogue record for this book is available from the British Library

ISBN 13: 978-1-138-23288-4

Typeset in Times New Roman
by RefineCatch Limited, Bungay, Suffolk

Publisher's Note
The publisher accepts responsibility for any inconsistencies that may have
arisen during the conversion of this book from journal articles to book chapters,
namely the possible inclusion of journal terminology.

Disclaimer
Every effort has been made to contact copyright holders for their permission to
reprint material in this book. The publishers would be grateful to hear from any
copyright holder who is not here acknowledged and will undertake to rectify
any errors or omissions in future editions of this book.

Contents

Citation Information		vii
Notes on Contributors		ix
	Introduction: Orality and translation *Paul F. Bandia*	1
1.	Speaking as Greeks, speaking over Greeks: Orality and its problems in Roman translation *Siobhán McElduff*	4
2.	Views of orality and the translation of the Bible *Lourens de Vries*	17
3.	Similarity and alterity in translating the orality of the Old Testament in oral cultures *Tshokolo J. Makutoane, Cynthia L. Miller-Naudé and Jacobus A. Naudé*	32
4.	Reviewing directionality in writing and translation: Notes for a history of translation in the Horn of Africa *Elena Di Giovanni and Uoldelul Chelati Dirar*	51
5.	Orality, trauma theory and interlingual translation: A study of repetition in Ahmadou Kourouma's *Allah n'est pas obligé* *Kathryn Batchelor*	67
6.	Translating orality, recreating otherness *Alexandra Assis Rosa*	85
7.	Translating orality in the postcolonial Arabic novel: A study of two cases of translation into English and French *Mustapha Ettobi*	102
Index		117

Citation Information

The chapters in this book were originally published in *Translation Studies*, volume 8, issue 2 (May 2015). When citing this material, please use the original page numbering for each article, as follows:

Introduction
Introduction: Orality and translation
Paul F. Bandia
Translation Studies, volume 8, issue 2 (May 2015), pp. 125–127

Chapter 1
Speaking as Greeks, speaking over Greeks: Orality and its problems in Roman translation
Siobhán McElduff
Translation Studies, volume 8, issue 2 (May 2015), pp. 128–140

Chapter 2
Views of orality and the translation of the Bible
Lourens de Vries
Translation Studies, volume 8, issue 2 (May 2015), pp. 141–155

Chapter 3
Similarity and alterity in translating the orality of the Old Testament in oral cultures
Tshokolo J. Makutoane, Cynthia L. Miller-Naudé and Jacobus A. Naudé
Translation Studies, volume 8, issue 2 (May 2015), pp. 156–174

Chapter 4
Reviewing directionality in writing and translation: Notes for a history of translation in the Horn of Africa
Elena Di Giovanni and Uoldelul Chelati Dirar
Translation Studies, volume 8, issue 2 (May 2015), pp. 175–190

Chapter 5
Orality, trauma theory and interlingual translation: A study of repetition in Ahmadou Kourouma's Allah n'est pas obligé
Kathryn Batchelor
Translation Studies, volume 8, issue 2 (May 2015), pp. 191–208

CITATION INFORMATION

Chapter 6

Translating orality, recreating otherness
Alexandra Assis Rosa
Translation Studies, volume 8, issue 2 (May 2015), pp. 209–225

Chapter 7

Translating orality in the postcolonial Arabic novel: A study of two cases of translation into English and French
Mustapha Ettobi
Translation Studies, volume 8, issue 2 (May 2015), pp. 226–240

For any permission-related enquiries please visit:
http://www.tandfonline.com/page/help/permissions

Notes on Contributors

Alexandra Assis Rosa is Assistant Professor in the Department of English at the University of Lisbon, Portugal, where she is also Associate Dean of the School of Arts and Humanities. Her main areas of research are descriptive translation studies, applied linguistics, and norms in both literary and media translation. She has recently co-edited 'Voice in Retranslation', a special issue of *Target* (27:1, 2015), and is editing 'East and West Encounters: Translation in Time', a special issue of the *Journal of World Languages* (due 2016) and 'Indirect Translation: Theoretical, Terminological and Methodological Issues', a special issue of *Translation Studies* (due 2017).

Paul F. Bandia is Professor of French and Translation Studies at Concordia University, Montreal, Canada, and Associate Fellow at the W.E.B. Du Bois Institute, Hutchins Center for African and African American Research at Harvard University, MA, USA. With interests in translation theory and history, postcolonial studies, and cultural theory, he has published widely in the fields of translation studies and postcolonial literatures and cultures.

Kathryn Batchelor is Associate Professor of Translation and Francophone Studies at the University of Nottingham, UK. Her recent publications include *Decolonizing Translation* (2009), *Translating Thought/Traduire la pensée* (a special issue of *Nottingham French Studies*, 2010, co-edited with Yves Gilonne) and *Intimate Enemies: Translation in Francophone Contexts* (2013, co-edited with Claire Bisdorff). She is a member of the International Association for Translation and Intercultural Studies and Chair of the Advancing Research in Translation & Interpreting Studies Steering Board.

Uoldelul Chelati Dirar is Associate Professor of African History in the Department of Political Science, Communication and International Relations at the University of Macerata, Italy. From 2010 to 2013 he was Director of the Centre for International Relations at the University of Macerata; since 2013 he has been appointed pro-rector for international relations. A historian by training, he has dealt with mainly the colonial history of the Horn of Africa, particularly Eritrea. His research interests focus on the processes of elites formation and the development of nationalism in the Horn of Africa.

Lourens de Vries is Professor of General Linguistics in the Faculty of Humanities and Professor of Bible Translation in the Faculty of Theology at the Vrije Universiteit Amsterdam, The Netherlands. His research interests include the anthropological and descriptive linguistics of New Guinea, linguistic aspects of Bible translation processes, the application of skopos approaches to Bible translation, and the history of Bible translation, especially in Asian contexts.

NOTES ON CONTRIBUTORS

Elena Di Giovanni is Associate Professor of English Translation at the University of Macerata, Italy, where she is also pro-rector for the development of linguistic competences. She has served as visiting lecturer at several universities, including Universitat Autònoma de Barcelona, Spain; Universidad Pablo de Olavide, Seville, Spain; Montclair University, NJ, USA; and, since 2009, Roehampton University, London, UK. Her research interests include translation in postcolonial contexts, audiovisual translation, media accessibility, and translation for children.

Mustapha Ettobi is a translator at the United Nations. He is interested in exploring the various aspects and repercussions of cultural representation in translation, and has focused mainly on the translation of postcolonial Arabic literature into English and French. His previous publications include articles on translators as mediators/creators and the effect of ideology and discourse on translation and the representation of foreign cultures.

Tshokolo J. Makutoane is Senior Lecturer in the Department of Hebrew at the University of the Free State, Bloemfontein, South Africa. He studies orality as a feature of Bible translations into African languages.

Siobhán McElduff is Associate Professor of Latin Language and Literature at the University of British Columbia, Vancouver, Canada. Her work focuses on issues of translation in the ancient Mediterranean, with an emphasis on Roman translation of Greek. Her most recent publication is *Roman Theories of Translation* (2013); she has also translated a selection of Cicero's speeches, *In Defense of the Republic* (2011); and co-edited a collection of essays on translation in the ancient Mediterranean, *Complicating the History of Western Translation* (2011).

Cynthia L. Miller-Naudé is Senior Professor in the Department of Hebrew at the University of the Free State, Bloemfontein, South Africa. She has been a consultant for Bible translators in Africa since 1992. She has published on the translation of biblical proverbs in African languages, religious translation in Africa, ideology and translation strategy in Bible translation, and on alterity, orality and performance in Bible translation.

Jacobus A. Naudé is Senior Professor in the Department of Hebrew at the University of the Free State, Bloemfontein, South Africa. He is a member of the Afrikaans Bible translation project for the South African Bible Society and serves on the advisory board of the Handbook of Translation Studies. He edited *Contemporary Translation Studies and Bible Translations* (2002), *Language Practice: One Profession, Many Applications* (2007), *Socio-constructive Language Practice: Training in the South African Context* (2008), and *Bible Translation and the Indigenous* (2009).

Introduction: Orality and translation

Paul F. Bandia

Department of French, Concordia University, Montreal, Canada

The relationship between orality and translation is intimate and intricate. The very act of speaking, which sets humans apart from other living species, involves the translating of thought into audible words or speech. The survival of such thought is made possible through oral transmission, recording or writing, which are all interfaces that depend on an act of translation across language or various communication media.

Therefore, as an important feature of human speech and communication, orality continues to enjoy a growing interest as a concept underpinning research in many disciplines, including translation studies. Orality has featured prominently in studies related to pre-modernist traditions, modernist representations of the past, and postmodernist expressions of artistry such as audiovisual media. Its conceptualization may vary according to the research objectives or preoccupations of particular disciplines. Anthropologists and historians conceptualize orality as the medium of expression and discourse of non-literate cultures, while colonialists and Christian missionaries explored orality as a means to understanding so-called primitive or heathen societies for purposes of proselytism and civilization. Modernists have shown an anaphoric interest in orality mainly as a sounding board for calibrating the privileges of modernity. In more recent times, postmodernist preoccupations with orality have explored issues related to the representation of otherness, the assertion of marginalized identities through a variety of art forms such as literature, cinema, music, painting and the spoken word. In these various disciplines or approaches, translation or interpretation is indispensable as the conduit for the recording, textualization, representation or appraisal of orality. Thanks to the influential work of scholars such as Albert Lord (*The Singer of Tales*, 1960), Jack Goody (*The Domestication of the Savage Mind*, 1977) and Walter Ong (*Orality and Literacy: The Technologizing of the Word*, 1982), orality has shed its negative image as primitive, unwritten, non-literate and exotic, and grown into a major field of scientific interest and the focus of interdisciplinary research including translation studies.

The increasing presence of research on orality in translation studies seems to follow two main trajectories that can be distinguished in terms of a pragmatic or metaphorical conceptualization of translation. From a pragmatic perspective, orality can be explored through the study of intra- and interlinguistic or intersemiotic translation practice. In this approach the focus is often on the treatment of the materiality of orality. This has opened up interdisciplinary work in various areas such as (post)colonialism, gender and cultural studies, intersemiotic and intercultural communication studies, or film and media studies. From a metaphorical standpoint, translation research on orality often deals with issues related to the representation of otherness or alterity, marginalized identities, minority or subaltern language cultures, etc., in the context of interculturality and transnationalism. The metaphorical conceptualization of translation allows for an investigation of the rapport between orality and translation in a variety of disciplines in the humanities and the social sciences, including the classics, history, theology, anthropology, sociology, archaeology and the fine arts. These research areas and disciplines are fertile ground for exploring the intersection between research on orality and translation studies.

The articles in this special issue are a testimony to the growing significance of orality and the various transdisciplinary research that showcase orality as an important research domain in translation studies. They explore orality from Antiquity to the present day and cover a wide range of practices and traditions. The intersection between orality and translation is explored in ways that highlight the importance of both in human history and in important cultural spheres such as literature, religion and historiography.

Siobhán McElduff's article acquaints us with the oral translation practices of Roman Antiquity and highlights the significance of oral performance in ancient Roman translation. It confronts orality and writing and shows how the art of rhetoric and speech was of prime concern for Roman translation, which was often conceived for public oratory. Lourens de Vries looks at the various conceptualizations of orality and the role they played in the theory and practice of Bible translation. These conceptualizations have evolved from a view of orality shaped by the main ideologies of nineteenth-century Germany to universalist constructions of orality based on a strict separation between oral and written communication in mid-twentieth-century linguistics, anthropology and philology, and ultimately to a definition of orality in late-twentieth-century biblical scholarship and linguistics based on a rejection of universalist constructs and an emphasis on the interconnectedness of the oral–written interface and the local specificity of such an interface. Cynthia Miller-Naudé et al. tackle the issue of translating between oral traditions with a significant distance in temporality and in culture. Using insights from biblical performance criticism, they explore through translation the similarities and differences between the orality of the Old Testament and the orality of Sesotho.

Elena Di Giovanni and Uoldelul Chelati Dirar discuss orality and translation in the Horn of Africa, an area that is rich in oral history, and its role in translation in precolonial, colonial and postcolonial times. The historical importance of this region outweighs its sparse representation in translation studies on Africa. This may account for the lopsided view of directionality in translation on the continent, which is often based on a strict division of horizontal translation practice as pre-colonial and vertical translation as (post)colonial. Focusing on orally transmitted knowledge among others, the authors highlight instances of multidirectional writing and translation processes from a historical perspective. Kathryn Batchelor proposes a new approach to reading orality-inflected literature in postcolonial contexts and illustrates its impact on the theory and practice of translating African literature. Drawing from trauma theory, Batchelor raises the possibility of reading orality in African literature not just as the result of a deliberate mining of African oral tradition, but also as a consequence of the writing and translation of trauma.

Using as a case study a novel on child soldiers, she shows how markers of orality can indeed be construed as markers of trauma. This enhances postcolonial translation criticism by blending the concepts of "translation-of-orality" and "translation-of-trauma", with significant implications for postcolonial translation theory.

Alexandra Assis Rosa takes a more pragmatic approach by viewing orality in terms of the orality-inflected discourse of characters in fiction, such as in speech and dialogue. Orality here becomes an important marker of social class and prestige, and defines sociolectal practices that highlight the inverse proportionality between orality and literacy. In other words, orality is a strong marker of identity and sociocultural value, which must be accounted for in interlingual transfer. The article explores the topic of linguistic variation in the context of the representation of language varieties in fiction and the problems the latter pose for interlingual translation. This article is unique in that it does not deal with orality as the fundament of the tradition or culture of a people, but rather views orality in light of the speech habits of a segment of a linguistic community. The metalinguistic characteristic of such speech as a marker of social class, prestige and level of literacy must be conveyed in translation by paying particular attention to the fictionalized oral aesthetics. This is demonstrated through a case study of the translation of Charles Dickens' *Oliver Twist* into European Portuguese.

Exploring various markers of orality in the North African novel, Mustapha Ettobi shows how these markers are unevenly dealt with in European-language translations. This provides the basis for confronting translation strategies such as assimilation versus non-assimilation, domestication versus foreignization, literal versus non-literal, and fluency versus opacity. Ettobi cautions that these dichotomies are not always clear-cut and the rationale for their use not always predictable. Furthermore, the choice of translation strategies for orality-inflected markers may not be neutral or innocent, but rather ideologically driven. The translation of Arabic literature into European languages has quite often been influenced by orientalist thinking, and this has been evident in the treatment of markers of orality that have variously been suppressed, enhanced, exaggerated or exoticized.

Judging from the variety of perspectives or approaches showcased in the articles in this special issue, the intersection of research on orality and translation is fertile ground for interdisciplinary work in the humanities and social sciences. Hopefully, this volume will set the groundwork for more collaborative endeavours between translation studies and those disciplines with an interest in orality as an important area for scientific research.

Speaking as Greeks, speaking over Greeks: Orality and its problems in Roman translation

Siobhán McElduff

Department of Classical, Near Eastern and Religious Studies, University of British Columbia, Canada

> This article explores the cultural and social background of oral and textual translation in Rome to discuss the profound effects that oral forms of translation, along with oral performance, had on ancient Roman translation. It examines the significance of speaking and writing "proper" Greek among the Roman elite, the anxieties that provoked in Rome, and the reasons why Roman texts elide the help of Greeks in their translations, even though the lack of dictionaries and other aids meant that their help was necessary. It also discusses the role of orality in Cicero's translations and, in particular, in his *On the Best Type of Orator*, and in Pliny the Younger's and Catullus' writings on translation.

Frequently, scholars approach oral translation as if it worked in the same ways that literary or textual translations do, or treat it as a poor cousin to literary translation (Cronin 2002). Here, for all I will talk about literary as well as oral translation practices in Ancient Rome, I do not wish to commit that error. However, as both oral and literary translation are embedded practices which take place in social environments and are affected by the habitus of a translator or interpreter,[1] it is necessary to examine and understand the particular circumstances of oral translation in a cultural system, and the case of Rome is not an exception to this rule. In this article I will use an examination of the cultural and social background of oral and textual translation in Rome to discuss the profound effects that oral forms of translation, along with oral performance, had on Roman translation, and how their impact may explain the forms it took (and, in one famous case, may explain Cicero's abandonment of a translation).

That said, it must be admitted that in dealing with antiquity we face the problem that oral translation was not a well-documented procedure and any picture we have of interpreters and interpreting (to take only one example of oral translation) is necessarily very fragmentary. It is also dominated by elite discourse, which frequently elides the presence of oral translation. Although, for example, we know that a great deal of interpreting must have happened in Roman courts and for the benefit of provincials who had to deal with the Roman administration and army,[2] we have little evidence of how it was practised, any norms it may have adhered to, or its practitioners. There is, as a result, a temptation to dismiss oral translation in Rome as unimportant in the role it played in shaping other translation practices, or to mark it as one of the many topics that, barring any further information being uncovered, we cannot discuss in any great detail.

Orality in Roman culture

However, Ancient Rome was very much a literate culture; it was also a profoundly oral one at the same time.[3] Those who created literary translations were deeply integrated into a cultural system where oral performance, especially in the courts and Senate, was also key to political, economic and literary success. Authors were expected to perform their works to friends and larger audiences as they were writing them and as part of their publication process. Let me stress, however, that I am not arguing that Roman texts were, for example, transmitted in the same manner as oral poetry in archaic Greece was or that Rome was an oral culture. Rather, I am stating that orality was an important component in literary production, even if only in terms of the language and the gestures that an author might make towards his audience[4] (even in the genre of oratory an initial first performance was often followed by the publication of a written text that might sometimes have little to do with the original version).[5] Translation and translating were part of this cultural environment: translating into and out of the right Greek and Greek texts *and* speaking the right sort of Greek were part of proving one belonged to the Roman elite.[6] Conversely, speaking the wrong sort of Greek, not speaking Greek or using it inappropriately marked you as the wrong sort of Roman (see below).

Orality and literary translation in Cicero and other Roman authors

The marks of orality can be found in a number of translations and texts on translation, but here I will focus on the Roman orator Cicero's *On the Best Type of Orator* (44 BCE), a text familiar to translation studies. This, a preface to a planned translation of two opposing Greek speeches of the fourth century BCE, Demosthenes' *On the Crown* and Aeschines' *Against Ctesiphon*, is best known for Cicero's comment "that he translated as an orator, not as an interpreter" (14). Less frequently cited is the final line of the preface, which introduces the translations. In this line Cicero announces to his audience: "but enough of me; now let us hear Aeschines himself (*ipsum*) speaking Latin".[7] It was extremely rare that Cicero said enough of himself: he clearly felt that hearing Cicero and about Cicero was a very good thing, and the more you got of him on a regular basis, the better.[8] However, it is not the unusual nature of this statement for Cicero that interests me, but how it highlights the intersection of the literate and the oral in Roman translation. Cicero's audience is not told to *read* Aeschines, but to *listen* to him *speaking* to them *in person*. The Latin grammar is very emphatic about this: this is Aeschines *ipsum*, himself, that Cicero's listeners will hear. The last word of the preface is *audiamus* – let us hear – a word that unites both the translator and his audience as listeners to the translated Greek orator, rather than marking Cicero out as the person who will be animating the voice of a Latinized Aeschines.

We are used to the invisible translator who elides themselves out of their text or performance; the Romans, however, were not.[9] Speaking *as* a Greek when one was a member of the Roman elite in the Late Republic was an act that carried considerable risks; speaking *over* Greeks, on the other hand, whether one did that through translation or some other means, was acceptable. (There were many Romans who thought the more you spoke over Greeks the better.) To understand why this is the case, I will examine the role of Greek and Greeks in Roman elite culture and translation before moving on to the issue of oral performance and the consequences of all these elements for Roman translation practices.

The Role of Greek and Greeks in Roman elite culture

Over the course of the third century BCE the Roman elite began a process of Hellenization that picked up speed and intensity as the centuries progressed and never vanished as a critical element in Roman aristocratic education (see e.g. MacMullen 1991). Speaking Greek, reading Greek, and knowing Greek literature – especially genres such as oratory and history – became a critical way to express elite status.[10] This did not occur without some pushback and there were attempts to restrict the influence of Greek culture, especially when it came into conflict with traditional modes of training and acculturating elite men. Cato the Elder (234–149 BCE) advised his son that

> I will tell you at the right point what I dug up on those Greeks in Athens, Marcus, my son: it is a good thing to browse their literature, not learn it off by heart. I will win my case that they are a worthless and unteachable people. Consider me a prophet in the following: as soon as that tribe hands over its literature, it will corrupt everything. (Cato, *To his son Marcus*, Fragment 1)

As a mark of his privileging of Latin over Greek, Cato the Elder used an interpreter when he spoke to the Athenian Assembly while a military tribune, supposedly causing the Athenians to admire the brevity of Latin when compared to Greek (Plutarch, *Cato the Elder* 12). The following comment by the imperial historian Valerius Maximus shows that issues about speaking Greek and when it was appropriate for Romans to do so lived on in the reign of Tiberius (14–37 CE):

> Long ago our magistrates acted to maintain the greatness of the Roman people; we can see this in how – along with other examples of how they preserved their dignified status – they guarded with great diligence the tradition of never giving responses (*responsa*)[11] to the Greeks in anything other than Latin. In fact, they even forced the Greeks to speak through interpreters not just in Rome, but even in Greece and Asia [Minor], stripping them of those smooth tongues through which they get their power. This certainly spread an increased sense of the dignity of the sound of Latin through all peoples. These magistrates were learned [i.e. in Greek], but they thought that the toga should not be subject to the *pallium*[12] in any area, and judged it was inappropriate that the importance and commands of empire should be handed over to the sweet nothings of literature.[13]

Although this passage is problematic,[14] we know from elsewhere that the Romans kept controls on the use of Greek in the Senate, including using interpreters to prevent Greeks from speaking directly to the Senate in formal situations.[15]

The Romans used Greek interpreters while representing Rome in an official capacity and avoided speaking the language in particularly fraught situations. The Roman general Scipio Africanus the Elder used an interpreter when speaking to the

Carthaginian general Hannibal before the battle of Zama in 202 BCE (Polybius 15.6, Livy, *From the Founding of Rome* 30.30). Although both were fluent in Greek, and Hannibal understood and spoke Latin (although with a strong accent), the presence of an interpreter marked their identities as generals leading armies of two powerful, non-Hellenistic states. The general Aemilius Paullus, who was also fluent in Greek, had his praetor[16] Gnaeus Octavius interpret for him when speaking to the defeated Greek army after his victory at the battle of Pydna in 168 BCE (Livy 45.29.1–3). Paullus spoke Greek to the Greek king while they were in Paullus' tent, but wasn't willing to speak it to him or the other Greek captives in public, and especially not before his victorious army.

At the same time, speaking and reading Greek was part and parcel of elite life and identity, and Romans embraced the language enthusiastically: the senator Fabius Pictor wrote the first history of Rome in Greek and the praetor Albucius was satirized by the poet Gaius Lucilius (c. 180–102/1 BCE) because he greeted everyone he encountered in Greek (Cicero, *On Moral Ends* 1.3). Lucilius himself mixed a great deal of Greek into his Latin poetry, and the poet Horace commented that "he achieved (*fecit*)[17] much because he mixed Greek with Latin words" (*Satires* 1.10.20). Romans eagerly imported Greek scholars to Rome and flooded to Athens to perfect their Greek and study philosophy and rhetoric.[18] And, despite his railing against the Greeks and their corrupting literature, Cato the Elder kept a Greek tutor in his own household to teach his children, so he was also aware of the need for Romans of his class to know the language and know it well.

When talking about elite ability in Greek we are *not* talking about an ability to throw out a few Greek phrases here and there; the ideal was to be fluent in Greek at a very high level. Cicero's command of Greek was apparently so perfect that it reduced Molon, his teacher of rhetoric in Rhodes, to tears because he was better than the Greeks even in Greek oratory (Plutarch, *Life of Cicero* 4.6–7).[19] Cicero was exceptional, but he represented a standard to which young, elite Romans were meant to aspire. However, even Cicero used interpreters when acting as a governor in Cilicia and his inappropriate speaking of Greek could cause him trouble, as when he was attacked for speaking Greek when he addressed the Syracusan Assembly in Sicily (Cicero, *Against Verres* 2 4.147). He also avoided Greek when speaking to the Roman Senate and people (Wallace-Hadrill 2011, 84), knowing it would send the wrong signals to his audience.

It is clear from the above that the situation in Rome regarding Greek was extremely complicated. While it became a building block of Roman elite identity and Greeks were imported as slaves, teachers and authors (sometimes these were one and the same) and found enthusiastic audiences in Rome,[20] it had to be treated with care. There were rules about when and where it was acceptable to speak it and how to use it in Roman literature – and breaking those rules had political and personal consequences, as in the case of Cicero cited previously. Elite Romans also spoke and read a very particular form of Greek: Attic Greek, the dialect of Attica and Athens, although Greeks of this period spoke *koiné*. Romans also learned a version of Attic that was not in current use, as much of their education involved reading and studying authors from the fifth and fourth centuries BCE, such as Demosthenes, Aeschines, Thucydides and Plato. We might compare learning to speak and read English from eighteenth- or nineteenth-century English: you would most likely be understood by many English speakers, but your speech would be

ORALITY AND TRANSLATION

marked as different to that of native speakers – which was probably the point for elite Romans.[21]

Greeks, their help in translation, and their elision in Roman texts

The situation was further complicated by the nature of ancient texts and the performative nature of Roman literary culture. First, ancient texts. These were not easy to negotiate; not only were they unwieldy because they were in scrolls and the Romans did not have writing desks, but, because words were not separated, letters were all the same height; there were no section headings, indexes, or, usually, tables of contents (see further Small [1997] on the nature of ancient texts and its effects on reading; on their effect on translation, see McElduff [2013, 7–8]). There were, even more importantly, no Greek-Latin dictionaries, with the exception perhaps of some technical ones (Horsfall 1979). This meant that when Romans sat down with a Greek text they usually needed some assistance, and that was particularly true for texts that used dialects other than Attic. In this situation the easiest thing was to turn to a Greek for help with specific language issues and with unfamiliar texts: translation was thus a collaborative process even for those whose Greek was excellent. Middlemen – Greek middlemen – were essential to help Roman readers through unfamiliar texts and dialects, and most translations surely involved some considerable amount of discussion and aid. However, these figures are *always* erased from published discussions of translation, even though we know they were used. In fact, our few mentions of the assistance of Greeks in Roman translation come from informal sources such as Cicero's letters, late asides or the Greeks themselves.

For example, a late, fifth-century CE source (Macrobius, *Saturnalia* 5.17.18) tells us that Virgil used the Greek poet Parthenius as a *grammaticus* to help him with Greek. Besides aiding Virgil with his Greek, Parthenius also produced the *Erotica Pathemata*, a sequence of prose stories in Greek about mythical figures suffering in exotic and improbable ways because of love, a work produced after he was brought to Rome as a slave in the late 70s or early 60s BCE. In his preface to the *Erotica Pathemata* he offered it to the Roman poet and politician Cornelius Gallus as a work that would be of use to both Gallus and himself. Greeks like Parthenius were vital in aiding Romans in their study of Greek and Greek literature, not just in Cicero's age (the Late Republic) but in all periods of Roman history, but, as I said above, are continually erased from our texts. Although we have little remaining from Gallus' poetry, I doubt that even if we had more, we would even find a hint of an acknowledgement of Parthenius' aid. We know from Cicero's letters that he had Greeks draw up epitomes of Greek texts from which he would work, which may help explain the phenomenal rate of his production of Latin versions of Greek philosophical thought,[22] but when he writes about translating he talks about Romans facing down and dominating Greek texts on their own. (A good example of this can be found at *On the Orator* 1.154–55, where the orator Crassus represents his translation from Greek into Latin as a solitary activity pursued to improve his ability in Latin.)

This erasure is not unique to Cicero, but also appears in his contemporary, the lyric poet Catullus. In poem 50, which is most likely a preface to the following poem in the collection (poem 51), a translation of a poem of the Greek poetess Sappho,[23]

Catullus talks of tossing poetry backwards and forwards with another member of the elite, Licinius Calvus:

> Yesterday, Licinius, we were at leisure and played a great deal on my writing tablets, as it suited us to be decadent. We both played, writing dainty little verse, now in one meter, now in another, returning like for like amongst the jokes and wine. I left so fired up by your charm and wit that even food did not aid me (poor me!), nor did sleep cover my eyes, but raging with passion I was tossed all over the bed, yearning to see the light of morning when I could see and talk with you. But when my half-dead body was lying exhausted by its labours on my little couch, I made this poem for you, you sweet thing, so you would understand my suffering from it. Now, you who are my eyes! Do not be too bold and be careful not to reject my prayer – otherwise Nemesis will demand a penalty from you. She is a vicious goddess: be careful not to offend her.

As stated above, the poem he sends to Licinius is, most likely, the following poem, a translation of Sappho 31. In negotiating an author like Sappho, who wrote in the Lesbian dialect, we can assume that some aid (and effort) would have been necessary, but none is mentioned, and all we have represented is Catullus, Calvus and a text. This is a poem that Catullus, half dead from the events of last night, tosses off in a state, we can assume, in which he is not fit for writing other forms of poetry – and, apparently, with no effort or assistance whatsoever.

Something similar occurs in Pliny the Younger's (61–c.113 CE) letter advising translation as a suitable exercise for a Roman senator who has retired to his country villa:

> The most useful activity and one which many people suggest is to translate from Greek into Latin or from Latin into Greek. This form of exercise produces ownership and brilliance in language and by imitating the best writers you gain a similar ability for invention. And also, what has escaped someone who is only reading cannot flee the grasp of someone translating. In this way understanding and judgment is acquired. It doesn't cause any harm, after you have read through something sufficiently to keep its main argument in your mind, to write as if in competition with it, and then compare your efforts with the original and consider carefully where your version is better or worse. There will be great congratulations if you are sometimes better, and great shame if the original is always better. You can sometimes select a very well known passage and try to compete with it. This is bold, but not shameless, since it will be a private struggle. And yet we see that many men have gained much praise for themselves in these sorts of competitions and have overcome those they merely thought to pursue, provided that they did not give up hope. (*Epistles* 7.9.3–5)

As we see from Pliny's final lines, although translation is a nice way to spend time at your villa, his addressee, Fuscus, will have to return to Rome and perform his translations to other members of the Roman elite if he wants to gain glory and recognition of his skill as a translator. The performance of translations is represented as a social and oral activity, even if here the production of the translations is not (though we should assume that Fuscus probably had a Greek slave or two on his staff in his villa to help him out with his work). The creation and presentation of translations was a collaborative experience, and their presentation was part of the fabric of elite social and literary life.

Why the Romans elide Greek help in translation

Where have the Greeks gone? It is not as if the Romans elsewhere elide the collaborative nature of literary production; Pliny writes about inviting others over to help him to edit his work for publication on a number of occasions. Some erasures may have to do with the slave status of many Greeks who aided Romans: slaves were tools and their presence was usually not worthy of note, but that cannot explain all of them. And even as slaves, Greek tutors had a higher status than other slaves: they were trained, sometimes famous before their enslavement (Parthenius, for example, was famous as a poet before he was taken to Rome), and could usually look forward to being freed, sometimes very quickly. Some Romans also kept free Greeks on staff whom they would bring out at dinners to debate with: the Greek satirist Lucian (second century CE) pitied those who had taken positions in the houses of Romans who kept them around as status symbols and to bolster their reputations as members of the intelligentsia even though they knew nothing.[24]

One answer may lie in the performative nature of Roman literary production and anxieties about showing oneself as in control of Greek texts, anxieties which were particularly high in performance (itself a fraught event under any circumstances). Roman literature was intended to be performed; as a first stage of production of many texts, authors recited their material to groups of friends; acting on their advice, vigorous editing took place.[25] Pieces were performed and re-performed as the process continued; final products were also recited, sometimes to large audiences who might be reluctant to come. Poets who were not good at performing poetry tried to find workarounds: Pliny, after discovering that he was not good at reciting his poetry, arranged to have one of his freedmen recite it, but wondered if he should stand behind him and mime out the words, something he indicates was quite common. He abandoned that plan as he was not particularly good at miming, not because it would have been awkward for his audience to watch him mimic the performer (*Epistles* 9.34). Roman literature was not published in our sense, but released (Small 1997, 40).[26]

Cicero, oral translation and its marks on his work

I now return to Cicero and will work my way back to the final line of the *On the Best Type of Orator* via some of his other translations. Cicero's philosophical translations were in the form of dialogues, a replication of orality, as well as a gesture to Plato's dialogues. The interlocutors were always Romans and usually (though not always) Cicero and his friends: he rewrote *On the Republic*, an imitation of Plato's *Republic*, to feature himself and his circle as speakers rather than a previous generation of Romans at the urging of a friend (*Letters to his Brother Quintus* 3.5.1–2). The friend, Sallustius, had argued that it would give the text more authority for Cicero to speak in his own voice, as he was a man of consular rank and worth hearing. Elsewhere, Cicero is careful to assure his audience that even if he is reworking Greek philosophy, he speaks as Cicero, not as a mouthpiece for any Greek philosopher, no matter how famous. We see this in *On the Laws* (53–50 BCE), a Ciceronian dialogue which imitates Plato's *Laws*. There, Cicero's brother Quintus comments that Cicero only seems to wish to imitate Plato stylistically and not literally translate him. Cicero replies:

> I may wish it – who is able or ever will be able to imitate (*imitari*) him stylistically? For it is easy to literally translate (*interpretari*) thoughts; that I could do if I did not wish to be myself. For what effort is there in speaking (*dicere*) the same thoughts translated (*conversa*) in almost the same words? (2.17)

When Cicero was creating these translations, Latin did not have a philosophical vocabulary, and he and other translators had to forge their own, either by repurposing existing vocabulary or creating new Latin words. Translating Plato into Latin in any form that approached the literal would be a very difficult task. However, if anyone had the command over both languages to do that, it was Cicero; that was not what held him back. He did not translate literally because he wanted to be heard in his text, to speak (*dicere*) in his own voice. He even has Quintus answer by insisting that he would prefer Cicero to speak as Cicero, representing the (purported) desires of a Roman reader. To further highlight the issues of orality and speech in this passage, Cicero does not just speak about translating, but uses *interpretari*, the Latin verb that indicates oral translation.[27] The passage suggests that it would be easy for Cicero to act like an *interpres*, an oral translator, but that he will not because that would be a disappointment for the Roman reader. The *interpres* is a complex figure in Cicero's text (see McElduff 2009), but here he is both a straw man that stands in for all the wrong forms of translation *and* represents the many oral interpreters that existed in Rome.

All oral performances in Rome were carefully scrutinized and bad performances were mocked; this was true not just for rhetoric, but for other types of literary production.[28] How you performed and how you spoke marked you as the right or wrong type of Roman male,[29] and even in a written text Cicero needed to acknowledge that he knew what type of performance was expected from him and would deliver it in his own voice, not that of some Greek, even if the Greek was Plato. As Rome's greatest orator, Cicero was keenly aware of the importance of oral performance and speaking in his own voice; after all, his career as a politician and lawyer depended on his ability to manage his performances and to convince others using not just speech but gesture, movement and emotive appeals (such as bursting into tears; see, for example, his breakdown at *In Defense of Milo* 105). As a new man, the first in his family to hold high political office in Rome, the performance of his speeches, whether in the court, the Senate or the Forum, was critical to his career and reputation.

Both Cicero's political[30] and literary reputation were under threat during the period he produced *On the Best Type of Orator*. His oratory was under attack by a group of self-proclaimed Atticist orators (who included the Licinius Calvus mentioned in Catullus' poem above), who labelled Cicero an Asianist, which meant a speaker of what the Atticists saw as a florid, overly rhythmic, and unmanly style of oratory. The insults between Cicero and this group flew thick and fast and involved attacks on opponents' masculinity,[31] as to speak the wrong type of oratory was to be the wrong type of Roman male, especially as the form of language that you used was considered to be embodied in your person and your character. Faced with these attacks, Cicero produced a range of oratorical treatises which were intended to secure his oratorical legacy. *On the Best Type of Orator* was one of these, and aimed to reclaim for Cicero two of the Atticists' most important Greek models: Demosthenes and Aeschines. By providing himself as Demosthenes and Aeschines, or, rather, a Latin Demosthenes and Aeschines called up from the dead and speaking to a Roman audience, he would stop the Atticists from going back to these models and claim them for himself.

In animating Aeschines as he does in the final line of *On the Best Type of Orator*, Cicero was using a rhetorical technique, prosopopoeia, which he had previously used to devastating effect in the *Defence of Caelius* (56 BCE). In this technique, orators spoke to their audiences in another persona or even as an object. In the *Defence of Caelius* Cicero spoke in the persona of Appius Claudius Caecus, a famous ancestor of one of the prosecutors and of the aristocratic woman that Caelius (among other charges) was accused of trying to poison. The particular form of prosopopoeia that Cicero used in *On the Best Type of Orator*, however, is unparalleled in extant Roman oratory in that Cicero animated not the ghosts of Romans, but of Greeks. By translating Aeschines and Demosthenes and animating them for a Roman audience, Cicero was trying to claim them as his rhetorical ancestors and pull them away from the grasp of the Atticists, making Calvus and the Atticists illegitimate figures trying to lay illicit claim to this tradition.

To achieve this, Cicero emphasized that he would speak as Aeschines *himself* (*ipsum*), embodying the ancient Greek orator in his person as the Roman Atticists could not. As stated above, the *ipsum* is not necessary for understanding the meaning in Latin, but is there for emphasis, to stress the fact that this is the *real* Aeschines performing for the Roman reader. However, this was a risky manoeuvre and would only work if Cicero convinced his audience that these translations were so authentic that they were what Aeschines would speak if he spoke Latin. In other words, he must convince them that when he speaks as Aeschines they are hearing the Greek orator and not Cicero. To do this Cicero would have to erase himself from his own translation, making himself an invisible translator. But for an elite Roman translator becoming invisible was not a positive outcome: he should speak in his own voice, no matter whom he was translating. A Roman audience would not be impressed by Cicero subsuming himself into the role of Aeschines, no matter how pleasing or convincing the translation he produced. The problem would be particularly acute if Cicero were to actually perform the speeches, as he would appear to mouth the words of Greeks, a slavish aide to alien orators. In other words, to *speak* as a Greek in translation was not an acceptable proposition for Cicero, or indeed any elite Roman, just as it was not for any elite Roman in daily life, even though he[32] was expected, paradoxically, to be able to speak Greek. In the case of *On the Best Type of Orator* and the mystery of the missing translations that were supposed to follow this preface, I would like to suggest that the unique situation of spoken Greek in Roman elite culture and the rules of speaking and performing Greek explains why Cicero never produced the promised translations. For those translations to work the way he wanted them to, he would have had to

ORALITY AND TRANSLATION

break too many rules of Roman translation and risk erasing his own voice in the translated speeches.

Notes

1. See, for example, the innovative collection edited by Pym, Shlesinger, and Jettmarová (2003).
2. We know most about military interpreters, on which see Peretz (1996) and Kurz (1986). A range of ancient sources discuss different uses of interpreters, though not on a frequent or consistent basis. Some examples: on interpreters in the Senate, see Cicero, *On Divination* 2.131.6; on military and diplomatic interpreters, see Sallust, *Jugurthine War* 109.4; Julius Caesar, *Gallic War* 1.19, 1.46, 1.52; and Josephus, *Jewish War* 5.360–75, 6.96-8; on bad interpreters, see Ovid, *Letters from Pontus* 4.14.39–43. For further discussion (with more references) of the many roles that interpreters might play in Rome, see McElduff (2013, 24–30).
3. I am not talking about the oft-repeated canard that the Romans could or did not read silently, a myth long since put to rest, but rather the complex intersection between the spheres of orality, reading and writing, a subject too large to be more than touched on here. On reading in Rome, see especially Valette-Cagnac (1997); on writing as social performance and texts as embodiment of the author, see Habinek (1998, 103–121); for a wide range of perspectives on ancient literacies, see Johnson and Parker (2009).
4. So, for example, at *Epistles* 1.41–44 the Roman poet Horace refers to his audience and says he is ashamed to present his trifles in the recital hall. A critic then responds by insisting that Horace is keeping his poetry for Jupiter's (Augustus') ear, instead of that of the public. Tacitus discusses the influence of the audience in shaping contemporary oratory (*Dialogue On Oratory* 20); Juvenal talks about the misery of having patrons who would not pay for the cost of hiring a recital hall (*Satires* 7.39–47).
5. On the importance of oral performance in Catullus, see Skinner (1993); on oral elements in Catullus, see Clark (2008); on the language of social performance in Cicero and Catullus, see Krostenko (2001). Regarding reworked oratorical texts: Cicero's *In Defense of Milo* was a vastly revised version of his initial and unsuccessful speech; nearly all of his *Verrines* and *Philippics* were never given orally, circulating only in written form.
6. I should, however, point out that Roman translators also saw translation from Greek as a strategy to raise the status of Latin (see, for example, Cicero *Tusculan Disputations* 2.5–6; Copeland [1991, 11–13]; and McElduff [2013, 101–105]).
7. *Sed de nobis satis. Aliquando enim Aeschinem ipsum Latine dicentem audiamus.*
8. This was a particular problem after his suppression of the Catilinarian conspiracy in 63 BCE. According to Seneca the Younger, it was not that he talked of this feat without reason, but without end (*On the Shortness of Life* 5.1).
9. I speak here of literary translations; translations of official documents into Greek, which were posted in the Greek East, were usually anonymous.
10. Other genres like lyric poetry were more problematic; Cicero said that even if he had two lifetimes, he would not have time to read lyric poetry (Seneca the Younger, *Letters* 49.5); he did not seem to regret this.
11. *Responsa* is the term used for replies by jurists and magistrates, to be distinguished from the *edicta* and the *consulta* of the Senate. The relevant *consulta* were translated into Greek and posted around the Greek East.
12. A Greek cloak: just as Romans were marked by wearing the toga, so Greeks were marked by the *pallium*.
13. On this passage, see Rochette (2011, 550) and Wallace-Hadrill (2011).
14. In particular, Valerius may be projecting backwards anxieties about the roles of Greek and Latin prevalent in the era of Tiberius.
15. See, for example, Suetonius, *Tiberius* 71. This was not an absolute rule, however, and exceptions could be made (Suetonius, *Claudius* 42; Cassius Dio 60.17.4; see further McElduff [2013, 30–32]).

ORALITY AND TRANSLATION

16. Praetors were Roman officials, elected on a yearly basis. The praetorship was the second highest rank in the *cursus honorum*, the course of offices that Roman elites tried to complete by holding the office above this, the consulship. Most interpreters were not of this status; in this situation the importance of the situation and the status of the king required the use of someone of high rank.

17. This verb can be used as a translation verb (see, for example, Terence *Andria* 3; McElduff [2013, 89, 129]), so Horace may be suggesting that Lucilius engaged in translation.

18. As a result, when Brutus fled to Greece after the assassination of Julius Caesar in 44 BCE, one of the places he went to recruit officers for his army was Athens – Horace was recruited to fight for the Republican cause during this visit.

19. These were not tears of joy: Molon was crying because now the Greeks had nothing, as Cicero had stripped them of their pre-eminence in rhetoric. Valerius Maximus tells us that Molon was the first Greek to address the Senate without an interpreter, an honour granted to him because of his status as Cicero's teacher (2.2.3).

20. The poet Archias, defended by Cicero in *Defence of Archias* against charges of illegally claiming Roman citizenship, was one such Greek who came to Rome voluntarily and lived in a number of elite households; he was given Roman citizenship as a reward for his writings (in Greek) praising elite Romans.

21. Valette-Cagnac (2005) is an excellent discussion of precisely what type of Greek the Roman elite may have spoken. Horrocks (2010, 79–122) is a good introduction to the rise of *koiné* and its distribution throughout the Greek East and under the Roman Empire. We are not sure what ancient Greek actually sounded like or the precise sound difference between Attic and *koiné*, so we cannot be sure of just how different an elite Roman's Greek would have sounded to a contemporary Greek.

22. Cicero had a Greek draw one up for Posidonius' *On Duty* while he was getting ready to write his own *On Duties* (*Letters to Atticus* 2.6.1).

23. We do not know if our collection of Catullus' poetry is as Catullus arranged it or if it reflects the arrangement of a later editor or editors. Poem 50 is followed by Catullus' translation of Sappho 31; Catullus precedes another translation (poem 66) with a translation preface (poem 65; it is explicitly a preface to the following translation). Both 50 and 51 are also connected by the situation of the narrator and the language used by Catullus (see further Wray [2001, 98–99]; Clark [2008], 261–263, and McElduff [2013, 129–131] for further discussion on the connections between poems 50 and 51).

24. *On Paid Positions in Great Houses*. Greeks might also be kept as living aides-memoire. Calvisius Sabinus, a Roman with a notoriously bad memory, kept learned slaves because he could not remember any Greek poetry: one knew all of Homer; one all of Hesiod; another the nine canonical Greek lyric poets. He felt that their knowledge was automatically his (Seneca, *Epistles* 27.6–7).

25. For a complication of this model, see Parker (2011), who is more sceptical about the orality of Roman literary life.

26. The historian Tacitus talks of poets having to beg people to turn up to be members of their audience (*Dialogue on Oratory* 9), while Pliny speaks of audience members coming in late, slipping out early, and boldly walking out whenever they got bored (*Epistles* 1.13).

27. Like all Latin terms for translation, it is not exclusively used for that activity and can be used for other forms of interpretation, such as the interpretation of dreams, etc.

28. Even those of emperors. Suetonius talks of the difficulties the Emperor Claudius had when he performed, some of which were due to external issues over which he had no control, as when a bench collapsed under the weight of a fat man in the middle of one of his readings (Suetonius, *Claudius* 41).

29. On this, see especially Gleeson (1995).

30. Faced with the crisis in the Roman Republic brought about by Julius Caesar's total domination of the political scene after his defeat of Pompey the Great and the Senatorial cause in 49 BCE, Cicero turned to producing philosophical works which were intended to ensure that his vision of the ideal state was left as a legacy to future Romans. This occurred at the same time as he produced much of his oratorical theory.

31. Calvus called Cicero's oratory "loose and floppy" (*solutum et enervem*), while Brutus termed it "effeminate and wonky" (*fractum atque elumbem*; Tacitus, *Dialogue on Oratory*

18.5). In response, Cicero called Calvus "bloodless and dried out" (*exsanguem et aridum*) and Brutus "sluggish and disjointed" (*otiosum atque diiunctum*, ibid.).

32. Although many elite Roman women were familiar with and learned in Greek literature and Greek, there was no social expectation that they be so.

References

Clark, Christina A. 2008. "The Poetics of Manhood? Nonverbal Behavior in Catullus 51." *Classical Philology* 103: 257–281.

Copeland, Rita. 1991. *Rhetoric, Hermeneutics, and Translation in the Middle Ages.* Cambridge: Cambridge University Press.

Cronin, Michael. 2002. "The Empire Talks Back: Orality, Heteronomy and the Cultural Turn in Interpreting Studies." In *Translation and Power*, edited by Edwin Gentzler and Maria Tymoczko, 45–62. Amherst: University of Massachusetts Press.

Gleeson, Maud. 1995. *Making Men: Sophists and Self-Presentation in Ancient Rome.* Princeton: Princeton University Press.

Habinek, Thomas. 1998. *The Politics of Latin Literature.* Princeton: Princeton University Press.

Horrocks, Geoffrey C. 2010. *Greek: A History of the Language and Its Speakers.* New York: John Wiley.

Horsfall, Nicholas. 1979. "Doctus Sermones Utriusque Linguae." *Echoes du monde classique* 22: 79–95.

Johnson, William, and Holt Parker, eds. 2009. *Ancient Literacies: The Culture of Reading in Greece and Rome.* Oxford: Oxford University Press.

Krostenko, Brian. 2001. *Cicero, Catullus, and the Language of Social Performance.* Chicago: University of Chicago Press.

Kurz, Ingrid. 1986. "Dolmetschen im alten Rom." *Babel* 32: 215–220.

MacMullen, Ramsey. 1991. "Hellenizing the Romans." *Historia* 40: 419–438.

McElduff, Siobhán. 2009. "Living at the Level of the Word: Cicero and the Interpreter in Ancient Rome." *Translation Studies* 2: 133–146.

McElduff, Siobhán. 2013. *Roman Theories of Translation: Surpassing the Source.* New York: Routledge.

Parker, Holt N. 2011. "Books and Reading Latin Poetry." In *Ancient Literacies: The Culture of Reading in Greece and Rome*, edited by William Johnson and Holt Parker, 186–211. Oxford: Oxford University Press.

Peretz, Daniel. 2006. "The Roman Interpreter and His Diplomatic and Military Roles." *Historia* 55: 451–470.

Pym, Anthony, Miriam Shlesinger, and Zuzana Jettmarová, eds. 2003. *Sociocultural Aspects of Translating and Interpreting.* Amsterdam: John Benjamins.

Rawson, Elizabeth. 1991. "The Interpretation of Cicero's *De legibus*." In *Roman Culture and Society*, 125–148. Oxford: Clarendon Press.

Rochette, Bruno. 2011. "Language Policies in the Roman Republic and Empire." In *Blackwell Companion to the History of the Latin language*, translated and edited by James Clackson, 549–563, New York: Blackwell.

Skinner, Marilyn. 1993. "Catullus in Performance." *Classical Journal* 89: 61–68.

ORALITY AND TRANSLATION

Small, Jocelyn Penny. 1997. *Wax Tablets of the Mind: Cognitive Studies of Memory and Literacy in Classical Antiquity*. London: Routledge.

Valette-Cagnac, Emanuelle. 1997. *La lecture à Rome: Rites et pratiques*. Paris: Belin.

Valette-Cagnac, Emanuelle. 2005. "Plus attique que la langue des Athéniens': le grec imaginaire des Romains." In *Façons de parler grec à Rome*, edited by Florence Dupont and Emmanuelle Valette-Cagnac, 37–80. Paris: Belin.

Wallace-Hadrill, Andrew. 2011. "To Be Roman, Go Greek. Thoughts on Hellenization at Rome." *Bulletin of the Institute of Classical Studies* 42: 79–91.

Wray, David. 2001. *Catullus and the Poetics of Roman Manhood*. Cambridge: Cambridge University Press.

Views of orality and the translation of the Bible

Lourens de Vries

Department of Language, Literature and Communication, Vrije Universiteit, Amsterdam, The Netherlands

> This article presents an overview of constructions of orality that played an important role in the theory and practice of modern Bible translation. Three distinct perspectives can be distinguished. First we have the constructions of orality as articulated by Buber and Rosenzweig in the Interbellum period, a view of orality embedded in ideologies and patterns of thinking of nineteenth-century Germany. The second perspective focuses on universalist and dichotomous constructions of orality, informed by mid-twentieth-century linguistics, anthropology and philology that strictly separated, isolated and contrasted oral and written communication. The third perspective has roots in developments in late twentieth-century biblical scholarship and linguistics. It rejects the universal dichotomies of the preceding period as pseudo-universal and empirically false and emphasizes two things, the interconnectedness of oral and written dimensions and the local nature of oral–written interfaces in different linguistic, cultural and historical conditions.

The purpose of this article is to present an overview of theories and ideologies of orality that play an important role in the theory and practice of modern Bible translation (twentieth and twenty-first century). Translators of the Bible, including those who are not inclined to theoretical reflection on their translation practices, often use the term "oral" to explain what they are doing. They may call the Bible a product of an "oral culture" and discern "oral styles" in biblical texts. They may view some audiences, or even cultures as a whole, as "predominantly oral", or see the Hebrew and Greek texts of the biblical corpus as "oral literature" written down. They may even try to capture the "orality of the Bible" in their translations. The term "oral" has an innocent and technical ring to it. But notions of orality functioned as a vehicle for a wide range of ideologies, theologies and philosophies in the history of Bible translation. This implies that the terms "oral" and "orality" mean different things to different scholars and this led some scholars to avoid the terms altogether (Rodriquez 2014, 6–7). However, as with so many other scholarly terms, this multiplicity of meaning is less problematic once the contexts in which scholars use these terms are taken into consideration. This article aims to give an overview of the perspectives, views and contexts that have informed the usage and meanings of the terms "oral" and "orality" in the history of Bible translation. Many of these views of orality were (and are) surprisingly immune to later insights and evidence from biblical scholarship and linguistics. This explains why Bible translations of the twenty-first century can be shown to reflect constructions of orality of the nineteenth or early twentieth century.

Three main perspectives on orality and Bible translation may be distinguished that can be chronologically ordered. The first perspective is early twentieth century (Neo-)Romantic constructions of orality as articulated by Buber and Rosenzweig (*Gesprochenheit* or "spokenness" of the Bible and its translation). These views of *Gesprochenheit* were embedded in wider nineteenth-century ideologies and patterns of thinking (de Vries 2012, 2014): for example, primacy of diachrony, expressive and nationalistic theories of language centred around *Sprachgeist*, emphasis on roots as translational units and on root meanings.

The second perspective focused on universalist dichotomous constructions of orality (e.g. Ong 1982), informed by mid-twentieth-century linguistics, anthropology and philology. The second perspective strictly separated, isolated and contrasted oral and written communication (de Vries 2003). These dichotomies ascribed a range of linguistic, cognitive and cultural properties to orality and literacy. Orality was associated with a strong tendency towards paratactic, concrete, context-bound, formulaic, repetitive and mnemonic discourse; literacy with a tendency towards complex forms of embedded syntax, abstraction and logic, with non-redundant, non-mnemonic forms of discourse, not tied to the immediate context.

The third, most recent, perspective has roots in developments in late twentieth- and early twenty-first-century biblical scholarship, ancient studies and linguistics. It rejects the universal dichotomies of the preceding period as pseudo-universal and empirically false. And it emphasizes two things: the interconnectedness of oral and written dimensions (oral–written interfaces) and the local nature of oral–written interfaces in different linguistic, cultural and historical conditions (e.g. Carr 2005; de Vries 2012).

Of course, this overview deals with just three major perspectives on orality in the field of Bible translation and does not pretend to cover the whole literature and research on orality and Bible translation.

The first perspective: *Gesprochenheit*

Martin Buber (1878–1965) and Franz Rosenzweig (1886–1929), both born and raised in Jewish families, collaborated on their German translation of the Hebrew Bible, *Die Schrift* (Buber and Rosenzweig 1997).[1] After the death of Rosenzweig in 1929, Buber went on to complete his last version between 1954 and 1962. The idea of the *Gesprochenheit* or "spokenness" of the Hebrew Bible is the central theme of both their theorizing about Bible translation and their translation practices in *Die Schrift*. Buber, born in Austria, studied philosophy between 1897 and 1909, in Leipzig and other places in Germany. It was in those years that he came in contact with the philosophies of nineteenth-century Germany (Schmidt 1995; Askani 1997). Rosenzweig studied philosophy in Freiburg and wrote a dissertation on Hegel in 1908. Buber and Rosenzweig did not only absorb German philosophies of the nineteenth century in their younger years, but they kept interacting with contemporary German philosophy: for example, with Interbellum philosophers, especially Heidegger (Gordon 2003).

Four influences are important to understand Buber and Rosenzweig (de Vries 2014): first, Romantic views of translation; second, generally accepted linguistic ideologies of nineteenth-century Germany; third, the philosophical climate of the German Interbellum period; and fourth, the Jewish heritage of Buber and Rosenzweig.

Van der Louw (2006, 14) discusses links between the German Romantic ideas on language and translation of people like Schleiermacher and Herder on the one hand and those of Buber and Rosenzweig on the other. There are continuities in the notion of translation as deeply and directly felt experience of the individual otherness of the original writer and of the individual otherness of his or her language, its unique *Sprachgeist* [language-spirit]. In line with early nineteenth-century Romantic translators, Buber and Rosenzweig have an expressive and psychological rather than a representational theory of language. At the collective level language is viewed as an horizon of understanding of a *Volk*, inseparable from the world view of its speakers. At the level of the individual writer language is seen as inseparable from the inner world of the writer that it expresses. The term *Sprachgeist* plays a key role in the way Buber and Rosenzweig think about language, culture and translation (Reichert 1996). To capture the *fremdes Sprachgeist* [foreign language-spirit] of Hebrew grammar and the individual otherness of the foreign biblical writers they forced the German language *zu einer fremden Änlichkeit*[2] [towards a foreign likeness], combining neologistic German, invented on the spot (e.g. *königen*, *darnahen* and *Nahung*), with archaic and rare German words. For a more detailed discussion of the relationship between Buber and Rosenzweig and the early nineteenth-century Romantic turn in translation, see de Vries (2014).

The second influence of nineteenth-century Germany on Buber and Rosenzweig are general ideas on language and linguistic ideologies of that period, especially the primacy of diachrony and unity assumptions. Language was approached from a diachronic perspective in nineteenth-century Germany. Comparative linguistics reconstructed *Ur* languages from which modern languages had descended. Lexical semantics was about *Ur* meanings of words as revealed by etymologies and not about synchronic contextual meanings in various contexts of usage. This diachronic take on language dominates the translation theory and practice of Buber and Rosenzweig (de Vries 2014). Rosenzweig talks about the etymological *Tiefsinn der Worte* [the deep meaning of words]. He employs the metaphor of a mineshaft into which we have to descend to find the *Ur* meanings of recurrent Hebrew roots, using German terms as the *Wurzelschicht der Worte* [the shaft of the root of words] (van der Louw 2006, 4). An example of this etymologizing translation practice would be how Buber and Rosenzweig in the Psalms render the Piel forms of חלץ, "to deliver; to rescue", with *entschnüren* and *losschnüren*, "to unlace, to untie (of ropes)", based on a (contested) etymology (Botterweck and Ringgren 1980, 437): for example, in Psalm 6:5 and Psalm 60:7.

Buber and Rosenzweig understood the heritage of Schleiermacher, Hegel and Herder in terms of their own times, the period between the two world wars in Germany. The chaos, horrors and trauma of the lost First World War and its aftermath had shaken many absolute truths and certainties of the nineteenth century. Heidegger captured the spirit of the Interbellum that left little room for absolute truths beyond time and place. Philosophy could no longer find any foundation other than the temporal existence in the historical here-and-now of the individual, the

Dasein, an existential ontology that broke with nineteenth-century absolute meta-physical foundations of philosophy in an anti-idealistic and relativistic climate (Gordon 2003). Van der Louw (2006, 5) and Gordon (2003) describe the links between Buber, Rosenzweig and Heidegger: for example, in the emphasis on the existential function of language, but also a shared focus on roots and etymology. Gordon (2003, 266) discusses the translation decisions of Rosenzweig that he sees as reflections of the philosophical climate of the German Interbellum such as an existential ontology and anti-idealism.

Buber and Rosenzweig stood in Jewish theological traditions, and they combined the heritage of nineteenth-century Germany with theological thoughts about the unity [*Einheit*] of the Hebrew Scriptures, a rabbinic hermeneutic that connected Hebrew roots, words and phrases in very different parts of the Hebrew Bible. The Hebrew Bible was a unity, one Book (*Die Schrift*, Scripture, in the singular). They saw this unity as a result of an *Einheitsbewusstsein*, "awareness of unity" (Buber 1964, 1113), or *bibelstiftende Bewusstsein*, "Bible creating awareness" (ibid. 1186), that worked in Scripture itself before it was canonized (Schravesande, 2009, 262–263). One divine Voice spoke in all the Hebrew Scriptures. The problem was how to connect disillusioned and sceptical modern Germans to this Voice in their concrete individual existence here and now, in their *Dasein*. Buber firmly believed that the ears of modern Germans, Jews or Christians, formed the connection to the Voice: when Scripture was called out and read aloud to them, God would enter the existence, the temporality of individuals, through their ears (van der Louw 2006, 4).

This notion of *Gesprochenheit* or oral-aural spoken *Urwort* dimension of Buber and Rosenzweig must be seen against the background of the nineteenth- and early twentieth-century ideological and philosophical climate sketched in the previous paragraphs. "Buber and Rosenzweig based their approach on the Romantic nineteenth century notion that the Bible was essentially oral literature written down" (Fox 1995, x). The Voice breathes and speaks in this fundamentally oral Hebrew Bible. Buber and Rosenzweig divided the Hebrew text in cola or breath units, units that could be spoken in one *Atemzug* or one breath. These cola were breath units and meaning units at the same time (Buber 1964, 1176–1177). Colometric structuring distinguishes all translations in the tradition of Buber and Rosenzweig; the cola are small units of text and at first sight colometric formatting seems to fragment the translation. But thanks to the *Einheitsbewusstsein* [awareness of unity] that worked in Scripture, intertextual webs of audible linkages were formed between these breath units, by repetition of keywords and of roots, across the whole canon (ibid., 1177). These *Leitworte* [leading words] form audible clues: the listener hears the repetitions, reflects on their links and by doing so starts to experience unity and connections, threads of meaning that bind the cola together throughout the canon, in an audible unity of Scripture, a unity based on the one Voice. The listener is drawn into an inner-Scriptural dialogic encounter of *Leitworte*, spoken to by the Voice in his or her existence, then-and-there (de Vries 2012, 91–92).

The *Leitwort* approach of Buber and Rosenzweig is much more than a literary notion because it combines repetition as a literary device with theological aspects of the unity of Scripture, and of the unity of canon and rabbinic reading traditions. But philosophical themes of the Interbellum also resonate in the *Leitwort* approach (the *Leitworte* speak existentially to the listeners), as well as Romantic themes of direct experience (the *Leitworte* speak directly to the listener who thus experiences the

Voice) and general nineteenth-century etymological views of word meaning. It comes as no surprise then that the *Leitworte* became the cornerstone of the Buber-Rosenzweig tradition in Bible translation, in theory and in translation practices that tried to capture the "orality of the Bible". Consider the translation of the Hebrew consonant root קרב in Leviticus 1:2. Buber and Rosenzweig created new German words (*Nahung* = near-ing; *darnahen* = to near there) to reflect the deep meaning (*Tiefsinn*) of the repeated root קרב "near" and translated: "Ein Mensch, wenn er von euch IHM eine Nahung darnaht"[3] (de Vries, 2014). Recent Bible translations in the tradition of Buber and Rosenzweig reflect these views of the orality of the Bible in their translation practices, to varying degrees. For example, Fox (1995) also translates at root level in this passage of Leviticus 1:2, to make the repetition of the root קרב audible in the English version: "When (one) among you brings near a near-offering for YHWH".

The popular Dutch translation by Oussoren (2004), called the Naarden Bible, pays tribute to Buber's perspective on orality in its preface and applies the *Leitwort* strategy consistently in the translation of both the Hebrew Bible and the Greek New Testament, also at root and stem level. The same is true of the French Bible translation by Chouraqi (1974).

The difference between moderate followers of Buber and Rosenzweig such as Everett Fox in the USA and more hardcore practitioners of these views such as Oussoren in The Netherlands and Chouraqi in France is that moderate followers tend to use the *Leitwort* translation strategy within smaller, literary units of the biblical texts, and then only when there is clear evidence for writer-intended conscious use of root or word repetition. But more hardcore followers emphasize the audible unity of the whole Bible and accordingly apply *Leitwort* strategies across books, at the level of the Bible as a whole, and with a much higher frequency. Colometric division of the text (Buber's *Atemzug* or breath unit) and audible allusions in Hebrew names are found in all post-war Bible translations that practice Buber's perspective on orality. For example, Everett Fox translates the name ya'aqov, "Jacob", in Genesis 25:26 as "Heelholder", to capture the sound similarity in Hebrew between 'aqev, "heel", and the name ya'aqov.

The second perspective: Universalist dichotomies

The first perspective on orality and Bible translation, with *Gesprochenheit* as central notion, had its ideological roots in Europe, especially in nineteenth-century Germany and had most of its impact in the world of Bible translation rather than in other fields of translation.[4] The second perspective on orality has its roots in three academic disciplines (linguistics, anthropology and classical philology) in Europe and America. It lacks the strong connections with theology and philosophy of Buber's construction of orality and for a while the second perspective seemed to express an academic consensus on the nature of orality. The well-written and influential book *Orality and Literacy* by Ong (1982) summarized this consensus just before it would be shattered by new findings in linguistics, biblical scholarship and anthropology. Precisely because of its less obvious connections with theology and ideology and its strong links to academic disciplines such as linguistics, the second perspective had a far wider impact than the first. In fact, many of the present uses of terms such as "oral culture", "oral style" and "oral syntax" in translation studies, cultural studies, biblical scholarship and other fields of the humanities are still informed by the second perspective.

Two elements are central to that mid-twentieth-century consensus on the nature of orality. First, an almost impenetrable barrier was erected between oral communication and written communication, in the words of Carr (2005, 6): "Past studies of the oral and the written have been plagued by a frequent tendency to juxtapose orality and memory with written textuality." Orality and literacy were understood as two separate, contrasting worlds. This dichotomous thinking, the "Great Divide" of orality and literacy, was so strong that counterexamples did not break the paradigm; rather, this led to the recognition of "mixed" forms that were placed on an "oral–written continuum" that maintained the basic opposition between the oral and the written.

The second element was an essentialist and universalist dichotomy that ascribed a universal set of contrastive properties to orality and literacy. Oral syntax was supposed to be simple, mostly paratactic, coordinative and basically juxtaposing chunks of information, without much syntactic integration. Written syntax was highly integrated, with embedding and recursion and complex syntax. Oral discourse was concrete, context-bound, formulaic and repetitive, involving the listener, synthetic rather than analytic. Written discourse was abstract, distanced, analytic, non-redundant, non-formulaic, lacking mnemonic devices needed in oral cultures to memorize oral long-duration texts. Oral cultures were pre-logic whereas writing had introduced logic and abstract reasoning.

Where did all these properties ascribed to orality and literacy of the second perspective come from?[5]

Syntactic attributes came from the linguistic debate about oral and written discourse in English (de Vries 2003, 397). Linguists like Chafe linked oral communication with parataxis, a lack of syntactic integration and reliance on context to infer semantic relations, in contrast with the high degree of explicit syntactic integration in written styles. Chafe and Danielewicz (1987, 103) attributed this difference in the degree of syntactic integration to processing constraints: "In other words, there is a strong tendency for casual speakers to produce simple sequences of coordinated clauses, avoiding the more elaborate interclausal relations found in writing. Elaborate syntax evidently requires more processing effort than speakers ordinarily devote to it". Although Chafe based his argument on informal, casual speech (without claiming to generalize over all oral genres, let alone over languages other than English), parataxis became associated with orality in general (de Vries 2003, 399).

Cognitive attributes ascribed to orality and literacy in the second perspective originated in anthropology (de Vries 2003, 398): for example, cognitive dichotomies of pre-logical versus logical cultures (Lévy-Bruhl 1926), or cultures with thought processes tied to the concrete versus those that can abstract from concrete circumstances (Lévi-Strauss 1966). In the work of Goody (1977) and Olson (1994), such old cognitive dichotomies resurface as cognitive properties of oral and literate societies. Olson (ibid.) emphasizes that written language is "decontextualized" when compared to speech. Speakers expect their listeners to infer information by combining utterance and context. Writers do not share an immediate context of utterance with their readers and accordingly cannot rely on contextual implications to the degree that speakers can. Olson (ibid.) connects this explicitness and autonomy of writing with the emergence of analytical and critical thinking, a cognitive development that was less likely to take place in the contextualized, more implicit communication of primary oral cultures. The second element in Olson's view is the written text as a fixed object which the reader can compare to other texts, interpret, summarize and so on. Such operations on written texts as fixed objects would supposedly stimulate the distinction between text and interpretation, and create a different metalanguage consciousness, leading to grammars, lexicons and, ultimately, to the development of logic (de Vries 2003, 398).

Stylistic and literary attributes of orality and literacy of the second perspective originated in the philological debate on the oral nature and origin of texts from antiquity, as we find in the work of Parry (1928) and Lord (1960) on Homer (de Vries 2003, 399). Parry noticed the frequent use of epithets, formulas, standard themes and other formulaic elements in the metrical epics of Homer and attributed that formulaic nature to the orality of such texts. Performing artists produced their oral texts by drawing from a store of fixed formulas, standard themes and epithets that helped them, together with rhythm, metre and assonance, as mnemonic devices to memorize those traditions and perform them orally from memory.

Ong (1982) brought the notion of additive parataxis from the linguistic debate, the context-bound concreteness from the anthropological debate, and the formulaic, repetitive, mnemonic elements from the philological debate together in an accessible, coherent, but highly dichotomous picture of orality that influenced many Bible translators, especially in missionary and evangelizing contexts. After the Second World War hundreds of missionary Bible translators from Europe and the USA became active in minority languages in remote corners of the world, and they found themselves very often in what they considered to be oral contexts, with oral languages and oral cultures. Their views of orality were shaped by the "Great Divide" of the oral and written dimensions of the second perspective and they interpreted what they saw through that lens. When I was a translation consultant in Indonesian West Papua in the 1980s and 1990s, I met Bible translators who tried to "oralize" their translations, to adjust the translation to what they saw as the oral mode of communication of their audiences (de Vries 2008). In practice, this often meant frequent use of topic markers, the use of extra-clausal thematic phrases that were not syntactically integrated in the following clause, forms of repetition and recapitulation (e.g. tail-head linkages) and very long clause chains, strings of syntactically very simple clauses.

The problem with that strategy was that the "oralized" translations became more difficult to read, and to read aloud to listening audiences (de Vries 2008, 308). Renck (1990, 96–97) gives interesting data from the Yagaria area of Papua New Guinea. The New Testament has been translated into two dialects of Yagaria, in the Move dialect and the Kami-Kuluka dialect. Renck (ibid.) gives Mark 15:21 in both translations. The Kami-Kuluka version uses cohesive markers (and recapitulative tail-head linkage) as in oral Yagaria narrative genres: it has 17 cohesive markers in three sentences which are connected by tail-head linkage. The Move version does not use those devices in this fragment. Renck (ibid.) writes that the Kami-Kuluka version is harder to read than the Move version because of the high frequency of cohesive markers and other "oral" features. Notice that these were efforts in the 1970s and 1980s to adjust written translations to oral environments of interior New Guinea, not to produce audio versions.

When "oralizing" strategies did not really improve the effective communication of the Gospel through these written missionary translations, a logical next step within a dichotomous paradigm was to conclude that written Bible translations could not work in predominantly oral environments, and this explains the impact of so called "storying" approaches in the missionary communication of the Gospel. The content of the Bible is translated into a chronologically ordered series of oral stories that are recorded and played to audiences. Kalkman (2010) described the strong and explicit links between the second perspective, especially as popularized by Ong (1982), and the Chronological Bible Storying approach in missiology and Bible translation as proposed by Brown (2004) and Franklin (2008). A key assumption in these missiological approaches is that communication in oral cultures privileges narratives. Abstract notions in non-narrative types of discourse – for example, many passages in the Letter to the Romans – should be transformed into concrete and non-analytic narratives.

Obviously, these audio versions of Bible stories work better than written translations in getting basic biblical stories across in environments with low levels of literacy. They are relatively effective because they continue a long and effective tradition in the history of Christian missions: missionaries who transformed what they perceived as the central content of the Bible into stories that they told to listening audiences. These missionaries did not consider their oral Bible stories as something that could replace a written translation of the Bible, as a sacred text with authority in the community of the young Church. The same is true of young Churches themselves: audio cassettes or DVDs with Bible stories are not perceived as sacred base texts that speak with authority to their communities.

The third perspective: Local oral–written interfaces

Independent developments in linguistics, anthropology, ancient studies and biblical scholarship towards the end of the last century and in the first decade of this century led to the breakdown of the paradigm of the second perspective. But these developments also stimulated the emergence of new approaches to the relationships between oral and written forms of communication: for example, in biblical or ancient media criticism (Carr 2005; Rodriquez 2014), linguistics (Biber 1988; Besnier 1995), and anthropology (Scribner and Cole 1981; Foley 1997).[6]

Computers and statistical "big data" research changed linguistics and stylistics in the last two decades of the previous century. One of the great breakthroughs was the work of Douglas Biber (1988), who studied 20 properties associated with oral and written language in a digital corpus of texts (both oral and written). He found no absolute differences between written and oral texts. Whether a given text – for example, a shopping list, a sermon or a love song – scored high for a certain property could not be predicted on the basis of whether that discourse was oral or written. Biber's work dealt a blow to the whole idea of a style continuum with "typically oral" and "typically written" extremes. That notion was replaced by genre-determined configurations of stylistic characteristics. This does not make the medium (oral or writing) irrelevant but rather underscores that it is only one feature of a genre. Whether a genre of texts is oral or written is far less important for its stylistic and linguistics properties than the combined impact of other aspects of its genre. A shopping list is a written genre but it has most of the properties ascribed to orality: it is paratactic in syntax, concrete, context-bound. The properties associated with orality and literacy turned out to be not predictably distributed over the oral and written genres represented in the corpus (de Vries 2003, 398). Biber's work on English was replicated and confirmed for non-western languages by Besnier (1995), working with a corpus from the Polynesian language of Nukalaelae. Stylistically, personal letters form one cluster with conversations on Nukalaelae whereas written sermons cluster with political speeches and radio broadcasts. The genre of personal letters is determined by the cultural context of Nukalaelae in which kinship and exchange relations are crucial.

I have earlier discussed data from primary oral languages of interior New Guinea in communities where writing was completely unknown (de Vries 2003). These data did not show the properties that the second perspective would predict: for example, relative lack of syntactic integration or prominence of formulaic-repetitive styles in long-duration texts. There are well-documented oral languages in New Guinea that have subordination as the most frequent, unmarked way of clause combining: for example, Yimas of Papua New Guinea. According to Foley (1991, 497), Yimas is a language that "contrasts with many other Papuan languages in making less extensive use of clause chaining .... The most common type of clause linkage in Yimas involves nominalization, both finite and non-finite."

Empirical studies on primary oral languages – that is, languages spoken by people who did not have literacy practices in any form or any (contact) language – showed rich oral traditions and various genres of oral literature but these long-duration texts did not show verbatim or semi-verbatim performance of these oral texts; rather, non-verbatim memorization and performance, with the important exception of ancestral (spirit) names and ancestral genealogies, were found (de Vries 2012, 94–95). Crucially, the mnemonic "poetic prose" style attributed to orality did not have a special prominence in the oral literatures of primary oral communities (de Vries 2003; van Enk and de Vries 1997) and this makes sense when communities have no written reference point for their long-duration texts, in cultural conditions where the intentions, the content, of the texts is the focus of the tradition and not the wording (de Vries 2012, 83).

The mnemonic formulaic-repetitive style associated in the Lord-Parry tradition with oral literatures turned out to be not typical of primary oral societies but rather were found in societies that have a non-print technology of (re)producing written texts, with scribal traditions and with a hybrid oral–written interface in which semi-verbatim memorization of written long-duration texts is the key feature: for example, in ancient biblical worlds or in the ancient civilizations of Asia (de Vries 2012, 73). In these conditions written texts are designed for easy memorization and oral recitation, and that is why they have the mnemonic "poetic prose" style. The written texts function very much like a score for a musician who performs a piece of classical music: as a written background reference for a piece that primarily exists in the memory of the performer (Carr 2005).

The anthropological debate on universal cognitive dichotomies of oral and literate cultures also lost its relevance (de Vries 2003, 398). Relativistic theoretical developments left little room for universal, ahistorical dichotomies of oral cultures versus literate cultures. Empirical research in cognitive linguistics and anthropology on the cognitive effects of the introduction of writing did not find universal effects but a variety of local cognitive effects. Indeed, the effects of writing turned out to differ in crucial ways in literate cultures, and this supported the idea of different local literacies (see, for example, Scribner and Cole 1981). As for the relationship between logic and writing, highly abstract logic and codification of rules for logical reasoning emerged in oral religious contexts to establish rules for doctrinal discussions: for example, in the Buddhist schools of Tibet (Foley 1997, 419).

Perhaps the most radical shift away from the second perspective occurred in the fields of classics and biblical scholarship. Two elements were fundamental in that paradigm shift: the emphasis on the interdependence and interaction of oral and written forms of communication and the emphasis on the local nature of that interaction. These two elements come together in the notion of local oral–written interfaces to which we now turn.

Local oral–written interfaces in antiquity

To present the new insights into orality and literacy in the field of ancient studies I will summarize findings by David Carr (2005) in his book *Writing on the Tablet of the Heart: Origins of Scripture and Literature*, a brilliant application of the new orality-literacy paradigm on biblical literatures that shows how local oral–written interfaces in ancient worlds help explain the origin, transmission, nature and performance of Hebrew, Aramaic and Greek Scriptures.[7] For Carr (ibid.) the key element in the transmission of long-duration texts in antiquity was the transmission *from mind to mind* in a process of indoctrination/education/enculturation of an elite minority of literati (6). The traditional texts were "written on the tablet of the heart" (127) and the goal was to plant the values and ideals of the ancient texts in those hearts along with the words. "Thus, the minds stood at the centre of the often discussed oral-written interface" (6).

Written copies of texts were not designed for instant reading off a page, certainly not for silent reading,[8] but rather "stood as a permanent reference point for an ongoing process of largely oral recitation" (Carr 2005, 4) based on memorization. This explains many striking aspects of ancient manuscripts: for example, the absence of word and/or sentence separation, leaving out vowels or sometimes giving only the first word of a verse in full, with just the first letter of each succeeding word of that verse and other forms of ancient "stenographics" (5). We can only understand these characteristics of manuscripts in the context of a specific type of local oral–written interface. Only when people were already very familiar with a text, on the basis of memorization, could they read it: reading was a kind of recognition. The written copy of long-duration texts, if at all present at the performance scene, functioned as "a musical score does for a musician who already knows the piece" (4). This analogy with a musical score is helpful to grasp the relationship between the written and oral dimension: they are interconnected aspects of the performative condition, linked via memorization practices.

Manuscripts that in their visual form assume this type of oral-written hybrid also occur in traditional cultures in other parts of the world (de Vries 2012, 73). The Makassarese of Sulawesi, Indonesia, wrote their long-duration texts on leaves of the Lontar palm. These Lontar manuscripts not only have no word spaces, but each syllable is represented by just the first consonant-vowel, deleting any consonant(s) that close the syllable (Evans 2010, 132). Cumming writes that "only by knowing the subject of a sentence can it be read. According to some Makassarese, the written script only 'becomes Makassarese when it is spoken aloud' " (2002, xii). The skills to perform texts in societies with these hybrid oral–written interfaces is limited to an elite minority who have the long-duration texts written on the tablets of their hearts during a prolonged period of training.

The central memorization aspect of ancient oral–written interfaces is the key to other important features of ancient long-duration texts. For example, the link with music: music, singing and chanting formed mnemonic aids to the memorization of these orally performed *written* traditions (Carr 2005, 94–96). Stylistic features such as inclusio, chiasmus, chain words, and other repetitive structures like parallelism, interpreted under the second perspective as oral residues in written texts of earlier purely oral traditions, may be reinterpreted as *writing* strategies designed to facilitate the memorization of the written text, to inscribe it more easily on the tablet of the heart, and to facilitate the oral performance of written texts by the mouth and lips in recitation. Carr writes in relation to Greek oral–written interfaces: "poetic and formulaic elements often pointed to by the oral-traditional school might be characteristics of *written* Greek epic that evolved to support its *oral* transmission within early Greek society" (ibid., 105). The frequent use of acrostics in ancient long-duration texts is a good example of a writing strategy aimed at memorizing and reciting the sequence of passages (73, 125).

Local oral–written interfaces and printed Bibles of early modern Europe

Technological and material changes stand at the heart of changing dynamics in local–written interfaces, and the materiality of the carriers of (translated) texts crucially shapes forms and functions of translations (Littau 2011).[9] The invention of print dramatically changed local–written interfaces in early modern Europe, and nowhere does this become more visible than in the Bible translations of early modern Europe.

The invention of printing by Gutenberg in 1440 led to a whole new oral–written interface. By 1500, printing presses were all over Europe, and millions of volumes had been distributed. Written texts entered the lives of countless individuals who read those books individually, in the privacy of their homes. Compared to the very small numbers of people who could read and write in ancient scribal cultures, early modern times saw a sharp increase of literacy rates, although nowhere near the literacy rates in modern, advanced societies. Mass production of Bibles led to individual reading of the Scriptures from a private copy. Memorization of long-duration texts became rare, and the primary mode of existence of long-duration texts was no longer in the minds of an educated, literate elite. Early modern mass-produced Bible translations of Europe show an explosion of visual paratextual elements in the text, compared to the Bible translations of antiquity: word spacing, indentation, pericopes with titles, chapters, verses, cross references to other texts in Scriptures, annotations and explanations. These paratextual features were designed to help individual readers to pick up the written text and start to read it, just read it off the page, without the aid of the memorized text stored in the brain, without assuming previous familiarity with the text prior to reading it, as in antiquity (de Vries 2012, 79). The pages of early modern Bible translations such as the Dutch *Statenvertaling* (1637) show an amazing system of paratextual links. Verses of Scripture are linked to other verses in different books and to theological reflections in the marginal notes. We have no direct proof of the effectiveness of these paratextual helps but we know they were in high demand. The *nota marginalia* of the Dutch *Statenvertaling*, its central paratextual feature, were translated into English to satisfy the demand among Protestants to be able to read and understand the Bible without the help and mediation of clergy or Church.

Concluding remarks

Notions of orality have played an intriguing role in the history of modern Bible translation, at all levels, from the way the biblical sources were understood as "essentially" oral to "oralizing" translation strategies and perceptions of audiences as "oral" in grammar, culture, style and cognition. To bring some order in the rich intellectual history of orality I distinguished three perspectives on orality and Bible translation, chronologically ordered from the nineteenth century to the early twenty-first century. The distinction of three perspectives on orality and Bible translation, although hopefully useful in an overview article like this, does not begin to do justice to many translators and works on orality and translation that do not fit this mould.

The first perspective on orality, of Buber and Rosenzweig, attracted translators and biblical scholars interested in the "oral" otherness of the Hebrew Scriptures. But the otherness of the Hebrew Bible, or any other text, is never a self-evident notion. To be identified and captured in translation, otherness needs to be theorized, constructed; this construction of otherness takes place in domestic terms and frameworks, and this is the irony of foreignizing translations (de Vries, 2014). Buber and Rosenzweig constructed the "oral" otherness of the Hebrew Scriptures in the terms, notions and ideologies of philosophies and ideologies that they had absorbed when educated as philosophers in Germany. Contemporary critics of Buber and Rosenzweig had a much sharper eye for this German layer of domestic inscription than later critics, after the Second World War, who tended to stress the Jewishness of Buber and Rosenzweig, and the Hebraicity of their translation, but ignored their roots in German philosophies and ideologies of language, culture and translation. An example of a contemporary critic sensitive to that German ideological side of Buber and Rosenzweig was Kracauer ([1926] 1963, 180), who used the term *völkische Romantik*, an expression translated by Maranhão as "racial Romanticism", to characterize the work of Buber and Rosenzweig (Maranhão 2003, 77; van der Louw 2006, 15).

This first perspective on orality had much less appeal for most missionary Bible translators who left Europe and the USA in great numbers after the Second World War to work in remote corners of the world, often with an evangelical American or European background. They were driven by a Protestant message-and-meaning perspicuity hermeneutics. The Bible was seen as a clear message from God in Hebrew and Greek that He wanted to be communicated as clearly as possible to all humans, to each in his or her own tongue. The exoticizing emphasis on Hebrew orality as part of a wider focus on Hebrew otherness and alterity of the first perspective did not fit their missionary, communicative *skopos*.

This does not mean that they did not notice or appreciate these Hebrew features. But rendering these features with the translation strategies of the Buber-Rosenzweig tradition (root concordance, colometric divisions, rare and highly infrequent words, difficult neologisms) did not have a high priority, given the missionary purpose.

Missionary translators did sometimes try to render the literary features focused on in the first perspective such as keyword repetition, sound effects or inclusio, by employing literary strategies of host communities with similar literary effects. Wendland (2011) is an example of such an approach that he calls literary functional equivalence.

Whereas the first perspective, of Buber and Rosenzweig, highlighted the orality of biblical source texts as an aspect of their otherness, the second perspective highlighted the orality of "target" cultures, as a form of otherness that Bible translations should take into account in order to successfully communicate with such "oral" audiences. Unfortunately, in portraying the orality of minority communities in the developing world as "paratactic" (that is, without complex syntax), "concrete and context-bound", "formulaic-repetitive", the second perspective had very little basis in empirical study of such communities, and came dangerously close to academic recycling of old stereotypes of "primitive" peoples as lacking abstract and logical thinking, with "oral" languages that supposedly lacked complex syntax and with simple, repetitive, coordinative forms of discourse (de Vries 2003).

Findings from anthropological linguistics, cognitive anthropology and especially the fields of ancient studies and biblical scholarship gave way, towards the turn of the millennium, to a third perspective on orality and literacy practices as historically situated, driven by local technologies and material conditions, local social practices of speaking and writing that can best be understood from the point of view of their interaction and points of contact. Key to this new approach is the historical situatedness of the interaction of orality and literacy practices. This means that we cannot generalize over the local oral–written interfaces in which the Hebrew sacred texts, the Septuagint or the writings of the New Testament functioned. Performance conditions, material culture, writing technology, the place of oral traditions; they all differed crucially in these three traditions. To give an example of a local–written interface, this article focused on the Hebrew Bible, following Carr (2005), who describes the place of scrolls, literacy, oral performance and memorization in ancient Israel in the comparative contexts of ancient Egypt, Mesopotamia and Greece. We lack such a comprehensive study of the Septuagint and the New Testament from the perspective of biblical media criticism. Further research of the Septuagint and the New Testament writings is needed to better understand the way in which oral and written dimensions interacted in the origin, performance and transmission of these traditions.

Notes

1. This section relies heavily on de Vries (2012, 87–93; 2014).
2. To use a characteristic phrase of Schleiermacher (1838, 277), quoted by Venuti (2008, 85), who also gives the translation by Lefevere (1977), "bent towards a foreign likeness".
3. This sentence exemplifies the very peculiar form of German that Buber and Rosenzweig used, often ungrammatical and with neologisms – very difficult to translate into English. A rather literal rendering would be: "A person, when he from among you brings-near to HIM a near-ing".
4. This section relies heavily on de Vries (2003).
5. I rely on Foley (1997, 417–434) for the origin of the properties ascribed to orality in the second perspective.
6. This section relies heavily on de Vries (2012).
7. This section is based on de Vries (2012, 71–79).

ORALITY AND TRANSLATION

8. This does not mean silent reading was unknown; it was known but not the default way to perform a text. See Carr (2005, 4) for the emergence of silent reading and more visually oriented reader-friendly teaching texts for use in early education in the Hellenistic period when literacy became more widespread.
9. This section is based on de Vries (2012, 79–82).

References

Askani, H. 1997. *Das Problem der Übersetzung-dargestellt an Franz Rosenzweig: die Methoden und Prinzipien der Rosenzweigschen und Buber-Rosenzweigenschen Übersetzungen.* Tübingen: Mohr.

Besnier, Nicholas. 1995. *Literacy, Emotion and Authority.* Cambridge: Cambridge University Press.

Biber, Douglas. 1988. *Variation Across Speech and Writing.* Cambridge: Cambridge University Press.

Botterweck, Johannes, and Helmer Ringgren (eds). 1980. *Theological Dictionary of the Old Testament.* Vol. 4. Grand Rapids: Eerdmans.

Brown, Rick. 2004. "Communicating God's Message in an Oral Culture." *International Journal of Frontier Missions* 21 (3): 122–128.

Buber, Martin. 1964. *Schriften zur Bibel.* Vol. 2 of *Werke.* Munich: Kosel.

Buber, Martin, and Franz Rosenzweig. 1997. *Die Schrift.* Gütersloh: Gütersloher Verlagshaus.

Carr, David M. 2005. *Writing on the Tablet of the Heart: Origins of Scripture and Literature.* Oxford: Oxford University Press.

Chafe, Wallace L., and J. Danielewicz. 1987. "Properties of Spoken and Written Language." In *Comprehending Oral and Written Language*, edited by R. Horowitz and S. J. Samuels, 83–113. New York: Academic Press.

Chouraqi, A. 1974. *La Bible.* Paris: Desclée de Brouwer.

Cumming, W. 2002. *Making Blood White: Historical Transformations in Early Modern Makassar.* Honolulu: University of Hawaii Press.

de Vries, Lourens. 2003. "New Guinea Communities Without Writing and Views of Primary Orality." *Anthropos* 98: 397–405.

de Vries, Lourens. 2008. "Appendix: Bible Translation and Primary Orality." In *Contextual Frames of Reference in Translation. A Coursebook for Bible Translators and Teachers*, Ernst Wendland, 297–310. Manchester: St Jerome.

de Vries, Lourens. 2012. "Local Oral-Written Interfaces and the Nature, Transmission, Performance and Translation of Biblical Texts." In *Translating Scripture for Sound and Performance*, edited by James Maxey and Ernst Wendland, 68–97. Eugene: Wipf and Stock.

de Vries, Lourens. 2014. "The Romantic Turn in Bible Translation." *Translation* 3: 123–149.

Evans, Nicholas. 2010. *Dying Words: Endangered Languages and What They Have To Tell Us.* Oxford: Wiley-Blackwell.

Foley, William A. 1991. *The Yimas language of New Guinea.* Stanford: Stanford University Press.

Foley, William A. 1997. *Anthropological Linguistics: An Introduction.* Oxford: Blackwell.

Fox, Everett. 1995. *The Five Books of Moses: A New Translation with Introduction, Commentary and Notes.* New York: Schocken.

Franklin, K. J. 2008. *Loosen your Tongue: An Introduction to Storytelling.* Dallas: SIL International.

ORALITY AND TRANSLATION

Goody, J. 1977. *The Domestication of the Savage Mind*. Cambridge: Cambridge University Press.

Gordon, Eli P. 2003. *Rosenzweig and Heidegger: Between Judaism and German Philosophy*. Berkeley: University of California Press.

Kalkman, Gino. 2010. "Het gebruik van Chronological Bible Storying in Bijbelcommunicatieprocessen in primair orale culturen." MA thesis, Vrije Universiteit.

Kracauer, S. [1926] 1963. "Die Bibel auf Deutsch. Zur Übersetzung von Martin Buber und Franz Rosenzweig." In *Das Ornament der Masse. Essays*, 173–186. Frankfurt: Suhrkamp.

Lefevere A. 1977. *Translating Literature: The German tradition from Luther to Rosenzweig*. Assen: Van Gorcum.

Lévi-Strauss, Claude. 1966. *The Savage Mind*. Chicago: University of Chicago Press.

Lévy-Brühl, Lucien. 1926. *How Natives Think*. New York: Knopf.

Littau, Karin. 2011. "First Steps towards a Media History of Translation." *Translation Studies* 4 (3): 261–281.

Lord, Albert. 1960. *The Singer of Tales*. Cambridge, MA: Harvard University Press.

Maranhão, Tullio. 2003. "The Politics of Translation and the Anthropological Nation of the Ethnography of South America." In Tullio Maranhão and Bernhard Streck (eds), *Translation and Ethnography: The Anthropological Challenge of Intercultural Understanding*, 64–84. Tucson: University of Arizona Press.

Olson, D. 1994. *The World on Paper: The Conceptual and Cognitive Implications of Writing and Reading*. Cambridge: Cambridge University Press.

Ong, Walter. 1982. *Orality and Literacy: The Technologizing of the Word*. London: Methuen.

Oussoren, P. 2004. *De Naardense Bijbel*. Vught: Skandalon en Plantijn.

Parry, Milman. 1928. *L'Epithète traditionelle dans Homère*. Paris: Société Éditrice Les Belles Lettres.

Reichert, K. 1996. "It Is Time: The Buber-Rosenzweig Translation in Context." In *The Translatability of Cultures: Figurations of the Space Between*, edited by Sanford Budick and Wolfgang Iser, 169–186. Stanford: Stanford University Press.

Renck, Günther. 1990. *Contextualization of Christianity and Christianization of Language: A Case Study from the Highlands of Papua-New Guinea*. Erlangen: Verlag der Ev. Lutheran Mission.

Rodriquez, R. 2014. *Oral Tradition and the New Testament: A Guide for the Perplexed*. London: Bloomsbury.

Schleiermacher, Fr. F. 1838. *Sämtliche Werke*. Section 3, Vol. 2. Berlin: G. Reimer.

Schmidt, Gerda G. 1995. *Martin Buber's Formative Years: From German Culture to Jewish Renewal, 1897–1909*. Alabama: University of Alabama Press.

Schravesande, Hans. 2009. *Jichud. Eenheid in het werk van Martin Buber*. Zoetermeer: Boekencentrum Uitgevers.

Scribner, S., and M. Cole. 1981. *The Psychology of Literacy*. Cambridge, MA: Harvard University Press.

van der Louw, Theo. 2006. "Vertalen volgens de Duitse romantiek (Schleiermacher, Buber) en soorten letterlijkheid." *Kerk en Theologie* 57 (1): 59–79.

van Enk, Gerrit J., and Lourens de Vries. 1997. *The Korowai of Irian Jaya: Their Language in its Cultural Context*. Oxford: Oxford University Press.

Venuti, Lawrence. 2008. *The Translator's Invisibility: A History of Translation*. 2nd ed. New York: Routledge.

Wendland, Ernst. 2011. *LiFE-style Translating: A Workbook for Bible Translators*. 2nd ed. Dallas: SIL International.

Similarity and alterity in translating the orality of the Old Testament in oral cultures

Tshokolo J. Makutoane, Cynthia L. Miller-Naudé and Jacobus A. Naudé

Department of Hebrew, University of the Free State, Bloemfontein, South Africa

> This article explores the relationship between the orality of the Old Testament as a source text and orality as a feature of the target culture. This relationship involves both alterity, the assertion of distance of culture, and similarity (or familiarity), the assertion of proximity of culture (Sturge 2007). However, because orality does not involve a fixed set of universal features, the similarities and differences between the orality of the Old Testament and the orality of a target culture are examined using the insights of Biblical Performance Criticism (Rhoads 2012). In other words, the process involves not just the translation *of* performance but also translation *for* performance (Maxey 2012). These concepts are explored through a performance translation of a liturgical psalm (Psalm 24) into Sesotho, a Bantu language of Southern Africa.

Beginning in the nineteenth century, biblical scholarship examined the orality of biblical texts as part of an attempt to discern the oral traditions that lie behind the written text, on the one hand, and the *Sitz im Leben* ("life setting") of the biblical traditions, on the other (Gunkel [1930] 1967; Morag 1969). Oral features were identified within a variety of genres, including narrative (Niditch 1996), prophecy (Culley 2000; Nissinen 2000) and the Psalms (Culley 1967). More recently, attention has shifted to the role of oral tradition and scribal activity in the composition and editorial shaping of the biblical text (Polak 1998; Millard 1999; Carr 2005).

Some Bible translations have attempted to portray the alterity of the oral features of the ancient Hebrew source text as is done, for example, in the Schocken Bible (Naudé 1999, 2005). Bible translations for oral societies have focused on incorporating oral features of language and perspective (Finnegan 1970) into the Bible as a target text (Noss 1981; Naudé and Makutoane 2006; Makutoane and Naudé 2004, 2008). The needs of illiterate, semi-literate and pre-literate hearers of Bible translations were often considered and incorporated into the translation brief (Makutoane 2011).

In this article we explore the relationship between the orality of the Old Testament as a source text and orality as a feature of the target culture. This relationship involves both alterity, the assertion of *distance* of culture, and similarity (or familiarity), the assertion of *proximity* of culture (Sturge 2007). Orality, however, does not involve a fixed set of universal features. As a result, the similarities and differences between the orality of the Old Testament and the orality of a target culture are examined using the insights of Biblical Performance Criticism (Rhoads 2012). In other words, we are interested in examining not just translation *of* performance but also translation *for* performance (Maxey 2012). These concepts are explored through a performance translation of a liturgical psalm (Psalm 24) into Sesotho, a Bantu language of Southern Africa.

Sesotho (Southern Sotho) is a Southern Bantu language of the Niger-Congo language family spoken by approximately 6,024,000 people, of whom 4,240,000 are in South Africa (the other speakers are in Lesotho and Botswana; *Ethnologue* 2013). Sesotho speakers were united by a common loyalty to the royal house of Mshweshwe (Moshoeshoe) in about 1822. He was able to create a Sotho identity and unity, both of which were used to repel the external forces that threatened their autonomy and independence (Rosenthal 1970, 45–46; see also Casalis 1977; Ellenberger 1997). Moshoeshoe welcomed the missionaries from the Société des Missions Évangéliques when they arrived at Thaba Bosiu in 1833 (see also Harries 2007). The complete Bible in Southern Sotho was published in France by the British and Foreign Bible Society in 1881, but because of the Basotho War it reached its prospective readers only in September 1883 (Smit 1970, 210). During this two-year delay, Mr Mabille, one of the indigenous translators, undertook a thorough revision, not only changing the orthography, but also improving the text. The first revision of the 1881 version was published in 1899 and an edition in revised orthography in 1909. A new Southern Sotho translation was published in 1989 by the Bible Society of South Africa. It was based on the principles of Nida and Taber (1974) and exhibits a dynamic equivalence translation (see Makutoane and Naudé 2009, 79–94 for a historical overview and features of the Sesotho translations).

Both Sesotho translations lean heavily on the reader's ability to understand a written text, which constitutes a very serious problem in a religious community made up of members not able to read. This was explored by a preliminary study of illiteracy in Bloemfontein's congregations in 2007 (Makutoane 2011, 1), which found that 11% of the church members could not read or write; presumably the figure would be higher in the rural communities. The study showed further that among the remaining 89% there are readers who found it difficult to understand the content of the Bible due to the complexity of its vocabulary and language structure, especially when it is read aloud.

The question to be investigated is how the Bible can be translated into Sesotho for performance in order to accommodate both kinds of users; that is, how the features of oral performance can be incorporated while translating the Scripture. An important factor in the translation of orality is the aesthetic representation of the alterity of otherness (Bandia 2011, 108); as a result, our aim is to work out aspects of an engagement model. The article has four sections. The first section presents a brief media history of the Bible with respect to translation. The second provides an overview of the field of Biblical Performance Criticism and examines its relationship to Bible translation. The third focuses on the relationship of oral performance and the representation of alterity. The fourth presents a performance translation of Psalm 24 in Sesotho.

Media history of the Bible

Recent research about the ancient literary cultures of the ancient Near East has implications for understanding better how the Bible was spoken, written and transmitted. Walton and Sandy (2013) utilize the operative contrast of hearing-dominant (traditions were passed on by word of mouth from generation to generation) versus text-dominant cultures (traditions were passed on by scribally produced texts). Furthermore, they differentiate the roles of documents (as essential records and solidified reference points to be read aloud as well as symbolic expressions of power) from the roles of scribes (who produced documents and maintained archives but were not the ones who recited the texts in public) (see also Redford 2000). These distinctions serve to nuance the categories of oral and written in important ways (see also Biber 1988; Chafe 1982). In the light of Ong (1982), Fowler (2009, 3–18) and Littau (2011), the media history or technologizing of the Bible can be adapted as follows:

Hearing-dominant

Oral/aural-written communication/verbal interpretive culture

   (i) Oral/aural communication (the oral/aural Bible)
  (ii) Handwritten manuscript communication (manuscript Bible)

Text-dominant

Print communication (printed Bible)/typographic interpretive culture
Electronic/media communication (electronic Bible)/digital-media interpretive culture

The oral and the written dimensions are intimately connected. The transmission of long-duration texts is from mind to mind in a process of indoctrination, education, and enculturation of an elite minority. Memorization (learning by heart) is central to oral tradition – oral performance from memory is the proof that ancient traditions have been mastered, thus setting the performer apart from those who have not internalized the tradition. Written copies of texts were not designed for instant reading off a page, but were a permanent reference point for an ongoing process of largely oral recitation. To be literate in antiquity meant that someone had internalized ancient texts and therefore had the ability to recite them and add to the tradition.

The invention of printing by Johann Gutenberg around 1440 changed the world in a dramatic way. Mass production of the translated Bible created the possibility for individual and silent reading from a private copy. Memorization of long-duration texts became an exception, and the primary mode of existence of long-duration texts ceased to be in the hearts and minds. The transition from the end of the age of printing into the new electronic age is currently under way.

Orality is concerned with cultural and aesthetic practices involved in the pre-modern traditions, in modernist representations of the past, or in postmodernist expressions of artistry, such as audiovisual media (Bandia 2011, 108). Concerning the visual aspect of the biblical text, it is also present in all phases. For example, the visual in the printed (or hand-drawn) fifteenth-century Pauper Bible lies closer to the frames, images and text of a web page than do the lengthy expositions of contemporary academic scholarship as represented, for example, in an academic journal (Adam 2009, 159–173). Many aspects of ancient orality have re-emerged in a communications environment of electronic-aided orality (Foley 2012).

Biblical Performance Criticism and translation

The new field of Biblical Performance Criticism (BPC) claims that because ancient Israel was a predominantly oral culture whose traditions were originally experienced as oral traditions, academic work on the Bible must shift from the mentality of a modern print culture to that of an oral/scribal culture in order to reframe the biblical materials in the context of traditional oral cultures (see Rhoads 2012 and Maxey 2012 for a summary as well as the review of Maxey and Wendland 2012 in Naudé 2014). Through constructing modern scenarios of ancient performances of the biblical text, BPC finds a new avenue for interpreting the traditions of the Bible as performance itself becomes a methodology of exegesis. When presented with two viable exegetical choices from a text, the act of performance can indicate which selection is more likely.

Similarly, choices of performance can inform and shape a translation. In translation for print, the focus is on the text rather than an oral performance; more on a single meaning of a text than the meaning potential; more on faithfulness to the original than creativity in the oral register of the receptor language; more on the intention of the author or text than the potential impacts upon an audience; more on an individual reader than the collective experience of a gathered community; more on the cognitive sense made by a reader than the emotional experience of the listeners (Rhoads 2012, 24). Through BPC, biblical exegesis moves toward an engagement model, which takes more seriously the potential impacts of oral translation on audiences (Rhoads 2012, 25). BPC, then, has particular relevance for Bible translation because it reconceptualizes the task of Bible translation as involving both translations *of* (ancient) performance and translations *for* performance (today) (Maxey 2012, 4).

Translation of performance

BPC emphasizes the essentially oral nature of ancient Israelite society. As noted above, biblical scholars have accepted the notion that oral traditions lie behind the written biblical tradition since the groundbreaking work of Gunkel ([1930] 1967) even though various opinions concerning the nature of those traditions have been put forward (Miller 2011). However, the nature of orality, in general, has been understood in a variety of ways.

Gunkel himself was acquainted with Wilhelm Wundt's folk psychology and so his research on the oral traditions of the Bible led to a universal, dichotomous characterization of oral cultures versus literate cultures; that is, a great divide between oral and written cultures and traditions. This view is prevalent in many of the definitions of the oral world, as for example, the view that the oral world describes societies which do not use any form of writing (Havelock 1986, 65) or who have never been introduced to writing (Jousse 2000).

In defining orality Finnegan's view is that oral culture began from the storytelling tradition and that the oral world is *by definition dependent on a performer who formulates it in words on a specific occasion* (Finnegan 1970, 2;

2007, 44). Similarly, Okpewho (1992, 4) defines the oral world as that which lays more emphasis on the notion that this form of knowledge comes from the past and is handed down from one generation to the other.

Other definitions of the oral world focus on the process of oral performance. Since the 1930s the oral formulaic theory has been associated with the work of Milman Parry and his student Albert Lord, as well as with the scholars Walter J. Ong and Jack Goody. The aesthetic qualities of oral performance as exhibiting accurate observation, vivid imagination and ingenious expression have also been highlighted (Nandwa and Bukenya 1983, 1). A similar process of oral performance in ancient Israel has been described by Rhoads (2012, 26–30) who suggests that originators of stories and speeches, like musical composers, probably would have composed in their imagination or sounded out what they were composing and later transcribed it. They likely visualized their whole embodied performance – gestures, movements and facial expressions – as they composed ahead of actually performing. The written records (scrolls) served mainly to assist a performer's memory to enable performances to be repeated on new occasions and in other locations, even though it is likely that compositions would also have passed in memory from oral performance to oral performance without the aid of a manuscript. The biblical writings preserved are like the fossil remains of living oral performances (ibid.).

As noted above, the simplistic binary of orality versus literacy has receded into the background as has a universalistic approach to oral cultures. De Vries (2012, 68–98) has criticized as "romantic" the pursuit of an exclusively oral context. By investigating a number of Bible translations from different cultures (seventeenth-century Dutch, twentieth-century translations for communities in Papua New Guinea and the German translation of the Hebrew by Buber and Rosenzweig) he has shown that orality is rarely absolute within a culture nor are the features of orality universal across cultures. Instead, the evidence is that many societies produced oral and written literature simultaneously. The oral and the written dimension are intimately connected, have many points of contact and coevolve. This interplay of written and oral dimensions is local in the sense that oral-written interfaces vary in time, place, context, and genre within communities (de Vries 2012, 74–75). On the basis of research by Carr (2005), de Vries argues that the literary features of the biblical text serve as reminders of a complex interplay of oral and literary strategies of communication.

Nonetheless, definitions of the oral world portray one common denominator and that is *performance*. This means that the oral world must be understood on the grounds that performing and translating the biblical text with its oral background involves the translation *of* performance.

Translation for performance

Marcel Jousse (1886–1967) was a French anthropologist who viewed performance as the main pivot around the development of the oral world where stories were told in a unique way for specific purposes and reasons (Jousse 2000). The basic element of the oral world is that the spoken words have no permanent or visual connotation, but they are seen as *events* or *gestes* or *actions of the universe* (ibid., 30) rather than as things (Loubser, 2007, 147). Influenced by Jousse, Finnegan (2007, 45) argued that performance encapsulates elements such as repetition, reduplication, mimicry, gesture, onomatopoeia and ideophones.

Jousse's anthropological, ethnological and psychological perspectives also influenced Ong in the development of his nine, well-known, systemic features of orality, which play a vital role in enhancing the memorability of an utterance or performance: additive rather than subordinative, aggregative rather than analytic, redundant or *copious*, conservative or traditionalist, close to the human life-world, agonistically toned, empathetic and participatory rather than objectively distanced, homeostatic, and situational rather than abstract (Ong 1982, 37–56, but see De Vries 2000 for a critique of Ong on the basis of primary oral cultures in Papua New Guinea). The importance of repeated formulas and performances for oral literature has been endorsed by Bandia (2008, 115) when he says: "Repetition and reduplication play an important role in African oral narrative ... and are often used for emphasis or semantic augmentation." The common denominators that Jousse, Ong and Bandia share encapsulate, amongst others: redundancy, repetitions, rhythms and memory/recollection. Furthermore, oral communication is not a one-way process, but a two-way process between the storyteller and the audience (see also Tedlock 1977). This implies that the performer takes his or her cues from the audience's moods and reactions.

In translating for performance, there are a number of features that have been identified. In this form of art, says Norrick (2000, 1), the storyteller introduces the story so as to secure listeners' interest, gain control of the floor and ensure understanding. That storyteller must then shape remembered materials into verbal performance designed for the prospective context. This means that stories are not merely a matter of verbal form or content, but of performance, and acting. In his view, memorization must be put alongside improvisation. This means that conservation and recalling of verbal material (be it recitations or clichéd parallelism) all facilitate memorization of long spontaneous improvised series. Furthermore, that storyteller must then shape remembered materials into verbal performance designed for the prospective context. This means that stories are not merely a matter of verbal form or content, but of performance and acting.

The role of sound in translation for performance cannot be underestimated, especially when one attempts to convey the oral/aural factor and sound play of the source text (Nässelqvist 2012, 49–67). In African languages, ideophones can play diverse functions in performance, as illustrated for the Gbaya language (Central African Republic) by Noss (2012, 99–118). Wendland's (2008) oratorical-performative approach to translation emphasizes that translations must facilitate oral reading/oral performance events in contemporary cultures in three areas, namely meaning, style and the rhetorical effects that the oration may have had on an ancient listening audience, in an effort to replicate a similar impact upon a listening audience in a particular modern culture. In this regard four aspects play a role, namely oral artistry, sound, memory, and context (see also Wendland 2012, 139–178).

Another method of producing a performance translation has been suggested by Mathews (2012, 119–138), who proposes starting with a literal translation aiming at lexical consistency with regard to verbal constructions, definite articles and particles. In this way, she aims to maintain the markers in the text for the audience, which understands the depth of these expressions from a shared cultural background. Her illustration using the biblical book of Habakkuk highlights the performance themes of embodiment, process and re-enactment.

Interpretation may function as oral performance of a written text. Karlik (2012, 179–216) describes the activity of interpreters of sermons in West African contexts in a case study of interpreter-mediation in the Guinea-Bissau language of Manjaku. The oral performance functions in the place of a written Bible translation.

Another approach is Maxey's (2009) translation-as-performance model. He facilitated an opportunity for storytellers from among the Vuté people (of Cameroon) to develop translations-in-performance. The end product is not necessarily a printed Bible to be reproduced and distributed, unless it is a working text that can change over time from performance to performance. A related approach is that of de Vries (2012, 87) who proposes a local oral–written interface approach for Bible translation based upon his experience as a translation consultant in Papua New Guinea. Local oral-written interfaces emerge when a primary oral culture becomes partly integrated in the course of the years in the wider nation state. This creates a small minority of indigenous literati who were exposed to education in the print-dominated environment of the national culture. These literati are able to read out translated Bible texts to listening communities in a liturgical setting just as they read out and translate government announcements or price lists at shops.

To summarize, Biblical Performance Criticism has the following characteristics:

(a)   it places a great value on memory; that is, it connects memory through story (this echoes Jousse's standpoint);
(b)   it not only involves storytelling, but creates the story through performance;
(c)   the audience not only hears the story, but experiences it; therefore the audience is not passive, but active (this has been endorsed by Jousse, Ong, Finnegan and Okpewho);
(d)   it understands that performance itself is translation. If translation is taking place in performance; the translation is taking place through sound, silence, gestures and interaction with the audience. These aspects are not just the add-ons, but are part of the one integrated act of delivery, that is, performance; and
(e)   translation for performance can include the use of the historical present (this is what Ong terms homeostasis).

To conclude, Bible translation involves both translation *of* performance and translation *for* performance when it takes into account both the original oral context of the source text and utilizes a performance modality for the target text.

Oral performance and alterity

Religious translation results in a kind of domesticity of texts which allows readers/hearers to feel at home with them by virtue of their familiarity even as they remain essentially foreign. Although religious translation is not explicitly discussed in his works, the philosopher Emmanuel Levinas (1906–1995) opens up a new way to view the foreign/the Other in religious translation through his discussion of the epiphany of alterity (Levinas [1995]/1999; [1972]/2006; see also Zimmerman 2013). His account of alterity (that is, an Otherness which is a dynamic experience of difference in human affairs and which cannot be circumvented) is embedded in a complex philosophical argument. For Levinas, alterity is based on the irreducibility of the other human person. An encounter with the Other, that is, with someone who does not fit neatly into our categories of understanding, confronts us with a unique ethical challenge. What does it mean to encounter someone who is the Other? Or, how should we respond to the Other? Levinas argues that the human life of the being or self takes place in the uncontrollable face of the Other. In particular, ethics, which makes human life human, is determined by how the space between one face and another face is bridged, for example by a caress, a blow, a touch of consolation or compromise, etc. For Levinas, then, to locate the origin of meaning in the human dimension means that its source lies in the irreducible and unsurpassable moral obligation to respond to the Other.

Without disregarding Levinas' emphasis on the significance of human relationships, Levinas' view of alterity can be applied to the translation of religious texts to provide a fresh perspective concerning their otherness. According to Levinas the narratives of biblical texts can only be read authentically in the light of their own logic and coherent with their original contexts; in other words, all contemporary interferences must be avoided when reading these texts (Zimmerman 2013, 35). The Levinasian turn towards the concrete face-to-face moment privileges the existence of the text to its interpretation, that is, the concrete form of the text over its interpretation. By emphasizing a simple but close reading of religious texts that acknowledges an authentic meeting with alterity, an authentic meeting with God occurs through the proximity of the other person (Zimmerman 2013, 110). The close reading implies an avoidance of the ambiguous, speculative or philological aspects of texts as well as the avoidance of the seeming glory of truth because comprehensive knowledge is not possible (ibid). Instead, a close reading must involve responsible activity that requires a self-effacing quality in the reader by responding ethically to one's responsibility for the Other (ibid). Meaning is derived from the language of the religious texts when they enter the service of ethics. To construct an authentically ethical community, it is necessary to study and interpret the biblical texts in the form of continual liturgical activity. In this way alterity is broken open to the simple believer.

In effect, Levinas' philosophical views cannot be used to argue for foreignization *or* for domestication of the text. Instead, Levinas' emphasis on the face-to-face quality of the text should rather be applied to the translation of religious texts as implying the oral presentation of alterity. In this way the hearer/reader meets a religious performance of the text with the same ethical significance as Levinas' face-to-face encounter with the Other. In other words, performance translation provides the translator of religious texts with a powerful means to accomplish Levinas' ideals concerning the epiphany of the Other—the translator of religious texts *presents* the face of the Other in as many facets as possible in order to *awaken* the face of the Other in the reader.

A performance translation of Psalm 24 in Sesotho

Psalm 24 has been understood by biblical scholars as part of a liturgy involving the entrance of the deity – or the ark of the covenant as representing the deity – into the sanctuary on Mount Zion. The precise circumstances in which the liturgy was

ORALITY AND TRANSLATION

performed in ancient Israel are not clear and have been understood as the return of the ark to the sanctuary following its use in battle at the head of the army (Sabourin 1974, 408) or as part of an autumn festival in which the climax is the appearance of the deity as king (Weiser 1962, 232).

The psalm is divided into two stanzas of two strophes each. In the first stanza, the creative power of the deity in the first stanza is followed by a question-answer sequence identifying the qualifications needed to meet the deity in his sanctuary. In the second stanza, the glory of the deity is described in military terms. Again there is a question-answer sequence used to identify the deity and describe his glory and military power. The deity who creates demands ethical behaviour of his worshippers. In turn, he creates stability in the universe through his military power.

In our performance translation of the psalm into Sesotho, we have been guided by the following principles. First, we have attempted to create a translation that maintains, as far as possible, the alterity of ancient Israel's liturgy and worldview. Second, we have worked to maintain those features of orality and performance that have been transcribed in the written version of the text as recorded in the traditional Hebrew text. Third, we have tried to produce a translation in Sesotho that exploits features of oral communication so that the translation appeals to the aural senses. Fourth, we have considered both the speaking voices as the psalm might have been performed in ancient Israel and the speaking voices within a modern performance of the psalm in a Sesotho context. In producing the translation, we have appropriated phrases from both the 1909 and the 1989 Sesotho translations, but the translation has been made with constant reference to the Hebrew source text. (For a performance translation of the same psalm into English and extensive discussion of the Hebrew source text, see Miller-Naudé and Naudé, forthcoming.)

[Mokoloko wa ba kukileng Areka ya Selekane ha o atamela Tempeleng/The procession of those carrying the Covenant Box as they arrive at the Temple]

Strophe A (verses 1–6). Mokoloko wa thabo ha ba nyolohela thabeng ya Sion/Festive procession of going up mount of Zion
(I) SEFELA SE RORISANG JEHOVA, MOHLODI WA TSOHLE/
   HYMN OF PRAISING THE LORD, CREATOR OF THE UNIVERSE
<u>**MOETAPELE WA SEHLOPHA SA DIBINI/CHOIR LEADER:**</u>

1. Lefatshe ke la Morena,
   earth is belong Lord
   The earth belongs to the Lord,

<u>**SEHLOPHA SA DIBINI/THE CHOIR:**</u>

Lefatshe le tsohle tse ho lona
earth and everything all.which in it
the earth and everything in it

Lefatshe le bohle ba ahileng ho lona
earth and all they.who live/dwell in it
the earth and all who live in it

ORALITY AND TRANSLATION

MOETAPELE WA SEHLOPHA/CHOIR LEADER:

2. Hobane ke yena ya le theileng
   For is he (the one) he.who it established
   For he is the one who has established it

SEHLOPHA SA DIBINI/THE CHOIR:

Ke yena ya le tiisitseng hodima mawatle le dinoka
is he (the one) he.who it made firm upon seas and rivers
he is the one who has fixed it upon the seas and the rivers

(II) KOPO YA HO DUMELLWA HO KENA KA TEMPELENG/ REQUEST TO GAIN PERMISSION TO ENTER IN THE TEMPLE MOKOPI/ENQUIRER:

3. Jwale ke mang ya tla nyolohelang thabeng ya Morena
   Now is who.it.is will ascend mountain of Lord
   Now who will ascend to the mountain of the Lord?

SEPHOLA SA DIBINI/THE CHOIR

mme ke mang ya ka emang sebakeng sa hae se halalelang
and is who.it.is will stand place his that which.is holy
or who will stand in his holy place?

JEHOVA/THE LORD:

4. Eo ke ya matsoho a hlokang molato;
   That one who has hands without guilt
   It is the one with clean hands

mme pelo ya hae e hlwekile,
and heart of one is pure
and with pure heart

ke eo ya sa neheleng moya wa ka lefeela la mafeela,
who that.one does not give away soul my meaningless [ideophone]
the one who does not give my soul to meaningless things

kapa ho hlapanyetseng leshano
or to swear lies
nor to swear by what is lies.

MOETAPELE WA SEHLOPHA/CHOIR LEADER:

5. Motho ya jwalo o tla iphumanela lehlohonolo ho Morena
   Person like that will receive blessing in/from Lord
   A person like that will receive blessing in/from the Lord

SEHLOPHA SA DIBINI/THE CHOIR:

o tla   iphumanela   le   ho loka   ho   Modimo Mopholosi   wa hae
will   receive   to be righteous in/from God   Saviour   of his
he will receive righteousness from God, his Saviour

MOETAPELE WA SEHLOPHA/CHOIR LEADER:

6. Ona   ke wona   moloko   o   mmatlang;
   This   the one   generation who seek (someone);
   This is the generation who seek (someone);

SEHLOPHA SA DIBINI/THE CHOIR:

o batlang   ho   bona   sefahleho   sa hao
who seek   to   see   face   your
who seek to see Your face

Oho   wena   Modimo   wa   Jakobo!
O   you   God   of   Jacob
O you God of Jacob!

Strophe B (verses 7–10)

(III) MOKOLOKO HA O KENA SIONE/
THE PROCESSION ON ENTERING ZION

(Ba batla hore Jehova ya emetsweng ke Areka ya Selekane a kene/Demands entrance for Yahweh who is probably represented by the Covenant Box)

MOETAPELE WA MOKOLOKO/
LEADER OF THE PROCESSION:

7. Lona   dikgoro, phahamisang dihlooho!   Bulehang!
   You   gates   raise   your.heads open!
   You gates, raise your heads! Open!

DITHO TSA MOKOLOKO/PILGRIMS:

lona menyako ya mehla ya boholo, iphahamiseng!   Ipuleng!
you doors   of time of old,   raise.yourselves open.yourselves
you doors of old times, raise yourselves! Open yourselves!

ho tle   ho kene   Kgosi   e   tlotlehang
so that may enter king   of honor
so that the King of Honor may enter.

BALEBEDI BA DIKGORO[BAPRISTA]/GATEKEEPERS[PRIESTS]:

8. Ke mang   Kgosi   ena   e   tlotlehang?
   Who is   king   this of   honor
   Who is this King of honor?

ORALITY AND TRANSLATION

DITHO TSA MOKOLOKO/PILGRIMS:

Kgosi ena e tlotlehang ke Morena ya matla, wa mohale;
king this of honor is Lord of powerful, the hero
This King of honor is the powerful Lord, the hero,

re re mohale ntweng
we say hero in war
we say the hero in the warfare.

MOETAPELE WA MOKOLOKO/LEADER OF PROCESSION:

9. Lona dikgoro, phahamisang dihlooho! Bulehang!
   You gates raise your.heads open!
   You gates, raise your heads! Open!

DITHO TSA MOKOLOKO/ PILGRIMS:

lona menyako ya mehla ya boholo, iphahamiseng! Ipuleng!
you doors of time of old, raise.yourselves open.yourselves
you doors of old times, raise yourselves! Open yourselves!

ho tle ho kene Kgosi e tlotlehang
so that may enter king of honor
so that the King of Honor may enter.

BALEBEDI BA DIKGORO [BAPRISTA]/GATEKEEPERS [PRIESTS]

10. Ke mang Kgosi ena e tlotlehang?
    Who is king this of honor
    Who is this King of honor?

DITHO TSA MOKOLOKO/PILGRIMS:

Morena wa mabotho ke yena Kgosi e hlomphehang
Lord of armies is the one king of honor
The Lord of the armies he is the Lord of honor.

One of the most prominent features of this performance translation into Sesotho involves a redivision of the Hebrew poetic couplets between two speaking voices, usually the choir leader and the choir. In Sesotho liturgical singing, as is the case in many traditions of indigenous African music, a leader sings a phrase or two and the larger group repeats the phrase or phrases before adding additional material. This oral technique of repetition is important as both a structuring technique and as a memory device, allowing the leader to direct the group by example and assisting the group in remembering what material should follow. However, by comparison to the Hebrew source text with its carefully balanced parallel lines, the Sesotho performance translation often seems lopsided, with material from the first poetic line of the source text moved to the second line and with increased repetition. This translation strategy can be illustrated using verse 1. In the Hebrew source text, there are only two poetic lines:

a. lyhwh hā'āreṣ ûməlô'āh
   to-YHWH the-earth and-fullness-its
   to the LORD [belongs] the earth and its fullness

ORALITY AND TRANSLATION

b. tēbēl wəyōšəbê   bāh
   world and-dweller.PL.of in-it
   world and those who dwell in it

In the performance translation of the Sesotho, the first Hebrew line has been divided into two:

a. Lefatshe ke la   Morena,
   earth   is belong Lord
   The earth belongs to the Lord,

b. lefatshe le   tsohle   tse   ho lona
   earth   and everything all.which in it
   the earth and everything in it

c. lefatshe le   bohle ba   ahileng   ho lona
   earth   and all   they.who live/dwell in it
   the earth and all who live in it

The Sesotho expands the two poetic lines of the Hebrew into three lines by dividing the first Hebrew line into two. The choir leader performs the basic statement in line a, while the choir expands the description of the earth in two aesthetically crafted lines in lines b and c.

A second feature found in Sesotho oral poetry involves rhythm, which is achieved through rhyming and through repetitions of words, phrases and sentences.[1] Both of these features are present throughout this oral translation of Psalm 24.

Rhyming occurs when one or more words have the same vowel and/or consonant endings. For example, in verse 1 the rhymes found at the ends of the lines can be indicated schematically as follows:

morena "Lord"   (A)
tsohle "everything" (B)
lona "it"   (A)
bohle "all"   (B)
lona "it"   (A)

Note that the rhyming pair *tsohle* "everything" and *bohle* "all" also translate a synonymously parallel word pair in the Hebrew. Rhyming can also be found both in verse 6 and in verse 7 with the ends of the words *o mmatlang ... o batlang*.

Repetition also contributes to the rhythm of the poem. Among the repeated elements are the following:

verse 1: *lefatshe* "the earth" (twice)
verse 2: *ke yena* "is the one" (twice)
verse 3: *ke mang?* "who?" (twice)
verse 5: *o tla iphumanela* "he will receive" (twice)
verses 7, 8a, 8b, 10a, 10b: *kgosi e tlotlehang* "king of honor" (five times)

Rhyming and repetition are used to show emphasis (the energetic stance) of the idea that is being conveyed.

ORALITY AND TRANSLATION

A third prominent feature of the performance translation of Psalm 24 is the addition of discourse markers that are appropriate to oral discourse. For example, in verse 3, the discourse marker *jwale*, "now", is added at the beginning of the question. The purpose of the discourse marker is to link the question to what precedes – on the basis of the preceding statements concerning God's creative activity, the question is asked. The discourse marker enhances the performance of the psalm by guiding hearers to connect the question to the statements that precede it.

Another oral discourse marker, *re re*, "we say", is added in verse 8. This discourse marker is an emphatic way of further specifying the nature of God as the hero. He is not just a hero, but, definitely, we want you to know he is a hero in warfare.

The most difficult verse in the psalm – and the one that presented the most challenges in translating – is verse 7 (which is repeated in verse 9). In order to describe how the Sesotho translation handled these problems, we begin with the Hebrew text:

a. śə'û   šə'ārîm   rā'šêkem
    lift.up.PL   gate.PL   head.PL.of-your.PL
    Lift up, O gates, your heads

b. wəhinnāś'û   piṭḥê   'ôlām
    and-be.lifted.up.PL   door.PL.of   eternity
    and be lifted up, O doors of eternity

c. wəyābô'   melek   hakkābôd
    and-he.will.enter   king.of   the-glory
    and the king of glory will enter

The verse consists of three poetic lines. The a and b lines have a number of parallel elements. The verb in each line is an imperatival form of the verb *nś* "lift up"; in the a line the verb is active (Qal stem formation) whereas in the b line it is passive-reflexive (Niphal stem formation). The pairing of active and passive verbal forms from the same lexical verb is a feature of Hebrew poetry (Berlin 1985, 36–40). Both lines are addressed to the same inanimate entity, which is described as "the gates" in line a and "the doors of eternity" in line b. The phrase "doors of eternity" can be understood as "eternal doors"; that is, "ancient doors" (Peacock 1981, 42). In the first line the vocative noun phrase "gates" intervenes between the verb ("lift up") and its object ("your heads"); this word order is common in biblical poetry but rare in biblical narrative (Miller 2010). The third line of the verse provides the reason for the command, namely that "the king of glory" (or "the glorious king") will enter after the gates lift up their heads.

The precise meaning of the notion that the gates will lift up their heads is debated. Crenshaw (2001, 166–167) understands the expression in a literal fashion. He describes this verse as having "bold poetic language" which "imagines the impossible, the raising of heavy gates like garage doors. Inanimate stone is addressed like a person; those seeking entry ask it to ascend so as no longer to present an obstacle" (2001, 167). Similarly, Peacock (1981, 42) understands the expression as indicating that the gates should open themselves up so that the great king can enter. As a literal expression, the "heads" of the gates could refer to the lintels, the

45

"horizontal pieces above the gates" (Bratcher and Reyburn 1991, 241). The implication, then, could be that "the gates are too small for such a great king, the Lord, to enter, and so they are commanded to raise their heads in order to make room for the king to enter" (242).

Similar expressions involving the lifting of the head have been identified in Ugaritic (a language related to Hebrew, which is attested in texts earlier than those of the Bible) with a metaphorical meaning. Dahood (1965, 152–153) points to an Ugaritic text in which the ploughmen lift up their heads; that is, they rejoice at the coming of rain after a drought (see also Luke 11:28 in the New Testament). Craigie notes another Ugaritic text in which the gods who cower before the threat of chaos are told to lift up their heads; that is, to be encouraged: "Lift up your heads, O gods" (1983, 214). He therefore understands the expression in Psalm 24 to be a transformation of the ancient Ugaritic mythology – it is the gates of the temple which are commanded to lift up their heads, that is, to rejoice at the approach of the creating and conquering king. In the verses that follow, the language is further transformed so that the "gates"/"doors" represent metonymically the gatekeepers of the temple who ask the identity of the one who is coming to enter the temple.

Both the 1909 and the 1989 Sesotho translations used only the word *menyako*, "doors", for the words "gates"/"doors" in the Hebrew source text. However, Sesotho does have another word, *dikgoro*, which refers to the gates of a traditional Sesotho village; this word is known, but it is not commonly used for modern gates. However, it does seem to convey what the Hebrew intends by the expression "gates of eternity" and, furthermore, it lends a sense of alterity to the translation. In the parallel lines, the common Sesotho word *menyako*, "doors", is used but in this line it is modified by the same descriptor used in the Hebrew text – "doors of ancient times". In this way, both lines are referring to the traditional gates/doors of a wall or enclosure, thus accurately reflecting the Hebrew source text.

The second problem in this verse involves the image of the gates raising their heads so that the King of Glory may enter. The 1909 translation retained this image, thus allowing the interpretation that the gates raise "their heads" as an expression of joy. By contrast, the 1989 translation substituted the verb *bulehang*, "open", to explicitate one meaning of the Hebrew expression. In this performance translation in which we wish to convey the alterity of the Hebrew, we decided to combine these approaches with first the image and then the explicitation of the image: "Raise your heads! Open!" parallel to "Raise yourselves! Open yourselves!"

Conclusions

A performance translation that strives for similarity to the source text and respect for the alterity of both the world view and the literary shape of the original can nonetheless incorporate oral features of the target language for performance by the target audience. In so doing, the performative nature of the source text is maintained even if the precise contours of the performance cannot be recreated in the sense that it is sometimes impossible to know how the text would have been performed in ancient Israel. Furthermore, performing the text in a modern African society recreates the religious experience from ancient Israel and allows a modern worshipping community to participate in the creation of a similar liturgical moment. Through a performance translation that incorporates both similarity and alterity of

ORALITY AND TRANSLATION

the source text, modern worshippers sense both their closeness to and distance from their counterparts in ancient Israel.

Acknowledgements

This work is based on research supported in part by the National Research Foundation of South Africa (Jacobus A. Naudé UID 85902). The grantholder acknowledges that opinions, findings and conclusions or recommendations expressed in any publication generated by the NRF supported research are those of the author, and that the NRF accepts no liability whatsoever in this regard.

Note

1. We are grateful to Mrs Moleboheng Lena Qhena, a Sesotho school teacher in Botshabelo (Free State, South Africa) for her assistance in analysing the poetic features of this performance translation of Psalm 24 in the light of the usual features of Sesotho poetry.

References

Adam, A. K. M. 2009. "Interpreting the Bible at the Horizon of Virtual New Worlds." In *The Bible in Ancient and Modern Media: Story and Performance*, edited by Holly E. Hearon and Philip Ruge-Jones, 159–173. Biblical Performance Criticism 1. Eugene: Cascade Books.

Bandia, Paul F. 2008. *Translation as Reparation: Writing and Translation in Postcolonial Africa*. Manchester: St Jerome.

Bandia, Paul F. 2011. "Orality and Translation." In *Handbook of Translation Studies: Volume 2*, edited by Yves Gambier and Luc van Doorslaer, 108–112. Amsterdam: John Benjamins.

Berlin, Adele. 1985. *The Dynamics of Biblical Parallelism*. Bloomington: Indiana University Press.

Biber, Douglas. 1988. *Variation across Speech and Writing*. Cambridge: Cambridge University Press.

Bratcher, Robert G., and William D. Reyburn. 1991. *A Handbook on Psalms*. UBS Handbook Series. New York: United Bible Societies.

Carr, David. 2005. *Writing on the Tablet of the Heart: Origins of Scripture and Literature*. Oxford: Oxford University Press.

Casalis, Eugène. 1977. *The Basutos*. Lesotho: Morija Printing Works. Originally published 1861 by James Nesbit, London.

ORALITY AND TRANSLATION

Chafe, Wallace. L. 1982. "Integration and Involvement in Speaking, Writing, and Oral Literature." In *Spoken and Written Language: Exploring Orality and Literacy*, edited by Deborah Tannen, 35–53. Norwood, NJ: Ablex.

Craigie, Peter C. 1983. *Psalms 1–50*. Word Biblical Commentary 19. Waco: Word Books.

Crenshaw, James L. 2001. *The Psalms: An Introduction*. Grand Rapids: Eerdmans.

Culley, Robert C. 1967. *Oral Formulaic Language in the Biblical Psalms*. Toronto: University of Toronto Press.

Culley, Robert C. 2000. "Orality and Writtenness in Prophetic Texts." In *Writings and Speech in Israelite and Ancient Near Eastern Prophecy*, edited by Ehud Ben Zvi and Michael H. Floyd, 45–64. SBL Symposium Series 10. Atlanta: Society of Biblical Literature.

Dahood, Mitchell. 1965. *Psalms I*. Anchor Bible 16. Garden City, NY: Doubleday.

De Vries, Lourens J. 2000. "Bible Translation and Primary Orality." *Bible Translator* 51 (1): 101–113.

De Vries, Lourens J. 2012. "Local Oral–Written Interfaces and the Nature, Transmission, Performance, and Translation of Biblical Texts." In *Translating Scripture for Sound and Performance: New Directions in Biblical Studies*, edited by James A. Maxey and Ernst R. Wendland, 68–98. Biblical Performance Criticism 6. Eugene: Cascade Books.

Ellenberger, David-Frédéric. 1997. *The History of Basuto: Ancient and Modern*. Lesotho: Morija Printing Works. Originally published 1912.

Ethnologue. 2013. 17th ed. www.ethnologue.com.

Finnegan, Ruth. 1970. *Oral Literature in Africa*. World Oral Literature Series 1. Cambridge: Open Book.

Finnegan, Ruth. 2007. *The Oral and Beyond: Doing Things with Words in Africa*. Chicago: University of Chicago Press.

Foley, John Miles. 2012. *Oral Tradition and the Internet: Pathways of the Mind*. Urbana: University of Illinois Press.

Fowler, Robert M. 2009. "Why Everything We Know about the Bible is Wrong: Lessons from the Media History of the Bible." In *The Bible in Ancient and Modern Media: Story and Performance*, edited by Holly E. Hearon and Philip Ruge-Jones, 3–18. Biblical Performance Criticism 1. Eugene: Cascade Books.

Gunkel, Hermann. (1930) 1967. *The Psalms: A Form-Critical Introduction*. Philadelphia: Fortress Press.

Harries, Patrick. 2007. *Butterflies and Barbarians: Swiss Missionaries and Systems of Knowledge in South-East Africa*. Oxford: James Currey.

Havelock, Eric. A. 1986. *The Muse Learns to Write: Reflections on Orality and Literacy from Antiquity to the Present*. New York: Vail Ballou Press.

Jousse, Marcel. 2000. *The Anthropology of Geste and Rhythm*. 2nd rev. ed. Translated by Edgar Sienaert and Joan Conolly. Durban: Mantis.

Karlik, Jill. 2012. "Translation and Performance: Interpreter-Mediated Scriptures in Manjaku." In *Translating Scripture for Sound and Performance: New Directions in Biblical Studies*, edited by James A. Maxey and Ernst R. Wendland, 179–216. Biblical Performance Criticism 6. Eugene: Cascade Books.

Levinas, Emmanuel. [1995] 1999. *Alterity and Transcendence*. European Perspectives: A Series in Social Thought and Cultural Criticism. New York: Columbia University Press.

Levinas, Emmanuel. [1972] 2006. *Humanism of the Other*. Translated by Nidra Poller. Champaign: University of Illinois Press.

Littau, Karin. 2011. "First Steps towards a Media History of Translation." *Translation Studies* 4 (3): 261–281.

Loubser, J. A. (Bobby). 2007. *Oral and Manuscript Culture in the Bible: Studies on the Media Texture of the New Testament*. Stellenbosch: SUN Press.

Makutoane, Tshokolo J. 2011. "Re-animating Orality: The Design for a New Translation of the Bible into Sesotho." PhD diss., University of the Free State.

Makutoane, Tshokolo J., and Jacobus A. Naudé. 2004. "Reanimating Orality: The Morality Play *Everyman/Elkerlijk* in Southern Sotho." *Journal for Semitics* 13 (2): 159–185.

Makutoane, Tshokolo J., and Jacobus A. Naudé. 2008. "Towards the Design for a New Bible Translation in Sesotho." *Acta Theologica* 28 (2): 1–32.

Makutoane, Tshokolo J., and Jacobus A. Naudé. 2009. "Colonial Interference in the Translation of the Bible into Sesotho." In *The Bible and Its Translations: Colonial and Postcolonial Encounters with the Indigenous*, edited by Jacobus A. Naudé, 79–95. Acta Theologica Supplementum 12. Bloemfontein: SunMedia.

Mathews, Jeanette. 2012. "Translating Habakkuk as a Performance." In *Translating Scripture for Sound and Performance: New Directions in Biblical Studies*, edited by James A. Maxey and Ernst R. Wendland, 119–138. Biblical Performance Criticism 6. Eugene: Cascade Books.

Maxey, James A. 2009. *From Orality to Orality. A New Paradigm for Contextual Translation of the Bible*. Biblical Performance Criticism 2. Eugene: Cascade Books.

Maxey, James. A. 2012. "Biblical Performance Criticism and Bible Translation. An Expanding Dialogue." In *Translating Scripture for Sound and Performance: New Directions in Biblical Studies*, edited by James A. Maxey and Ernst R. Wendland, 1–21. Biblical Performance Criticism 6. Eugene: Cascade Books.

Millard, Alan. 1999. "Oral Proclamation and Written Record: Spreading and Preserving Information in Ancient Israel." In *Michael: Historical, Epigraphical, and Biblical Studies in Honor of Prof. Michael Heltzer*, edited by Yitzhak Avishur and Robert Deutsch, 237–242. Tel Aviv: Archaeological Center.

Miller, Cynthia L. 2010. "Vocative Syntax in Biblical Hebrew Prose and Verse: A Preliminary Analysis." *Journal of Semitic Studies* 60 (2): 347–364.

Miller, Robert D. 2011. *Oral Tradition in Ancient Israel*. (Biblical Performance Criticism 4) Eugene: Cascade Books.

Miller-Naudé, Cynthia L., and Jacobus A. Naudé. Forthcoming. "Alterity, Orality and Performance in Religious Translation." In *Key Cultural Texts in Translation*, edited by Kirsten Malmkjaer.

Morag, Shelomo. 1969. "Oral Traditions and Dialects: Towards a Methodology for Evaluating the Evidence of an Oral Tradition." In *Proceedings of the International Conference on Semitic Studies held in Jerusalem, 19–23 July 1965*, 180–189. Jerusalem: Israel Academy of Sciences and Humanities.

Nandwa, Jane, and Austin Bukenya. 1983. *African Oral Literature for Schools*. Nairobi: Longman.

Nässelqvist, Dan. 2012. "Translating the Aural Gospel: The Use of Sound Analysis in Performance-Oriented Translation." In *Translating Scripture for Sound and Performance: New Directions in Biblical Studies*, edited by James A. Maxey and Ernst R. Wendland, 49–67. Biblical Performance Criticism 6. Eugene: Cascade Books.

Naudé, Jacobus A. 1999. "A Descriptive Translation Analysis of the Schocken Bible." *Old Testament Essays* 12 (1): 73–93.

Naudé, Jacobus A. 2005. "On the Threshold of the Next Generation of Bible Translations: Issues and Trends." *Translators' Journal META* 50 (3).

Naudé, Jacobus A. 2014. "Review of Maxey and Wendland 2012." *Journal for Semitics* 23 (1): 279–284.

Naudé, Jacobus A., and Tshokolo J. Makutoane. 2006. "Reanimating Orality: The Case for a New Translation in Southern Sotho." *Old Testament Essays* 19 (2): 723–738.

Nida, Eugene A., and Charles R. Taber. 1974. *The Theory and Practice of Translation*. Leiden: Brill.

Niditch, Susan. 1996. *Oral World and Written Word: Ancient Israelite Literature*. Louisville: John Knox Press.

Nissinen, Marti. 2000. "Spoken, Written, Quoted, and Invented: Orality and Writtenness in Ancient Near Eastern Prophecy." In *Writings and Speech in Israelite and Ancient Near Eastern Prophecy*, edited by Ehud Ben Zvi and Michael H. Floyd, 235–271. SBL Symposium Series 10. Atlanta: Society of Biblical Literature.

Norrick, Neal R. 2000. *Conversational Narrative: Storytelling in Everyday Talk*. Amsterdam: John Benjamins.

Noss, Philip. A. 1981. "The Oral Story and Bible Translation." *Bible Translator: Technical Papers* 32 (3): 249–318.

Noss, Philip A. 2012. "Sound and Meaning in the Gbaya Bible: Ideophones, Performance, and Bible Translation." In *Translating Scripture for Sound and Performance: New Directions in*

Biblical Studies, edited by James A. Maxey and Ernst R. Wendland, 99–118. Biblical Performance Criticism 6. Eugene: Cascade Books.

Okpewho, Isidore. 1992. *African Oral Literature: Backgrounds, Character, and Continuity*. Bloomington: Indiana University Press.

Ong, Walter. 1982. *Orality and Literacy: The Technologizing of the Word*. London: Methuen.

Peacock, Heber F. 1981. *A Translator's Guide to Selected Psalms*. Helps for Translators. London: United Bible Societies.

Polak, Frank H. 1998. "The Oral and the Written: Syntax, Stylistics, and the Development of Biblical Prose Narrative." *Journal of the Ancient Near Eastern Society* 26: 59–105.

Redford, Donald B. 2000. "Scribe and Speaker." In *Writings and Speech in Israelite and Ancient Near Eastern Prophecy*, edited by Ehud Ben Zvi and Michael H. Floyd, 145–218. SBL Symposium Series 10. Atlanta: Society of Biblical Literature.

Rhoads, David. 2012. "The Art of Translating for Oral Performance." In *Translating Scripture for Sound and Performance: New Directions in Biblical Studies*, edited by James A. Maxey and Ernst R. Wendland, 22–48. Biblical Performance Criticism 6. Eugene: Cascade Books.

Rosenthal, Eric. 1970. *Encyclopaedia of Southern Africa*. London: Frederic Warne.

Sabourin, Leopold. 1974. *The Psalms: Their Origin and Meaning*. New York: Alba House.

Smit, A. P. 1970. *God Made It Grow: History of the Bible Society Movement in Southern Africa*. Cape Town: Bible Society of South Africa.

Sturge, Kate. 2007. *Representing Others: Translation, Ethnography and the Museum*. Manchester: St Jerome.

Tedlock, Dennis. 1977. "Toward an Oral Poetics." *New Literary History* 8 (3): 507–519.

Walton, John H., and Brent Sandy. 2013. *The Lost World of Scripture: Ancient Literary Culture and Biblical Authority*. Downers Grove: Inter-Varsity Press.

Weiser, Artur. 1962. *The Psalms*. Old Testament Library. London: SCM Press.

Wendland, Ernst R. 2008. *Finding and Translating the Oral-Aural Elements in Written Language: The Case of the New Testament Epistles*. Lewiston: Mellen.

Wendland, Ernst R. 2012. "Comparative Rhetorical Poetics, Orality, and Bible Translation: The Case of Jude." In *Translating Scripture for Sound and Performance: New Directions in Biblical Studies*, edited by James A. Maxey and Ernst R. Wendland, 139–178. Biblical Performance Criticism 6. Eugene: Cascade Books.

Zimmerman, Nigel. 2013. *Levinas and Theology*. London: Bloomsbury.

Reviewing directionality in writing and translation: Notes for a history of translation in the Horn of Africa

Elena Di Giovanni[a] and Uoldelul Chelati Dirar[b]

[a]*Department of Humanities, University of Macerata, Italy;* [b]*Department of Political Sciences, University of Macerata, Italy*

> Bringing together history and the study of translation, this article focuses on Christian missionary activities in Eritrea and Ethiopia, with special reference to the nineteenth and early twentieth centuries. It presents and discusses their impact on the shaping and reshaping of cultures and identities in a dynamic interrelation with the African agenda. Though focusing on relatively recent events, this article also takes into account the traditions of evangelization and translation that populated the cultural and religious landscape of the region over a timespan of more than 16 centuries. Focusing on orally transmitted knowledge, written documents, the advent of printing in the area, and all the other activities which have made the dissemination of the missionaries' Christianity possible, this article aims to overcome the common assumption that colonialism stands as an absolute historical divide, and to suggest a revision of the notion of directionality typically applied to the observation of translation phenomena in Africa and other colonial contexts, whereby horizontality is associated with *before* and verticality with *after* the colonial period. Reflecting upon instances of multidirectional writing and translation processes from a historical perspective, with special reference to Christian missionary activities in the Horn of Africa, the ultimate aim of this article is to highlight the importance of interdisciplinary research and its great potential in casting light over events and practices which are still largely unexplored.

Although translation studies has had a relatively short life, since its official debut in the 1970s (Holmes 1972), the history of translation and translations is as old as human communication itself. And although the work of translators has been generally shrouded in invisibility,

> [they] have been instrumental agents in the advancement of culture throughout history .... The function of these "unassuming artisans of communication" has included such far-reaching and transformative roles as inventing alphabets, enriching languages, encouraging the emergence of national literatures, disseminating technical and scientific knowledge, propagating religions and writing dictionaries. (Brodzki 2007, 16)

History, for its part, has been the object of discussion and investigation since the beginning of time, certainly with frequent reference to texts, translators and translations, just as translation studies has relied on historically relevant events and explanations for its development. The interdependence of the two areas of study can be traced in the writings of many scholars. Within translation studies, for instance, Stephen Quirke (2006, 270), mainly with reference to ancient Egypt, remarks that "translation or transfer marks the start of five millennia of history". In his many articles on the history of translation and interpretation in Africa, Cameroonian scholar Charles Atangana Nama refers to the need for a true interplay between the two disciplinary approaches; he goes as far as suggesting that "it would be interesting, particularly for a student of ancient African history, to coordinate a research team with a contemporary scholar of translation, to trace the kinds of translation and interpretation patterns which took place in precolonial times" (1993, 415).

Although mutually essential, the disciplines have hardly ever come together in systematic investigations, and, perhaps more significantly, the studies that have been carried out have so far enjoyed limited circulation. Wishing to adopt a truly interdisciplinary approach in this study, we shall employ sources and resources from both history and translation studies in an effort to merge them, thus creating a thorough observation of phenomena which are, in fact, impossible to separate on either of the two disciplinary fronts.

Such an approach spells out the need to adopt a broad and flexible definition of translation, where writing, transmitting, codifying, interpreting and retelling (Inggs and Meintjes 2009) all have a place. As Brodzki puts it, especially with reference to colonial settings, their pre- and post-included acts of translation are "processes of intergenerational and intercultural transmission" (2007, 14); that is, instruments of historical consciousness that cannot be levelled out by reductionist postcolonial frameworks. With reference to the African continent, one of the few volumes currently available on translation in Africa, *Translation Studies in Africa* (Inggs and Meintjes 2009) contains creative and broad definitions of translations by all its contributors, be they scholars, writers or translators (Di Giovanni 2013). Atangana Nama (1993) had already argued in favour of a broader definition of the term "translation" with reference to Africa, calling, among other things, for the study of phenomena of "transmutation" (414). In this article, translation will be discussed precisely in these terms, with orality, its transmission and its relation to literacy playing a crucial role throughout.

This article will, therefore, follow the long path of *inter*linguistic and *inter*cultural exchanges in the Horn of Africa before, during and after colonization, bringing together history and the study of translations and referring to translation broadly speaking, with a view to painting a larger picture of all these activities and gauging their impact on the shaping and reshaping of cultures, identities and social relations. Moreover, our aim is also to enrich current theories of translation in Africa, first and foremost by acknowledging Africa's great diversity and highlighting its agency, generally overlooked since the colonial period.

Why the Horn of Africa?

The Horn of Africa, more specifically the territory corresponding to today's Eritrea and Ethiopia, stands out as an interesting case. This area had seen the flourishing of a host of oral but especially written traditions well before the advent of colonization.

The Horn, which has always been characterized by the presence of a written language for intra- and intercultural communication, had established a complex network of interactions with other African, Asian and European languages for almost two millennia, with Sabean, Greek, Ge'ez and Amharic in turn constituting the status of the most powerful written languages. Besides these, the presence and role of Arabic as a written vehicle for Islamic culture in the Horn as well as the whole of Africa should not be underestimated, as evidenced by hundreds of thousands of Arabic manuscripts still available to the scholarly community (Gori 2007; Ahmed 2009).

Although the first evidence of a standardized use of Ge'ez can be traced back to the second century AD, it only later developed as a fully fledged language for political and religious purposes. In fact, until the fourth century the dominant diplomatic and commercial language was Greek, as is proven by many archaeological remains (Avanzini 2005). Scholars agree that Ge'ez developed as a literary language from between the fifth and seventh centuries AD and connect this with Christianity's introduction into the region, which occurred in the fourth century. Thus, the development of Ge'ez language and literature can also be seen as the result of intense translation processes, mainly effected for religious purposes.

The translation into Ge'ez of various literary works from Greek and Arabic, for example, is attested from the fourth century BC. Needless to say, translation of the Holy Bible into Ge'ez constitutes the bulk of these activities, offering many interesting elements for linguistic as well as theological debate. It is also worth noting that these translation processes involved many books which are not part of the biblical tradition in Western Christianity and that, to date, the oldest sources for many crucial documents on the history of Western and Eastern Christianity are mainly available in Ge'ez translations (Bausi 2008). Moreover, as has been recently pointed out by Alessandro Bausi, these translation processes were not linear and involved the interaction and merging of different textual materials. As Bausi (2014, 18) states, by way of example, "Mediaeval Ethiopian scribes, much like their European brethren, used multiple textual sources (referred to as 'contamination')."

From the twelfth century, major political turmoil led to a shift in the centre of power from the areas where the Ge'ez civilization and culture had originally developed towards the South, namely towards areas where Amharic was the dominant language. Therefore, at least until the sixteenth century, there was a regime of linguistic dualism whereby Ge'ez was still the language of education, literacy and religion, whereas Amharic gained ground as the language spoken by most subjects of the empire – a sort of lingua franca confined to the domain of orality and flanked by a host of exclusively oral languages.

The hierarchical relationship among local languages in the region was also deeply influenced by translation processes. For instance, Amharic reached the status of a fully fledged written language around the seventeenth century, mainly as a reaction to Portuguese missionary encroachment. The Portuguese had landed on the African shores of the Red Sea in 1541 with the aim of joining forces with the Abyssinian Empire and containing the Ottoman presence in the Red Sea Region. Portuguese forces were soon followed by Jesuit missionaries, who launched an intense proselytizing campaign aimed at converting local Orthodox Christians to Catholicism. Translation of Ge'ez literature into Latin and dissemination of Catholic theological notions were the cornerstones of Jesuit activities in the region.

To counter the challenge to its spiritual hegemony, the Orthodox Church took a decisive step and started using Amharic to write its religious texts for catechism (Cerulli 1968). In fact, although Ge'ez remained the official language at court and was used until the nineteenth century for various religious and secular literary genres (hagiographies, royal chronicles and poetry), around the tenth century it gradually stopped being spoken and understood by the largely illiterate majority of the population. The Orthodox Church, therefore, started to translate the basic tenets of its theological thought into Amharic, freeing them from the elitist rarefactions of Ge'ez. After this, written Amharic was intensively used for religious teaching, which led to the development of a new literary genre. The so-called *andemta* (Cowley 1974) – that is, biblical commentaries – became increasingly diffused as a translation of the translation: they paraphrased and explained the Bible in Amharic based on the Ge'ez translation.

As a result, hierarchical relations among languages in the region were based on the predominance of Ge'ez and Amharic as written languages, while the others remained long confined to the domain of orality. Eventually, the nineteenth century was to mark the advent of Amharic as the dominant language used for both political and religious purposes, and also the slow development of written traditions for other languages.

Translation studies and Africa

The coexistence and reciprocal influence of so many languages across the vast continent of Africa has led to the multiplication of activities relating to translation in the broad sense defined above. Interlingual transfer processes within Africa as a whole and specific regions have often involved interaction between orality and literacy, in different ways. This may be one of the reasons why little attention has so far been devoted to the study of African translation practices in Western academia. Thus, the difficulties of mapping often uncodified processes of transfer, between languages themselves uncodified, has been a thorny issue for researchers.

Even today, the wealth of interlingual activities throughout Africa is inversely proportional to the attention they have received by translation studies scholars. In Europe and North America, the number of volumes devoted to the exploration of issues of translation pertaining to the African continent can be counted on one hand, while contributions by African scholars in Africa have only occasionally reached continental or even national borders. There have been, of course, several exceptions, as in the work of scholars from Cameroon (University of Buea) and South Africa. The latter has seen the flourishing of undergraduate and postgraduate translation courses at several universities, matched by intense research activities.[1] And yet, by and large, Africa still constitutes unexplored territory in terms of translation research, encouraging an overall tendency to consider it in monolithic terms. Among the aims of this article is the desire to counter such an attitude, highlighting not only Africa's great diversity from a historico-translational point of view, but also its agency in terms of interlingual and intercultural communication processes, which is often overlooked in studies born out of postcolonialism.

There is a growing body of writings from African diasporic intellectuals and thinkers concerning African literature, philosophy and cultural studies. Although imbued by postcolonial hybridity and sometimes personal/cultural bitterness, their contribution to enlivening the international debate is undeniable, as is the revival of African folklore which occasionally emerges as part of their work. The connections between orality and literacy, the role of translators (missionaries, informants, writers, ethnographers, intellectuals, all included) and the interactions between languages and cultures within and across the Horn of Africa will be discussed from a historical perspective in the next sections. More specifically, our analysis will proceed by referring to, and redefining, writing as translation and directionality.

Writing as translation

Valuable and varied contributions to the study of translation in Africa have been made by Paul Bandia (2008) in numerous essays as well as in the book *Translation as Reparation*. A key notion for Bandia (2006, 2008, 2009) is that of writing as translation in Africa. Referring almost exclusively to the postcolonial period and not specifically to any region or country, Bandia attaches a twofold meaning to this concept.

In his 2009 chapter in *Translation Studies in Africa*, Bandia says: "there is no doubt that translation has played an important role in ensuring communication and exchanges between the numerous linguistic and ethnocultural groups on the African continent", adding that "given the continent's vast oral traditions and the many non-alphabetized languages, the writing of these cultures can be viewed in terms of translation" (2009, 2). In this first definition, Bandia concentrates on written codification – that is, the textualization of orally transmitted languages, traditions and folklore on the part of missionaries, ethnographers and colonizers – while also referring to contacts between local cultures. His second definition of writing as translation concerns the writing of African europhone literature by African-born authors; that is, their transfer of values, ideas, traditions and attitudes originating in African contexts through a European language.

For his first definition, he draws inspiration from the long tradition of ethnographers, whose efforts were often, and are still, seen as translations. As John Sturrock (2010) observes in his essay "Writing Between the Lines: The Language of Translation", the work of ethnographers often revealed multiple writing-as-translation processes with the language of the indigenous people, which, being codified in writing, were subject to investigation. This occasionally led to spontaneous writing that was then translated into other languages. Sturrock cites the linguist/ethnographer Bronislaw Malinowski:

> We shall have in the first place to produce the texts, phrases, terminologies and formulae in native. Then we shall have to face the task of translating them. A word for word rendering is necessary to give a certain direct feeling of the language, which a free translation can in no way replace. But the literal translation is not sufficient. (1935, 10–11)

Through Malinowski's words, Sturrock highlights the multifarious and important translational work carried out by ethnographers. As Bandia (2009) also points out, they were essential for the codification of languages and cultures, although, as we shall see, they did not play a major role in the Horn of Africa as in other regions. Moreover, the first, systematic ethno-linguistic efforts are to be ascribed to the missionaries, the forerunners of recognized ethnographers and ethnography-as-translation.

Returning to Bandia's twofold definition and more specifically to its second part, the writing of europhone literature in Africa, or by African-born diasporic writers, undeniably implies multiple translation processes. Moreover, this activity has been constantly on the increase, taking up new forms and meanings, unforeseeable nuances and increasing visibility worldwide. A large number of African-born writers could be quoted here, writers who have more or less struggled with the acceptance of the use of English, French or other European languages as tools for cultural translation.

With reference to English, amongst those writers and intellectuals who have discussed their use of European languages, we have the contrasting attitudes of Nigerian-born Chinua Achebe and Kenyan Ngũgĩ wa Thiong'o. Achebe, who passed away in 2013, wrote repeatedly about his use of, and relationship with, English. If we refer to Schmied's (1991, 121) classification of the attitudes of non-European, postcolonial writers using European languages in their work, he may be classed among the so-called "adaptionists" – that is, those who accept English in Africa as a historical fact and consider it as a tool in their own hands. Achebe's attitude is aptly summarized as follows:

> Is it right that a man should abandon his mother tongue for someone else's? It looks like a dreadful betrayal and produces a guilty feeling. But for me there is no other choice. I have been given the language and I intend to use it. (1975, 55)

Perhaps the use of the word "adaptionist" is reductive. Achebe does not simply "adapt" to English, but actively seizes the language and makes it a tool for expression, for the sharing of experiences and feelings, bending it to his own expressive needs. Ngũgĩ wa Thiong'o, on the other hand, has frequently expressed his rejection of colonial/imperial languages, advocating a revival of African languages for all forms of expression. However, he has often written in English – he lives and works in an English-speaking country – which he uses for the purpose of a close, almost literal translation of his African culture and language:

> As a writer who believes in the utilization of African ideas, African philosophy and African folklore and imagery to the fullest extent possible, I am of the opinion the only way to use them effectively is to translate them almost literally from the African language native to the writer to whatever European language he is using as a medium. (1986, 8)

In addition, and perhaps more interestingly for our purposes, wa Thiong'o has recently dedicated several works to the appreciation of orality:

> There's a tendency to assume that knowledge, education, jurisprudence, and especially philosophy, come from the pen. This is because knowledge, the world over, reaches us through books.... Words don't come out of our mouths in written form; they come out as voice, spoken. The pen imitates the tongue. The pen is clerk to the tongue. It draws pictures of the spoken. The pen speaks the already spoken. (2013, 159–160)

In this vivid apology for orality, we can identify his wish to bring to light and revive the origins, and the richness, of African languages and cultures. He aims to promote their appreciation and study in an era in which colonialism and its aftermath seem to outshine any other aspect and period.

To sum up, the twofold definition offered by Bandia points to the enormous complexity of cross-lingual and cross-cultural interactions in Africa during and after colonization. This has been confirmed by the brief reference to the postcolonial anglophone writers Achebe and wa Thiong'o, whose attitudes hint at a very dynamic and complex domain, where translation processes are as frequent as they are diluted. However, there seems to be an overall tendency to see writing as translation largely as a vertical process, where the European ethnographers first, then writers and translators – and their languages – are always at the top of the axis. The next section aims to provide a wide spectrum of examples of writing as translation in the Horn of Africa, where verticality appears in complex forms and is far from being the exclusive structure that can be identified in translational processes.

Writing as translation in the Horn

In the Horn of Africa, the work of ethnographers-as-translators has always been marginal, overruled by the presence and influence of linguists, mainly belonging to the tradition of oriental studies. A special focus on the Christian Orient has been developed over the decades, this declination of the term "orientalism" having little in common with the more recent, Saidian-inspired approach.

As mentioned earlier, this region had already developed its own alphabet and its own written tradition by the fourth century AD. The language used at that time at court in town states such as Aksum, Adulis and Yeha was Ge'ez, which belongs to the South-Semitic branch of the Afroasiatic family like other languages still spoken in the Horn – Argobba, Gurage, Harari, Tigre and Tigrinya, for instance (Voigt 2005). Accordingly, Western scholars interested in the Horn of Africa could connect to the cultures of the region through the rich and long-established scholarly tradition of Semitic studies with its wealth of glottological, philological, palaeographic and comparative research. This led to the use of disciplinary tools that were not rooted in the conventional ethnographic method used in colonial Africa, but that echoed orientalist discourses. We would even go so far as to suggest that orientalist discourses were actually preceded by "Ethiopicist" experiences.

By way of example, consider the keen interest in Ge'ez and Amharic languages by German scholar Hiob Ludolph as early as the seventeenth century, when he came in contact with pilgrims from the Horn of Africa who travelled to Rome. Seminal works such as the *Grammatica Aethiopica* (Ludolph 1661, [1699] 1702), *Historia Aaethiopica* (Ludolph 1681), *Grammatica Linguae Amharicae* (Ludolph 1698a, 1698b), *Lexicon Amharico-latinum* (Ludolph 1698) and *Lexicon Aethiopico-latinum* (Ludolph 1699) all resulted from this experience. Ludolph's work has since represented a crucial, authoritative source for Western scholars interested in the Horn and constitutes evidence for the dialectic, horizontal nature of the exchange between European and African cultures in pre-colonial contexts. A crucial role in the development of Ludolph's linguistic and historical expertise in the region was played by S. Stefano Maggiore, a church in Rome that has received Ethiopian pilgrims since the fourteenth century (Leonessa 1929). Pilgrimage was instrumental in connecting Ethiopian Christianity with other Eastern and European forms, a custom that can be traced back to the tenth century. Pilgrims who originally ventured only to Jerusalem's holy sites began to opt for much longer itineraries, particularly to Rome (Cerulli, 1943–47).

In this regard, pilgrimage can be considered not only as a spiritual experience, but also as a process of exposure to, and translation of, cultures. Abba[2] Tesfatsion Malhaso, an Ethiopian priest who arrived in Rome at the beginning of the sixteenth century, was an exemplary pilgrim in this sense. A close friend of Pope Marcellus II and Pope Paul III, and trusted advisor to Ignatius Loyola, Abba Tesfatsion was instrumental in shaping the European vision of Ethiopian culture and politics. Moreover, impressed by the huge potential of the printing press, he designed the Ge'ez fonts that were used to print and publish the Ethiopian version of the New Testament. He also promoted the translation and publication of the Ethiopian liturgical canon in Latin. These texts reached the court at the Vatican and made a strong impression on Pope Paul III, to the extent that he sent copies of these books as presents to the major European royal courts of the day (Lefevre, 1969–70). With reference to the colonial context, the orientalist influence that partly shaped the encounter between Europe and the Horn of Africa also helps to explain why the overall majority of colonial (and not only colonial) scholars then active in the region had a background in Semitic and Oriental studies, and many were the product of the prestigious and still existing Istituto Universitario Orientale (originally established as "Collegio dei Cinesi" in the eighteenth century) in Naples.

To conclude, the considerable emphasis placed on the written traditions of the region and the consequent development of orientalist narratives point to yet another instance of verticality. Colonial scholars have tended to pay less attention to cultures and languages that did not have a written tradition, thus reinforcing internal verticality from powerful, written languages down to the unwritten but widely spoken local languages.

Directionality

This leads us naturally to the second of the two concepts expressed in translation studies with reference to Africa. Although not explicitly referred to as "directionality", this term appropriately sums up the issue raised by several scholars, in and outside translation studies, referring to the directions taken by the interlingual processes of textual and cultural transfer in Africa, before and after colonization. According to Bandia, directionality is expressed through the concepts of verticality and horizontality, the latter belonging to the pre-colonial period, and the former characterizing translation, and writing-as-translation processes, during and after colonization. As he writes:

> European colonization added another dimension to the vibrant intercultural activity on the African continent. In addition to the horizontal translation and intercultural activity among Africans themselves, and to some extent including the Arabic tradition, there was now a vertical translation practice, based on unequal power relations, between European and African language cultures. In this vertical relationship, translation became much more than a mere exchange of cultures or texts, and assumed an ideological basis which determined and influenced the orientation of translation in the recording and transcription of African oral culture in European languages, as well as in the conveyance of Western civilization in African society. (2009, 5)

Although referring to the "vibrant intercultural activity" characterizing the African continent before colonization, Bandia locates it, with its complexity and vibrancy, along a horizontal axis, thus suggesting that the pre-colonial period was generally characterized by egalitarian linguistic and cultural exchanges. On the other hand, as has been argued above, virtually all the complex processes of writing as translation that occurred during and after the arrival of the colonizers are seen as vertical, with European languages and cultures always occupying the top position. Thus, directionality seems to have been largely reduced to a perpendicular axis, so that it seems to be reductive even when viewed purely in light of the examples of interlingual and intercultural exchanges so far presented, and solely with reference to the Horn of Africa.

In our view, directionality in translation processes in Africa, and more specifically in the Horn, has to be seen in more complex terms that not only imply the possibility of *reversed* directionality, but must also cater for countless other relations and connections, intermediaries on the perpendicular axis, stretching beyond it, and often not even represented as straight lines.

As far back as 1993, Atangana Nama, advocating a thorough study of translation in Africa, spelled out some of the reasons for the development of mainly perpendicular approaches to the observation of translation processes. Stating that such a thorough study is not only ambitious, but virtually impossible if not developed "country by country" (1993, 414), he goes on to remind his readers that much more has been written since the advent of colonialism and that, unfortunately, what remains in written form tends to be seen as testimony to the past much more than the unwritten. In short, he seems to support the idea that translational interactions have come to be discussed much more with the arrival of the Europeans and their languages, and that the body of writings produced during and after colonization is relatively easier to obtain and study than precolonial writings. Secondly, Atangana Nama says that "the myth that translation and interpretation in Africa began with the advent of imperialism seems to have been embraced and concretized even in intellectual circles" (ibid.), suggesting that, even in Africa, the strength of Western-driven, postcolonial perspectives has sunk in, somehow levelling out the study of these and other phenomena and fuelling a certain disregard for pre-colonial, African history. In our opinion, if the concept of translation is to be expanded when looking at African interlingual and intercultural activities, by the same token the research horizon must be broadened, pushed well beyond colonization and observed in all its complexity, which has to be represented more like an array of straight and curved lines than as a perpendicular axis. The next section provides further evidence of the rich and complex directionality of interlingual and intercultural processes within the Horn of Africa, also highlighting the fact that, even during colonization, the colonizers' language and culture did not often play a dominant role.

The Horn of Africa: Directionality revisited

Verticality and horizontality in translation processes had been seen in the Horn of Africa well before colonization, taking on a multitude of different forms. In terms of horizontality, beyond the overall pattern identified by Bandia, we might recall the translations of texts from Latin into Ge'ez and from Ge'ez into Latin that were carried out by the Portuguese Jesuits during the sixteenth and seventeenth centuries.

Although these translation activities were mainly instrumental to the religious community to resolve internal conflicts (Pennec 2003), they nonetheless contributed to the dissemination of religious and linguistic traditions in the region. We have already pointed out concerning verticality that the hegemonic role firstly of Ge'ez, and later Amharic, had a strong influence on the other African languages spoken in the region, which were long confined to ordinary domestic spheres. Furthermore, these other African languages were codified largely in the colonial period, proving that the strong, vertical pressure from Ge'ez and Amharic on these languages came to be reviewed and progressively subverted with the influence of colonialism, but not necessarily with the intervention of the colonizers' language and culture.

When discussing directionality in the Horn, we cannot avoid referring to the religious sphere. If Ge'ez and Amharic have been essential for the spreading and support of Christianity (Tamrat 1972; Crummey 2000), which was dominant in the region, Islam was also widespread as a result of centuries-long contacts with the Muslim world (Gori 2006). The strong identification of Ge'ez and Amharic as languages of Christian power has, for a long time, led Muslim communities, particularly those where Amharic was not their mother tongue, to try and overcome this regime of verticality by resorting to Arabic. In fact, the common feeling was that the overwhelming predominance of Ge'ez and Amharic with their wealth of written texts could not be countered with languages that still did not enjoy the status of written languages and that, even when they did, could not compete fairly. Therefore, for these Muslim communities, Arabic was perceived as the only successful alternative, also by virtue of its prestigious written tradition, which was richer and more widespread than that of Ge'ez and Amharic.

Interestingly enough, this centuries-long overlap of religious and linguistic identities was increasingly subverted from the end of the nineteenth century, when scholars noticed a new pattern of Muslim proselytism that resorted to Amharic instead of Arabic (Cerulli 1926). This dramatic change in attitude has been explained as the result of the development of Amharic as a lingua franca well beyond its original boundaries, and therefore much more useful to illiterate audiences for whom Arabic was unintelligible (Drewes 2007).

Western modernity[3] in the Horn was characterized by the preservation of age-old verticality as well as by the introduction of new forms of directionality. With reference to missionaries and colonial authorities, let us recall here that, in their official communications, they complied with pre-existing vertical relationships by using Amharic and Arabic rather than their own languages. However, this also implied introducing a new, somewhat paradoxical form of horizontality: by using Amharic and later Tigrinya for official correspondence, the colonizers put their own language – that is, Italian – on the same level as those languages, acknowledging their usefulness. There is ample evidence (Chelati Dirar, Gori, and Taddia 1997) of the use of local languages even well past the colonial occupation, at a time when one would have expected the implementation of Italian as the language of power and official communication.

On another front, the intensive normative activity carried out by first missionaries, and then colonial authorities, dramatically reshaped the region's linguistic landscape. This process started from the early nineteenth century, with the leading role of Protestant missionaries, particularly from the Swedish Evangelical Mission (Evangeliska-Fosterlands Stiftelsen), and resulted in the production of grammars, manuals and the translation of religious material including the Bible. In this process, besides Amharic – with its first translation of the Bible, previously accessible only in Ge'ez – other languages spoken in the Horn moved from the oral to the written world. This was the case with Tigrinya and Tigre, both languages belonging to the Afro-Semitic tradition just as Kunama and Oromo belonged to the Nilo-Saharan and Cushitic families respectively. However, writing grammars and translating religious and pedagogical material was not a neutral intervention. First of all, missionaries wrote grammars and translated texts into one of the many varieties of the local language, normally that used in the area where they were based. By so doing, they also introduced verticality within the same language, giving prominence to one variety over the others. Moreover, the linguistic activities carried out by missionaries altered inherited relations of verticality among the local languages, which also implied a challenge to linguistic and political identities. It is interesting to note here that, in some cases, local communities were not enthusiastic about the introduction of new relations of horizontality among their languages. For centuries, only certain languages had been deemed appropriate to convey religious messages, for instance, whereas others were perceived as suitable only for mundane and more trivial purposes. As pointed out by the Swedish historian Gustaf Arén, with reference to the debate on the translation of the Bible into Tigrinya, many of the Eritrean priests as well as informants and assistants of the Swedish Mission "protested that Tigrinya was devoid of theological concepts and thereby unfit for religious use; Amarinya was by far to be preferred as a vehicle of spiritual truth" (Arén 1978, 332).

On the colonial front, an interesting example comes from Eritrea. Alongside the introduction of Italian for teaching in colonial/missionary schools, the colonial administration deliberately pushed for the strengthening of Tigrinya as a local language so as to counter the influence of Imperial Ethiopia through its lingua franca, Amharic. Martino Mario Moreno, one of the most important Italian scholars and colonial administrators, states:

> In old Eritrea the largest part of the Christian population speaks Tigrinya. When we occupied the country, this language was hardly ever found in written form, due to the overall illiteracy as well as to the dominant role played by the official language of the rulers: Amharic. Italy has drawn it out of the shadows, teaching how to read and write it. The Franciscan Catholic Mission, which runs a large number of schools, has collaborated with the Government by publishing a large number of schoolbooks and religious texts that have aroused passion among many readers. (Moreno 1939, 35, our translation)

All these examples and reflections would indicate the need for a wider approach to directionality in translation processes, in the Horn as well as in Africa as a whole.

A closer look at a few texts

To further support the claims made above, and bring our interdisciplinary analysis forward, we shall now focus on three outstanding instances of translation processes recorded in the Horn of Africa well before colonization and after its onset. A first example is provided by the *The Fisalgwos*, a Ge'ez translation of the Greek *Physiologos* attested to have been produced during the fifth century. The *Physiologos* (originally written between the end of the second century and the beginning of the third in Alexandria) was a description of animals, stones and plants, each assuming symbolic or moral values, and was extremely popular in both Eastern and Western Christendom. It has been one of the main sources of Christian symbolism (e.g. the phoenix as symbol of Christ's resurrection), which made it the most translated book after the Bible throughout the Middle Ages. The Ge'ez version is the closest to the Greek original and was probably completed in Egypt by an Ethiopian monk in a Skete monastery. The translation of this book had a twofold impact. On the one hand, it fitted successfully with the cultural landscape of Ethiopian Christianity deeply imbued as it was with a culture of symbolism, while, on the other, this religious tradition was linked with a larger community both in the Eastern and Western Christendom, with whom their religious values and symbolism were shared.

A second example is *The History of High Ethiopia or Abassia (Historia de Ethiopia a Alta ou Abassia)*,[4] by Manoel de Almeida, a Portuguese Jesuit missionary who had travelled to Ethiopia in 1624. This book was largely an interpretation and rewriting (recodification) of a previous work, *Historia de Ethiopia*, written by Father Pero Paez around 1622 and never published (Pennec 2003).[5] De Almeida relied heavily upon Ge'ez materials such as the Royal Chronicles and a *History of the Galla (Zēnāhū lagāllā)*, written in 1593 by Bahrey, who was an Orthodox monk. Bahrey's book was a history of the Oromo people, referred to at the time as Galla. This text has been greatly appreciated because, although reflecting the Amharas' (people speaking Amharic) perception of the Oromo, it went beyond the conventional genres of the time (hagiography and chronicles), producing a detailed historiographic reconstruction of the Oromo expansion in the sixteenth century and constituting a major source of knowledge concerning this people until the eighteenth century and beyond (Gusarova 2009). In translational terms, De Almeida's book can be seen as a double translation. On the one hand, as mentioned above, it is a rewriting of Paez's *Historia de Ethiopia*, in terms that were more appropriate for the Jesuit hierarchy and their missionary goals; on the other, he relies heavily on Ge'ez sources and therefore tends to project an image of Ethiopia that is heavily influenced by the Ge'ez-Amhara-Christian discourse.

A third example is offered by Johannes Kolmodin, a Swedish orientalist and linguist (and therefore not involved in Italian colonial administration),[6] who transcribed Tigrinya oral traditions pertaining to the history of the populations of the rival villages of Hazzega and Tsazzega never previously codified. Kolmodin's (1912) *Traditions de Hazzegaet Tsazzega*[7] remains a seminal work for the history of Eritrea from the seventeenth to the nineteenth centuries and an outstanding example of ethno-linguistic and philological research (Negash 1999; Gebremedhin 2011). From the perspective of our discussion on directionality, Kolmodin's work is also extremely relevant as it raises important issues. One issue deals with methodology, and is treated in great detail in the introduction, which he wrote in French. Kolmodin begins by explaining his method, based on fieldwork among local communities with the support of local informants and advisors, whom he acknowledges individually,[8] something that was not particularly common in those years. Kolmodin then points out that when transcribing the oral traditions, he had consciously adopted a Tigrinya standard based on the language used by his informants, differing from that used by both Catholic and Swedish missionaries active in other areas. By so doing, he raises another important issue, that of the written codification of Tigrinya, which could be seen as a challenge to the supremacy of Amharic through a variety of this vernacular language that came directly from its speakers. Finally, Kolmodin's book is also relevant as he ignores (or challenges) existing notions of verticality within the Italian colony, and after having been published in 1912 the Tigrinya version of his *Traditions de Hazzega et Tsazzega* was published in a French translation in 1914 (Kolmodin, 1915), thus ignoring the language of the colonial ruler.

Conclusion

The last three examples seem to confirm that the approach defined within this article is appropriate for the analysis of translation processes in Africa, or part of it, whether these processes involve what is normally assumed to be "translation proper" (from one language into another), the writing of orally transmitted languages and cultures, or the production of europhone literature in and on Africa. The strength of such an approach lies in its interdisciplinary nature, whereby translation phenomena, broad though they are, are seen as embedded in historical events, or as historical landmarks themselves.

One of the aims of this article has been to push the observation spectrum beyond the all-too-commonly discussed colonial context, examining the rich history of interlingual and intercultural exchanges in the Horn and the whole of Africa over the centuries before colonialism. Another aim, which goes hand in hand with the first, has been to highlight African agency in translation processes, before but also *during* and *after* colonization. As a further development, these aims could be pursued by looking at today's landscape; namely, at the way in which directionality in translation is yet again challenged by the penetration of African languages within European countries, cultures and languages, what Ali and Alamin Mazrui refer to as "linguistic counter-penetration":

> Yet another factor that may aid the continued survival of some indigenous African languages is a more global one: *linguistic counter-penetration* engendered by the African diaspora. Just as Western languages have penetrated deep into the African continent, the growth of the African diaspora in Canada, Europe and the USA has enabled African languages to begin counter-penetrating the West. (1998, 47, emphasis added)

Although perhaps not consciously, linguistic counter-penetration does involve African agency, which other scholars are also emphasizing, in other forms and on other fronts. Ghirmai Negash, for instance, like many other contemporary African writers and translators, advocates the systematic translation into Western languages of literary works written in African languages,

> for indeed, although most of the great postcolonial writings in African literature are coded in European languages, and African-language literatures are not habitually associated with "serious" writing, [they] demonstrate the capability of African-language literatures to carry the larger "political" and "quotidian" realities of Africa as they evolve across historical time and – often fiercely contested – social space(s). (2009, 87)

However, in addition to looking at today's directionality in translation and writing-as-translation in Africa and on Africa and the desire never to lose sight of African agency, interdisciplinary studies like this one ought to promote the systematic investigation of interlingual and intercultural exchanges "country by country", to use Atangana's phrase, thus building a solid history of translation in Africa.

Notes

1. Consider, among others, the teaching and research activity carried out at Stellenbosch University, North-West University, University of South Africa and University of the Witwatersrand in Johannesburg.
2. In Ge'ez, Amharic and Tigrinya, *abba* means "father". In religious terms, it is commonly used to address priests and monks.
3. With Western modernity we refer to the complex interplay of missionaries, explorers, scholars and colonial administrators who were active in the region starting from the late eighteenth century. Moreover, with this broad, open-ended term we aim to refer to processes and events that are much wider than those usually implied by "colonialism".
4. De Almeida's book was published posthumously in an abridged version in 1660.
5. Pero Paes' book was published only three centuries later, in 1903, by the Jesuit Camillo Beccari (Beccari, 1903). It was commissioned from Paes by his superiors as a Jesuit answer to two previous works written 1610–11 by Dominican theologian Luis de Urreta, who maintained that Ethiopian Christians were not schismatic but belonged de facto to the Catholic Church. This declaration was considered by the Jesuit leadership to constitute a dangerous challenge, and Urreta's argument delegitimized their argument in favour of deep missionary involvement in the Horn. However, Jesuit authorities did not appreciate Paes' handling of his task and asked De Almeida to rewrite the book. In this regard, see Pennec (2003, 245–248, 264–268).
6. Eventually Kolmodin was recruited as an advisor by the Ethiopian Emperor Haile Selassie and worked in this capacity in Addis Ababa at the Ministry of Foreign Affairs from 1931 until his death in 1933 (Halldin Norberg 1977).
7. Kolmodin (1914) also published a critical edition of Ge'ez manuscripts dealing with the history of the Tsazzega and Hazzega families.
8. Kolmodin (1912) mentions Bahta Tesfa Yohannes and Tewolde Medhin Gebremedhin. The latter was to play a crucial role in the development of the Tigrinya language as well as in the cultural and political history of Eritrea and Ethiopia.

References

Achebe, Chinua. 1975. "The African Writer and the English Language." In *Morning Yet on Creation Day*, edited by Chinua Achebe, 55–62. London: Heinemann.

Ahmed, Hussein. 2009. "The Coming of Age of Islamic Studies in Ethiopia: The Present State of Research and Publication." In *Proceedings of the 16th International Conference of Ethiopian Studies*, edited by Svein Ege Harald, 449–455. Trondheim: Norwegian University of Science and Technology.

Arén, Gustav. 1978. *Evangelical Pioneers in Ethiopia: Origins of the Evangelical Church MekaneYesus*. Stockholm: EFS.

Atangana Nama, Charles. 1993. "Historical, Theoretical and Terminological Perspectives of Translation in Africa." *META*, 38 (3): 414–425. doi:10.7202/003693ar.

Avanzini, Alessandra. 2005. "Gəʿəz Inscriptions in Ethiopia/Eritrea in Antiquity." In *Encyclopaedia Aethiopica*, vol. 2, edited by Siegbert Uhlig et al., 159b–162a. Wiesbaden: Harrassowitz.

Bandia, Paul. 2006. "African Europhone Literature and Writing as Translation. Some Ethical Issues." In *Translating Others (Vol. 2)*, edited by Theo Hermans, 349–364. Manchester: St. Jerome Publishing.

Bandia, Paul. 2008. *Translation as Reparation: Writing and Translation in Postcolonial Africa*. Manchester: St Jerome.

Bandia, Paul. 2009. "Translation Matters: Linguistic and Cultural Representation." In *Translation Studies in Africa*, edited by Judith Inggs and Libby Meintjes, 1–20. London: Continuum.

Bausi, Alessandro. 2008. "La Tradizione Scrittoria Etiopica." *Segno e Testo*, 6: 507–557.

Bausi, Alessandro. 2014. "Writing, Copying, Translating: Ethiopia as a Manuscript Culture.' In *Manuscript Cultures: Mapping the Field*, edited by Jörg Quenzer and Jan-Ulrich Sobisch, 35–75. New York: Walter de Gruyter.

Beccari, Camillo. 1903. *Notizia e Saggi di Opere e Documenti Inediti Riguardanti la Storia di Etiopia durante i Secoli XVI, XVII e XVIII*. Roma: Casa editrice Italiana.

Brodzki, Bella. 2007. *Can These Bones Live? Translation, Survival and Cultural Memory*. Stanford: Stanford University Press.

Cerulli, Enrico. 1926. "Canti Amarici dei Musulmani di Abissinia." *Rendiconti della Reale Accademia Nazionale dei Lincei*, serie 6, 2: 433–47.

Cerulli, Enrico. 1943–47. *Etiopi in Palestina. Storia della Comunità Etiopica a Gerusalemme*. Roma: Libreria dello Stato.

Cerulli, Enrico. 1968. *La Letteratura Etiopica*. Milano: Sansoni.

Chelati Dirar, Uoldelul, Alessandro Gori, and Irma Taddia. 1997. *Lettere Tigrine. I Documenti Etiopici del Fondo Ellero*. Torino: l'Harmattan Italia.

Cowley, Roger. 1974. "Old Testament Introduction in the Andemta Commentary Tradition." *Journal of Ethiopian Studies* 12 (1): 133–175.

Crummey, Donald. 2000. *Land and Society in the Christian Kingdom of Ethiopia: From the Thirteenth to the Twentieth Century*. Urbana-Champaign: University of Illinois Press.

Di Giovanni, Elena. 2013. "Writing as Translation in Africa: The Case of Hama Tuma." *TEXTUS, Global Literatures and Translation* 26 (3): 77–96.

Drewes, Abraham Johannes. 2007. "Amharic as a Language of Islam." *Bulletin of the School of Oriental and African Studies* 70 (1): 1–62.

Gebremedhin, Ezra. 2011. "Zanta Tsazzegan Hazzegan: Johannes Kolmodin's Contributions to an Understanding of Eritrean Highland Culture." In *The Last Dragoman: Swedish Orientalist Johannes Kolmodin as Scholar, Activist and Diplomat*, edited by Elizabeth Ozdalga, 71–82. Istanbul: Swedish Research Institute in Istanbul.

Gori, Alessandro. 2006. *Contatti Culturali nell'Oceano Indiano e nel Mar Rosso e Processi di Islamizzazione in Etiopia e Somalia*. Venezia: Cafoscarina.

Gori, Alessandro. 2007. "Arabic Manuscripts." In *Encyclopaedia Aethiopica*, vol. 3, edited by Siegbert Uhlig et al., 744–749. Wiesbaden: Harrassowitz.

Gusarova, Ekaterina. 2009. "The Oromo as Recorded in Ethiopian Literature." In *Proceedings of the 16th International Conference of Ethiopian Studies*, edited by Svein Ege, Harald Aspen, Birhanu Teferra, and Shiferaw Bekele, 1323–1332. Trondheim: Norwegian University of Science and Technology.

ORALITY AND TRANSLATION

Halldin Norberg, Viveca. 1977. *Swedes in Haile Selassie's Ethiopia (1924–1951)*. Uppsala: Nordiska Africainstitutet.

Holmes, James. 1972. *The Name and Nature of Translation Studies*. Amsterdam: Translation Studies Section, Department of General Literary Studies, University of Amsterdam.

Inggs, Judith, and Libby Meintjes, eds. 2009. *Translation Studies in Africa*. London: Continuum, 2009.

Kolmodin, Johannes. 1912. *Traditions de Hazzega et Tsazzega*. Textes Tigrigna. Roma: C. De Luigi.

Kolmodin, Johannes. 1914. *Traditions de Hazzega et Tsazzega*. Annales et documents. Uppsala: Berling.

Kolmodin, Johannes. 1915. *Traditions de Hazzega et Tsazzega*. Traduction française. Uppsala: Appelberg.

Lefevre, Renato. 1969–70. "Documenti e Notizie su TasfäSeyon e la sua Attività Romana nel Secolo XVI." *Rassegna di Studi Etiopici* 24: 74–133.

Leonessa, Mauro da. 1929. *Santo Stefano Maggiore degli abissini e le Relazioni Romano-etiopiche*. Città del Vaticano: Tipografia Poliglotta.

Ludolph, Hiob. 1661. *Grammatica Aethiopica*. London: Roycroft.

Ludolph, Hiob. (1699) 1702. *Grammatica Aethiopica*. 2nd ed. Frankfurt am Mainz: Zunner.

Ludolph, Hiob. 1681. *Historia Aethiopica*. Frankfurt am Mainz: B. C. Wust für J. D. Zunnerum.

Ludolph, Hiob. 1698a. *Grammatica Linguae Amharicae*. Frankfurt am Mainz: Martinus Jacquetus.

Ludolph, Hiob. 1698b. *Lexicon Amharico-latinum*. Frankfurt am Mainz: Martinus Jacquetus.

Ludoph, Hiob. 1699. *Lexicon Aethiopico-latinum*. Frankfurt am Mainz: J. D. Zunnerum.

Malinowski, Bronislaw. 1935. *Coral Gardens and their Magic*. Vol. 2. London: Allen & Unwin.

Mazrui, Ali A., and Alamin M. Mazrui. 1998. *The power of Babel : language & governance in the African experience*. Oxford: James Currey.

Moreno, Martino Mario. 1939. "Evoluzione dei Linguaggi Indigeni a Contatto della Civiltà e Formazione delle Lingue Indigene Letterarie e Ufficiali in Africa." In *Atti del convegno Internazionale sul Tema: L'Africa, Roma 4–11 Ottobre 1938, Reale Accademia d'Italia*, 571–591. Roma: Fondazione A. Volta.

Negash, Ghirmai. 1999. *A History of Tigrinya Literature in Eritrea: The Oral and the Written 1890–1991*. Leiden: Research School of Asian, African and American Studies (CNWS), Universiteit Leiden.

Negash, Ghirmai. 2009. "Native Intellectuals in the Contact Zone: African Responses to Italian Colonialism in Tigrinya Literature." *Biography* 32 (1): 74–88.

Ngũgĩ wa Thiong'o. 1986. *Decolonizing the Mind: The Politics of Language in English Literature*. London: Longman.

Ngũgĩ wa Thiong'o. 2013. "Tongue and Pen: A Challenge to Philosophers from Africa." *Journal of African Cultural Studies* 25 (2), 158–163.

Quirke, Stephen. 2006. "Translation Choices across Five Thousand Years: Egyptian, Greek and Arabic Libraries in a Land of Many Languages." In *Translating Others*, edited by Theo Hermans, vol. 2, 265–282. Manchester: St Jerome.

Pennec, Hervé. 2003. *Des Jésuites au Royaume du Prêtre Jean*. Paris: Centre Culturel Calouste Gulbenkian.

Schmied, Joseph. 1991. *English in Africa: An Introduction*. London: Longman Linguistics Library.

Sturrock, John. 2010. "Writing Between the Lines: The Language of Translation". In *Critical Readings in Translation Studies*, edited by Mona Baker, 49–64. London: Routledge.

Tamrat, Taddesse. 1972. *Church and State in Ethiopia (1270–1527)*. Oxford: Clarendon Press.

Voigt, Rainer. 2005. "Ethio-Semitic." In *Encyclopaedia Aethiopica*, vol. 2, edited by Siegbert Uhlig et al., 440–444. Wiesbaden: Harrassowitz.

Orality, trauma theory and interlingual translation: A study of repetition in Ahmadou Kourouma's *Allah n'est pas obligé*

Kathryn Batchelor

Centre for Translation and Comparative Cultural Studies, University of Nottingham, UK

> The use of stylistic devices based around repetition in Ahmadou Kourouma's *Allah n'est pas obligé* is usually taken as one of the markers of the novel's link to oral storytelling traditions. It is, however, equally feasible to read such devices as markers of trauma, linking them, for example, to therapeutic storytelling and to the development of inner schemata adequate to the traumatic experience. This article presents a reading of *Allah n'est pas obligé* that seeks to combine the concepts of translation-of-orality and translation-of-trauma, thus contributing to ongoing discussions around the postcolonializing of trauma theory. It also explores the implications of such a reading for postcolonial translation theory, and particularly the theorization of the translation of orality-inflected literature.

The relevance of oral storytelling traditions to Ahmadou Kourouma's oeuvre has long been acknowledged, not only by a large number of critics, but also by Kourouma himself. For many critics, the simple fact that Kourouma's novels are works of African literature is sufficient to link them to oral traditions, since in their view African European-language literature can be viewed as "a hybrid product which is looking inward into African orature and outward into imported literary traditions" (Zabus 2007, 5). Peter Vakunta (2010, 78), for example, whilst acknowledging the multiplicity of genre and performance styles in the oral tradition, argues that "orality functions as the matrix of African mode [sic] of discourse", and offers an extended analysis of the oral poetics of Kourouma's first novel, *Les Soleils des indépendances*. Kourouma himself repeatedly stressed the relevance of *oralité* to his work, both in terms of the overall structures adopted in his novels and in the details of syntax and lexis. In an interview accorded to Jean Ouédraogo, for example, he outlines the specific oral narrative technique adopted in each of his first three novels:

> In *The Suns of Independences* I follow the model of the *palabres*.... In *Monnew*, we are dealing with an epic, the main protagonist is a king, and in Africa, this domain belongs to the *griot*. Hence my borrowing of the *griot's* technique. With regard to ... *En Attendant le Vote des Bêtes sauvages*, I chose to situate the action in the midst of a hunting society. I am, therefore, using the technique of what we call the hunters' *griot* or *sèrè*. Each time, there was a correlation to the protagonist. (Ouédraogo 2000, 1338–1339)

ORALITY AND TRANSLATION

While the link between *Allah n'est pas obligé* and a particular African narrative technique is not as clear in this fourth novel as it is in Kourouma's first three novels – the protagonist is a child and, as the narrator himself acknowledges, children invariably fulfil the role of listener, rather than speaker, in traditional Malinke society – the fictionalized construction of an oral context for the novel is no less present. It is fully revealed in the final paragraphs of the novel, when the protagonist Birahima is invited to tell his older cousin all that he has seen and done, and Birahima explains that he settled down comfortably and started to "conter [ses] salades" [tell his stories] (Kourouma 2000, 224) "for a couple of days" (Kourouma 2006, 215).[1] His final words turn out to be the opening words of the novel, revealing that the whole tale has been told in response to the cousin's invitation. This fictionalized construct of the text's oral nature is evoked at various points elsewhere in the novel, with Birahima commanding his audience to "sit down and listen" (Kourouma 2006, 12) before launching into the main part of his tale, and declaring at various points that he is too tired, or can't be bothered to say any more "today" (42). Many of the lexical and syntactic features identified by Kourouma (1997a, 1997b), Gyasi (2006), Bandia (2008), Vakunta (2010) and others as being characteristic of the oralization of written literature and more specifically as being markers of oral discourse in Kourouma's earlier novels are also present in *Allah n'est pas obligé*: these include direct interaction with the reader, exclamations, ideophones, proverbs, refrains, evocations of the trickster figure (most obviously in Yacouba, Birahima's companion), parallelism and repetition.

In these respects, it is undoubtedly appropriate to view *Allah n'est pas obligé* as an instance of what Bandia terms "intercultural writing as translation" or, in other words, as an example of "translation from an oral-tradition discourse into a written one" (2008, 38). However, it is equally feasible to read Kourouma's novel under another critical paradigm that has drawn on the metaphorical notion of translation, namely that of the translation of trauma, or pain, into writing. This paradigm is developed by Madelaine Hron in connection with representations of immigrant experiences in literature: drawing on Roman Jakobson's (1959) typology, she argues that "pain can be conceived of as a system of signs ... the translation of pain may be deemed to be a form of 'intersemiotic translation' " (Hron 2009, 40). Hron argues that this kind of translation, which she also refers to as a "rhetorics of pain" (48) is "most apparent in the use of language – the grammatical syntax, style, and arsenal of literary techniques" (48). Her indicative list of the kinds of techniques associated with a rhetorics of pain shows a clear overlap with many of the stylistic features that are often linked to translations of orality in African writing, and includes "exclamations, rhetorical questions, or repetitive declarative statements ... [r]epetition, fragmentation, or the use of ellipses ... [t]he *epimone*, or frequent repetition of a phrase or question for emphasis" (48–49).

This overlap in what we might term the "surface features" of translations from two different kinds of source text, or "metatext" (Tymoczko 1999, 24) – orality in the first case, trauma or pain in the second – is undoubtedly relevant to Kourouma's *Allah n'est pas obligé*, telling as it does of a child's experiences in one of the most brutal civil wars of the twentieth century. Furthermore, the fictionalized construction of an oral context for the novel, outlined above, offers a significant impulse for reading the novel as a translation-of-trauma rather than simply as a translation-of-orality, for when Birahima tells the reader to sit down and listen, he follows this with a further command: "And write everything down" (Kourouma 2006, 5). This command goes some way to explaining the apparent inconsistency in the supposed oral nature of his tale which emerges when Birahima states: "The dictionaries are for looking up big words .... I need to be able to explain stuff because I want all sorts of different people to *read* my bullshit" (3, my emphasis). This scenario, according to which the tale is not simply an instance of oral storytelling, but more precisely an instance of dictation, evokes the possibility of reading Birahima's story as testimony.[2] This possibility is further supported by Birahima's repeated assertions that what he is saying is true, as well as by the occasional expression of anxiety that he will not be believed.

In this article, I shall first explore the potential for reading *Allah n'est pas obligé* along these lines, working primarily within a trauma theory framework, and focussing in particular on aspects of the text that are characterized by repetition, a stylistic device that, in African fiction at least, has a strong tendency to be interpreted as a marker of oral discourse. In its attempt to theorize an orality-inflected narrativization of trauma, this article may be viewed as a continuation of Craps and Buelens' project which sought to "examine where and how trauma studies can break with Eurocentrism" (2008, 2). In the second part of the article, I shall explore the implications of this "'postcolonializing' [of] trauma studies" (3) for postcolonial translation theory, asking whether reading texts such as *Allah n'est pas obligé* in this way alters our evaluations of the relative success or failure of efforts at interlingual translation of orality-inflected literature.

Trauma theory

Within the broad body of approaches to the study of trauma that make up the diverse field of trauma studies, it is the "therapeutic current" (Visser 2011, 274) associated most notably with Judith Herman's (1992*)* *Trauma and Recovery* as opposed to the "aporetic current" developing out of the view that trauma is in essence unspeakable, that is most obviously relevant to a reading of *Allah n'est pas obligé*. Birahima is chatty, voluble or, in his own words, a child who "talk[s] too much" (Kourouma 2006, 3); his narrative is characterized by an excess of words, rather than a retreat into silence; and when he consigns an episode to silence he states not that the episode *cannot* be spoken about, but that he does not *wish* to speak about it.[3] This emphasis on control is apparent from the very opening words of the novel, in which Birahima declares: "Je décide le titre définitif et complet de mon blablabla" [I'm deciding the full and definitive title of my blablabla] (Kourouma 2000, 9), and is characteristic of the novel as a whole. His narrative thus tallies with Herman's vision of storytelling as a way of restoring "a sense of efficacy and power", reversing the "helplessness [that] constitutes the essential insult of trauma" (2001, 41). Herman's view of therapeutically successful storytelling as being "an organized, detailed, verbal account, oriented in time and historical context" (177) as opposed to a confusion of "frozen imagery and sensation" (175) also ties in with the kind of account presented in *Allah n'est pas obligé*, even if some elements of what Herman would view as earlier, unsuccessful attempts are nevertheless present in Birahima's rendition.

Furthermore, Herman's locating of trauma in the event itself, rather than in the response to an event – a definition preferred by scholars such as Cathy Caruth (1996) – provides a more convincing justification for a trauma theory-based analysis of

ORALITY AND TRANSLATION

Birahima's narrative, allowing us to start from the premise that the events described by Birahima, which include "exposure to extreme violence" and "witnessing grotesque death", are among those "certain identifiable experiences" (Herman 2001, 34) that increase the likelihood of psychological trauma. In other words, it is not the identification of a trauma-inflected response that justifies the use of the critical paradigm, but rather the nature of the narrated events themselves and the positing of the narrative as testimony. To some extent, this represents a way out of the conundrum of depending on Eurocentric formulations of textual strategies deemed appropriate for the representation of traumatic experiences – many of which may not be appropriate to African novels whose primary links may be to oral traditions rather than modernist and postmodernist forms – in order to justify the use of the trauma theory paradigm.[4]

According to Herman's model, the transformation of trauma into restorative storytelling can only take place once safety has been established for the trauma survivor. Here, too, there are resonances with *Allah n'est pas obligé*, even if the kind of safety that Birahima achieves is rather more flimsy than the kind of safety achieved by survivors in Herman's Western model: Birahima is seated in his wealthy cousin's four-wheel-drive car, putting ever more physical distance between himself and the war zone; his return to safety is marked not only by the thrice repeated "la route était rectilingue" [the road was straight] (Kourouma 2000, 222–223), but also by the older cousin's tender term of address, "petit Birahima" [little Birahima] (224), and his gentle invitation, "dis-moi, dis-moi" [tell me, tell me] (ibid.).

Other aspects of Herman's theory, which is elaborated primarily in terms of its relevance to psychotherapeutic practice, and includes discussion of survivor–therapist interaction during the storytelling process, are clearly less directly relevant to *Allah n'est pas obligé*. Nevertheless, Herman's paradigm offers a useful framework within which to analyse Birahima's narrative, and in the section that follows I shall draw on it to propose an alternative trauma-based reading of specific features of the narrative – notably, features involving some element of repetition – that are usually taken as indicative of the underlying orality of Kourouma's work.

Repetition as therapeutic storytelling

Parallelism and the closely related device of anadiplosis are frequently taken as markers par excellence of oral discourse. Ruth Finnegan (1977, 127), for example, notes that some scholars "unequivocally regard repetition (including parallelism and formulaic expressions) as characteristic of oral literature [and] even the yardstick by which the oral text can definitely be distinguished from written literature". In *Allah n'est pas obligé*, Kourouma makes striking use of parallelism and anadiplosis in Birahima's narrations of particularly traumatic experiences. The first of these concerns Birahima's account of the burning of his arm as a child:

> Je suis allé trop vite, trop loin, je ne voulais pas me faire rattraper. J'ai foncé, j'ai bousculé dans la braise ardente. La braise ardente a fait son travail, elle a grillé mon bras. Elle a grillé le bras d'un pauvre enfant comme moi parce que Allah n'est pas obligé d'être juste dans toutes les choses qu'il fait sur terre. (Kourouma 2000, 14–15).
> [I went too quickly, too far, I didn't want to get caught. I tore along, I fell into the burning embers. The burning embers did their work, they grilled my arm. They grilled the arm of a poor child like me because Allah is not obliged to be fair in all the things he does on earth.]

ORALITY AND TRANSLATION

In this passage, Kourouma accumulates parallel syntactic structures in the build-up to the burning ("Je suis allé trop vite ... je ne voulais pas ... J'ai foncé, j'ai bousculé"), and draws on anadiplosis to speak of the burning event itself ("la braise ardente. La braise ardente ... elle a grillé mon bras. Elle a grillé le bras"). That this event is particularly traumatizing for Birahima is signalled explicitly in his account: it is the first thing that he thinks to relate about his life story, it continues to dominate his thinking, in the manner of the "indelible image" (Herman 2001, 38) described by trauma theorists,[5] and he has a physical reaction, reliving his feelings of pain and fear, when he tells the story.

Another tale that is narrated by drawing heavily on the devices of parallelism and anadiplosis is that of one of Birahima's child-soldier friends, Kik. The events that lead to Kik's death are told as part of the more general narrative of the child-soldiers' journey to the ULIMO (United Liberation Movement of Liberia for Democracy) camp, and are then retold in the context of the funeral oration that Birahima decides to tell for his friend. It is in this retelling that repetitive structures dominate, and, as in the story of the burnt arm, parallelism is used during the build-up, and anadiplosis during the climax:

> Dans le village de Kik, la guerre tribale est arrivée vers dix heures du matin. Les enfants étaient à l'école et les parents à la maison. Kik était à l'école et ses parents à la maison. Dès les premières rafales, les enfants gagnèrent la forêt. Kik gagna la forêt. Et, tant qu'il y eut du bruit dans le village, les enfants restèrent dans la forêt. Kik resta dans la forêt. C'est seulement le lendemain matin, quand il n'y eut plus de bruit, que les enfants s'aventurèrent vers leur concession familiale. Kik regagna la concession familiale ... Kik est devenu un soldat-enfant. Le soldat-enfant était malin. Le malin small-soldier a pris un raccourci. En prenant le raccourci, il a sauté sur une mine. ... Nous l'avons abandonné mourant dans un après-midi, dans un foutu village, à la vindicte des villageois. A la vindicte populaire parce que c'est comme ça que Allah a voulu que le pauvre garçon termine sur terre. Et Allah n'est pas obligé, n'a pas besoin d'être juste dans toutes ses choses, dans toutes ses créations, dans tous ses actes ici-bas. (Kourouma 2000, 96–97)
> [In Kik's village, the tribal war arrived at about 10 o'clock in the morning. The children were at school and the parents at home. Kik was at school and his parents at home. As soon as the firing started, the children ran into the forest. Kik ran into the forest. And, for as long as there was noise in the village, the children stayed in the forest. Kik stayed in the forest. It was not until the next morning, when there was no noise anymore, that the children ventured into their family compounds. Kik went back to his family compound ... Kik became a child-soldier. The child-soldier was clever. The clever child-soldier took a shortcut. When he took the shortcut, he stepped on a mine. ... We abandoned him as he was dying one afternoon, in a fucked-up village, to the villagers' condemnation. To public condemnation because that is how Allah wanted the poor boy to end his days on earth. And Allah is not obliged, doesn't need to be fair in all his things, in all his creations, in all his actions here below.]

In her analysis of *Allah n'est pas obligé*, Annik Docquire Kerszberg (2002, 112) links anadiplosis with the oral character of the narrative, observing that the same device features heavily in Camara Laye's *L'Enfant noir*, and suggesting that it may be connected specifically with the oral storytelling traditions of the Malinke people. It is certainly present elsewhere in *Allah n'est pas obligé*, notably in Birahima's account of Yacouba's life, or in his description of the background to Prince Johnson's murder of Samuel Doe.[6] While Kerszberg argues that "cette pléthore de répétitions confère au texte l'apparence de l'oralité de même qu'une fausse

71

ORALITY AND TRANSLATION

simplicité" [this plethora of repetitions confers on the text the appearance of orality as well as a false simplicity] (113), and stresses the importance of this false simplicity for the satirical humour of the novel, I would suggest that the use of these repetitive structures can also be seen as a means for Birahima to tame and gain mastery over traumatic events, allowing this act of storytelling to function as a therapeutic narrative of the kind envisaged by Herman. For, by drawing on devices associated with traditional storytelling structures, or, in other words, by drawing on the same patterns as those employed for more ordinary biographies or tales, Birahima is "reconstruct[ing] the traumatic event as a recitation of fact" (Herman 2001, 177), creating a line of continuity that helps to integrate the traumatic event into the fuller narrative of his life. The translation of orality and the translation of trauma here work hand in hand, the presence of the oral markers highlighting the degree of success with which the traumatic memory has been transformed into a coherent narrative.

Repetition as the development of a new schemata

In both of the extracts cited above, Birahima concludes his account by citing the titular leitmotif, "Allah is not obliged to be fair about all the things he does here on earth" (Kourouma 2006, 1). This leitmotif, or a variation on it, is cited more than ten times across the novel as a whole, and is joined by two other leitmotifs that are repeated with comparable levels of frequency: "Allah never leaves empty a mouth he has created" (35), and "that's the way it is with tribal wars" (98). Once again, these repetitive devices, which function as refrains, can be viewed as markers of oral discourse, typical as they are of traditional oral tales. Yet when the novel is read within a trauma theory framework, these refrains can also be linked to trauma theory's postulation of a "completion principle" (Horowitz, 1986), summarized by Regal and Joseph (2010, 15) as "an inherent drive to make our mental models coherent with current information". Horowitz's theory is constructed on the premise that our inner schemata will need alteration in order to be made adequate to account for traumatic events, a premise that is echoed in Herman's model when she argues: "Traumatic events ... undermine the belief systems that give meaning to human experience. They violate the victim's faith in a natural or divine order and cast the victim into a state of existential crisis" (2001, 51). What is striking about the three refrains used by Birahima is that they are *not* subject to overt questioning as a result of the traumatic events experienced by the narrator; if we take them as representative of Birahima's belief system or inner schemata, it would appear that his belief system remains intact, contra the theories of trauma developed by Horowitz, Herman and others.[7] The only instance of overt questioning of a belief system relates to the use of grigris, an essential part of Yacouba's trade but never clearly adopted as part of Birahima's own schemata. Following two events in which failure or success is ascribed to improper or proper use of the grigris, Birahima reflects:

> It was about this time that I realised I didn't understand this fucking universe, I didn't understand a thing about this bloody world, I couldn't make head or tail of people or society ... Was this grigri bullshit true or not true? Who was there who could tell me? Where could I go to find out? Nowhere. Maybe this grigri thing is true ... or maybe it's a lie, a scam, a con that runs the whole length and breadth of Africa. *Faforo!* (Kourouma 2006, 118)

This is the only example of questioning within the novel that might obviously fit Herman's (2001, 178) view that "the traumatic event challenges an ordinary person to become a theologian, a philosopher, and a jurist"; elsewhere, Birahima's inner schemata appears to remain largely unchallenged.

One possible explanation for this apparent failure of Birahima's narrative to include a "systematic review of the meaning of the event" (Herman 2001, 178) is that his original belief system was developed in a context in which trauma and pain were already an intrinsic part of life: growing up in his mother's hut surrounded by the intense, unremitting pain and stench of her ulcer, Birahima was forced to develop a world view that could take account of that undeserved suffering, as well as of his own, and was encouraged in this by his grandmother; "Allah is not obliged to be fair in all his things here below" represents just such a schemata as well as being compatible with popularized Muslim beliefs in an evening-out of suffering between now and the afterlife.[8] Such a line of reasoning suggests that tenets of trauma theory that are couched in universalist terms, such as Herman's assertion that "the arbitrary, random quality of her fate defies *the basic human faith* in a just or even predictable world order" (ibid., my emphasis), are shown to need modulation in contexts where religious, cultural or political factors mean that the predictability of events and justice on this earth are far from being basic, default assumptions.

While it is certainly true that explicit interrogation of the narrator's inner schemata is almost entirely absent from *Allah n'est pas obligé*, to state that Birahima's belief system undergoes no change as a result of the trauma he experiences would be to ignore the acerbic humour of the novel, as well as the details of the minor modulations that two out of the three leitmotifs undergo. The titular leitmotif, for example, often occurs in conjunction with the repeated swearwords with which Birahima punctuates his narrative, and occasionally even incorporates vulgar language into its own formulation. These vulgarizations undermine the apparent piety of the leitmotif, rendering it less an assertion of faith in the all-powerfulness of Allah than an expression of the narrator's bitterness, frustration and anger at his own lack of control over events. This undermining is confirmed by the contexts in which the second leitmotif, "Allah never leaves empty a mouth he has created", appears. Apparently an expression of faith in Allah's care for his creatures, these words are cited ironically at times when Birahima and Yacouba are forced to eat tree leaves and roots, steal, or when they have no means of subsistence other than their AK-47s.

Another significant way in which the validity of the titular leitmotif is called into question is through the apparent interchangeability of its subject – Allah – for another one. Birahima evokes the titular leitmotif not only with Allah in the subject position, but also with "the spirits of the ancestors" (Kourouma 2006, 13), and "God" (141). Although the syncretism expressed by these variations of the leitmotif is in some senses nothing more than the reflection of the various belief systems of those around Birahima – the Islam of his Muslim mother and grandmother, the animism of his stepfather, the Christianity of Marie-Béatrice and Prince Johnson – its effect is devastating: rather than being a reassuring expression of faith in a higher wisdom or good associated with a specific higher being, the letimotif becomes a terrifying expression of the view that human beings are at the mercy of whatever higher power they chose to believe in. The leitmotif thus does not so much serve to make trauma manageable or comprehensible, as it might first appear, but rather to make trauma infinitely possible. It suggests that, far from representing a schemata adequate to the trauma that he is describing, the first two leitmotifs are in fact an expression of the sense of helplessness that, as argued above, is viewed by trauma theory as lying at the heart of every traumatizing experience.

It is perhaps for this reason that Birahima begins to apply the leitmotif to himself, explicitly shifting from "Allah is not obliged" to "I am not obliged" on a number of occasions. Immediately after the conclusion of the Kik passage cited above, for example, Birahima states: "The same goes for me. I don't have to talk, I'm not obliged to tell you my dog's-life-story, wading through dictionary after dictionary. I'm fed up talking, so I'm going to stop for today. You can all fuck off!" (Kourouma 2006, 91). The titular leitmotif thus gradually becomes a means of justifying Birahima's right to control over his narrative, and is an important marker of the restoration of power through therapeutic storytelling.

An interesting point that emerges out of this modulation is that while Birahima's role in the conflict is by no means passive – he admits in the opening paragraphs that he has "killed lots of innocent victims" (Kourouma 2006, 4) – at no point in any of the specific conflicts that Birahima describes does he explicitly state that he has killed anyone. Where reprehensible actions are described, Birahima places himself within the role of passive recipient of decisions made by a higher force. One example of this was cited above in relation to the Kik passage: although Kik was abandoned by Birahima and his friends, he was abandoned not because of their decision, but because "that's how Allah decided he wanted poor Kik to end his days on earth" (91). Another example can be found in Birahima's description of how he got together a band of friends to go out and steal food: "We stole food, we pilfered food. Pilfering food isn't stealing because Allah, Allah in his inordinate goodness, never intended to leave empty for two whole days a mouth he created. *Walahé!*" (129). Such shifts of blame away from Birahima are also enacted through use of the third leitmotif; when Birahima describes how he and his fellow child-soldier colleagues chase two men, for example, he explains simply: "Nous les avons pris tout de suite en chasse. Parce que c'est la guerre tribale qui veut ça" [We immediately chased after them. Because that's the way it is with tribal wars] (93). The tribal wars refrain is also evoked when describing various atrocities such as the use of human skulls to mark out the limits of the soldiers' camps, or the systematic torturing of people from other ethnicities, or the equally systematic raping of women by rebel leaders. To some extent, the use of this third refrain could be seen as a new schemata, introduced to account for some of the traumatic experiences that Birahima undergoes – the civil war being in and of itself a sufficient explanation, demarcating an arena in which more usual codes of conduct do not apply. It is undoubtedly also the case, however, that it serves to deflect blame away from Birahima himself, and its usage and repetition thus function to highlight contentious issues around the victim versus perpetrator status of child-soldiers and sufferers of trauma.

From inter-semiotic to interlingual translation

This reading of *Allah n'est pas obligé* within a trauma theory-based framework raises a number of significant questions when brought alongside interlingual translation practice. Both the English and the German versions of *Allah n'est pas obligé* eliminate or dilute the repetitive patterns based on parallelism and anadiplosis analysed above. The opening of the Kik story, for example, is told in the German

ORALITY AND TRANSLATION

version using very little repetition: the sentence "Les enfants étaient à l'école et les parents à la maison" is omitted entirely, and elsewhere the parallels between the children's actions and Kik's are drawn either by simple summarizing phrases ("Kik war unter ihnen"; "Kik auch") or by a sentence that uses different vocabulary to the one that it is paralleling (the children "wagten sich", while Kik "lief"; the children went back to "die Grundstücke ihrer Familien", while Kik returned "zur elterlichen Hütte"):

> Der Stammeskrieg hatte Kiks Dorf gegen zehn Uhr morgens erreicht. Kik war in der Schule, seine Eltern hielten sich zu Hause auf. Schon bei den ersten Feuerstößen liefen die Kinder in den Wald. Kik war unter ihnen. Und solange Lärm im Dorf war, blieben die Kinder im Wald. Kik auch. Erst am nächsten Morgen, als keine Geräusche mehr zu hören waren, wagten sich die Kinder auf die Grundstücke ihrer Familien. Kik lief zur elterlichen Hütte. (Kourouma 2004, 96)
> [The tribal war reached Kik's village at about 10 o'clock in the morning. Kik was in school, his parents were at home. As soon as the first shots were fired the children ran into the woods. Kik was with them. And while there was still noise in the village, the children stayed in the woods. Kik too. It was not until the next morning, when there were no more sounds to be heard, that the children dared go to their families' homes. Kik ran to his parents' hut.]

Similarly, the anadiplosis structure that occurs later in the story is weakened in the German version, with just one of the sentence endings becoming the beginning of the next sentence, rather than three: "Nach und nach ist Kik ein soldatisches Kind geworden. Der kindliche Soldat war pfiffig. Der pfiffige *small soldier* hat eine Abkürzung genommen. Dabei ist er auf eine Mine getreten" [Little by little Kik became a soldierly child. The childish soldier was smart. The smart *small soldier* took a shortcut. In so doing he trod on a mine.] (Kourouma 2004, 96–97).

The English version of the Kik story dilutes the repetitions to a lesser degree, retaining most of the parallelism in the first section and two out of three anadiplosis devices in the second:

> The tribal wars arrived in Kik's village at about ten o'clock in the morning. The children were at school and their parents were at home. Kik was at school and his parents were at home. When they heard the first bursts of gunfire, the children ran into the forest. Kik ran into the forest. And the kids stayed in the forest all the time they could hear the gunfire from the village. Kik stayed in the forest. It was only the next morning when there was no more noise that the children dared to go back to their family huts. Kik went back to his family hut.... Gradually, Kik became a child-soldier. ... Kik was cunning. The cunning child-soldier took a shortcut. Taking a shortcut, he stepped on a mine. (Kourouma 2006, 90–91)

Elsewhere, the anadiplosis device is shown to be particularly vulnerable to dilution: the English and German versions of the other passage using anadiplosis cited above reveal partial and complete elimination of the device respectively:

> I made a dash and fell on to the glowing embers. The fire did its job and grilled my arm. It grilled the arm of a poor little kid because Allah doesn't have to be fair about everything he does here on earth. (Kourouma 2006, 7)

> Ich legte noch einen Zahn zu, und da fiel ich in die brennende Glut. Und die hat ganze Arbeit geleistet und meinen Arm orderntlich gegrillt. Sie hat mir armes Blag den Arm

geröstet, denn Allah ist nicht verpflichtet, in allen Dingen, die er auf Erden tut, gerecht zu sein. (Kourouma 2004, 14)

[I put on a bit of speed and fell into the burning embers. And they did a good job and grilled my arm really well. They roasted the arm of this poor brat, because Allah is not obliged to be fair in all the things that he does on earth.]

The repetition of the various leitmotifs shows less vulnerability to dilution overall in both the English and the German versions, with the titular leitmotif providing something of an exception to this generalization. The principle reason behind the weakening of the *Allah n'est pas obligé* refrain is that, whereas the original always draws on the verb "obliger" when citing the leitmotif and its modulations, the English and German versions each use two different terms for the main verb of the leitmotif, thereby rendering its repetition less obvious in the text. In the German version, although the verb selected for the title and for the first two introductory references to the leitmotif in the text is the modal verb "müssen" [to have to], later citations of the leitmotif draw on the verb "verpflichten" [to oblige]. Inversely, the English version uses the verb "obliged" in the title and in the introductory references, but frequently has recourse to the modal verb "to have to" on subsequent occasions. Although it is possible to argue that the leitmotif as a whole is still recognizable despite the synonymic variation in the English and German versions, there are a number of important occasions when statements may not be recognized as variations of the leitmotif because they are incomplete renditions of it and depend, in the original, on the presence of the word "obligé" to signal the link between the expression and the leitmotif. In the case of Birahima's explanation of his mother's life of suffering, for example, the link between the statement relating to Allah's and the spirits' lack of obligation to answer prayers and the titular leitmotif is less clear in the English version than in the French original:

Allah doesn't have to accept sacrifices and neither do the spirits of the ancestors. Allah can do whatever he feels like; he doesn't have to acquiesce to every prayer from every lowly human being ("acquiesce" means "agree to"). The spirits of the ancestors can do what they like; they don't have to acquiesce to all our complicated prayers. (Kourouma 2006, 13)

Similarly, one of the earliest shifts from the "Allah" to the "je" is likely to go unrecognized in the English version, due to the use of the modal verb rather than the verb "obliged": "whenever a child soldier dies, we have to say a funeral oration. That means we have to recount how in this great big fucked-up world they came to be a child-soldier. I do it when I feel like it, but I don't have to" (83).

Although the German version does use the same verb in these examples as in the title leitmotif, the decision to use the modal verb "müssen" rather than the more marked verb "verpflichten" in the leitmotif means that the signal given to the reader that these are instances of leitmotif repetition is much less clear. The verb "müssen" is, by its very nature, extremely common, and occurs in many other contexts in the text, meaning that the reader is much less likely to see it as a repetition of the title, or, even if s/he does recognize it as a repetition, to be sure that it is deliberate rather than accidental. The German translations of the passages discussed above are as follows:

ORALITY AND TRANSLATION

Allah und die Manen der Ahnen nehmen nicht immer unbedingt alle Opfer an. (Manen bedeutet: gute Geister, Seelen der Verstorbenen.) Allah macht, was er will; er muss nicht unbedingt den armen Menschen alle Bitten gewähren. Auch did Manen machen, was sie wollen; sie müssen nicht unbedingt den Betenden alle dringenden Wünsche erfüllen. (Kourouma 2004, 21)
[Allah and the manes of the ancestors don't always necessarily accept all sacrifices. (Manes means: good spirits, souls of the deceased.) Allah does whatever he wants; he doesn't necessarily have to grant poor humans all their requests. And the manes also do whatever they want: they don't necessarily have to fulfil all the urgent wishes of those who pray to them.]

Wenn ein Kindersoldat stirbt, muss man also eine Trauerrede auf ihn halten; das bedeutet, man muss sagen, wie er in dieser großen beschissenen Welt ein Kindersoldat werden konnte. Ich tue es nur, wenn ich es will, ich muss es nicht tun. (90)
[When a child-soldier dies, you have to hold a funeral speech for him; that means you have to say how he came to be a child-soldier in this big fucked-up world. I only do it if I want to, I don't have to do it.]

Overall, then, whereas in the original the pattern of leitmotif repetition and its modulation can be easily followed throughout the original text, in the English and German versions the repetition is less obvious, and the parallels between the statements involving "je" or "God" are partially blurred. The potential of the leitmotif to convey both the abdication of responsibility for trauma and the assumption of mastery over it is thus correspondingly weakened.

Contextualizing interlingual translation practice

When these alterations to the repetitive structures of the original are read in the wider textual and paratextual contexts of the English and German versions of *Allah n'est pas obligé*, a number of different points relating to motivation and effect emerge. The diminution of repetition in the English version occurs in the context of a fairly close rendering of the source text, along with the retention of other markers of orality within the text, such as exclamations, ideophones and proverbs. Paratextual evidence, notably in the form of the translator's note included at the beginning of the book, reveals a strong overall positing of the relevance of oral-tradition discourse by the translator. The translator indicates that he has been aided by "recordings of the oral narratives of child-soldiers" and states that "when all else has failed, I have been guided by my ear, and by the music of contemporary *griots* Abdul Tee-Jay, Usifu Jalloh and Bajourou" (Wynne 2006). Wynne's use of the term "oral narratives" – rather than "stories" or "testimonies" – to refer to the child-soldiers' accounts of their experiences is striking, and posits a line of continuity between traditional oral narratives and contemporary forms of communication that many would not take as a given. Another notable aspect of Wynne's view of orality that emerges here is its generality: in order to translate Birahima's voice well, Wynne has found useful the voices of a number of West African musicians, viewing these as present-day perpetuators of oral tradition ("contemporary *griots*"). Once again, through his phrasing, Wynne indirectly draws a line of continuity between centuries-old African oral traditions and the present day, between African oral literature canons and Kourouma's novel. Both the study of the translator's textual choices and his paratextual positioning thus indicate that the diminution of repetition in the translated version is not to be read as an effort to weaken the orality of the text, but rather as evidence that repetition is construed as one among a body of stylistic devices that convey orality, and as such may be reduced so long as the overall orality of the text is conveyed by other means.

This analysis indicates that Wynne's translation approach fits soundly within the interpretative paradigm outlined in the opening paragraphs of this article, according to which Kourouma's novel is to be read as a translation of an "oral-tradition discourse into a written one" (Bandia 2008, 38), or as part of an African mode of discourse that has orality as its "matrix" and as the "fundamental reference" of its "imaginative mode" (Irele 2001, 11). Wynne's citation of Kwaku Gyasi's article, "Writing as Translation", elsewhere in the note, further confirms the interpretative framework according to which the translation has been carried out.[9] While few would contest the relevance of orality to Kourouma's works in general, my analysis of the stylistic and thematic importance of the repetition-governed structures in *Allah n'est pas obligé* and their alteration in translation suggests that there are two dangers associated with such an interpretative framework.

Firstly, such a framework runs the risk of treating the relevance of orality to African fiction in overly general terms, ignoring the specific relation of the spoken word to the written one in individual works. To make this point is to take up an argument developed by Moradewun Adejunmobi in her examination of works by Amadou Hampaté Bâ. In her article, Adejunmobi (2000, 27) argues that "it is time to move beyond discussions of Hampaté Bâ's work whose objective it is to prove that orality accounts for the distinctiveness of his writing, and to begin considering other kinds of filiation between orality and writing in his texts", stressing Bâ's focus, in *L'étrange destin de Wangrin* and *Amkoullel, l'enfant peul*, on the moment of the transition to writing, rather than on invoking tradition for its own sake. In a similar vein, we might argue that the interplay between orality and writing finds very different expression in each of Kourouma's novels, and that in *Allah n'est pas obligé* the focus is not on traditional oral narrative structures or events, but rather on the importance of writing down Birahima's spoken words in such a way that many different kinds of people, speaking different varieties of languages, can read his story. Orality, in this case, is used not to valorize tradition, but to individualize experience, turning a "child-soldier" from a faceless, almost abstract, category into an individual with charisma and a sharp sense of humour.

Secondly, the dominance of the interpretative framework based around orality renders readers, critics and translators alike vulnerable to what might be termed interpretative "pigeonholing", encouraging them, when reading African fiction, to subsume features such as repetition, ideophones and exclamations under the broad heading "orality", rather than according each stylistic variation the interpretative attention it deserves. Such an approach means that alternative readings of "orality-inflected" passages are rarely considered, and translators are less likely to use style as "the basis and focal point for a translation" (Boase-Beier 2006, 112) or to view style as indicative of "the cognitive state of the speaker or writer" (114) than they might be for, say, literature originating in the West.

If the broader contexts of the English renderings of repetition-based passages indicate that their diminution may be a consequence of the dominance of an orality-based interpretative framework, the textual and paratextual contexts of the German renderings point to a rather different explanation. The German version of *Allah n'est*

ORALITY AND TRANSLATION

pas obligé contains a number of striking amendments to the original text, including a significant number of additions. Particularly noticeable among these are the inserted sentence, "Ich habe den Ausbruch des Bürgerkriegs nicht selbst miterlebt, aber ich höre immer gut zu, wenn ein anderer Kindersoldat oder unsere Kriegsherrn oder Yacouba etwas zu erzählen haben" [I didn't experience the outbreak of the civil war myself, but I always listen when another child-soldier or one of our leaders or Yacouba have stories to tell], before Birahima's historical summary of the development of the various factions involved in the Liberian civil war. This insertion appears to be an attempt to make Birahima's extensive knowledge of political events appear more plausible, an interpretation that is consistent with epitextual material in the form of an openly available letter from the German publishers defending decisions taken during the translation process. The relevant section of the letter offers valuable insights into the overall approach governing the translation:

> Es gibt in der Erzählung einen "Bruch" .... Es geht darum, dass plötzlich und unvermittelt der kleine Birahima seitenlange Erklärungen mit Fakten und Namen niederschreibt, die seinen Horizont völlig übersteigen. Die Perspektive des Erzählers droht dadurch ganz und gar unglaublich zu werden. Ich habe diesen Bruch nicht eliminiert; die gezielten Zusätze in diesen Passagen haben nur ein einziges Ziel: den Leser darauf aufmerksam zu machen, dass der Text selbst ... ein Bewusstsein für diesen Bruch hat. Auch hier galt es zu berücksichtigen, dass ein deutschsprachiges Publikum dieses Heraustreten aus der Erzählperspektive viel stärker wahrnimmt als jeder französischsprachige Leser. (Bracht, 2005)
> [There is a "break" in the narrative .... Suddenly and unannounced, little Birahima writes down explanations with facts and names that are pages long and that go well beyond his realm of knowledge. The narratorial perspective thus risks becoming completely implausible. I did not eliminate this break; the deliberate insertions around these passages have a single goal: to make the reader aware that the text itself ... is conscious of this break. This was another place where it was important to take into account that a German-speaking audience would perceive the departure from the narratorial perspective much more strongly than any French-speaking reader.]

This citation reveals the extent to which translation decisions – and it should be noted that the phrasing of the letter indicates that many of these were the publishers', rather than the translator's – were taken based on what the publisher perceived to be the target audience's needs and levels of tolerance. Other significant alterations in the German translation such as the omission of many of Birahima's bracketed definitions, and another even longer insertion in the final paragraphs of the text, are justified in the letter on the same basis, as is the elimination of "die bewusste sprachliche Unbeholfenheit" [the conscious linguistic awkwardness] (ibid.) that Bracht sees as a central characteristic of Kourouma's text. As an example of such awkwardness, Bracht gives the tenfold repetition of "avant" [before] on a single page, arguing that the French reader would take such repetition as evidence that "das fictive Ich des Textes eben die Sprache nur mühsam beherrscht" [the fictional I of the text speaks the language only with some difficulty] (ibid.); a German reader, by contrast, would read such repetition as "eine lästige Unbeholfenheit, die er instinktiv der Übersetzung angelästet hätte" [an irritating awkwardness, which he would have blamed instinctively on the translation] (ibid.). The dominant interpretative paradigm that appears to have governed the German publisher's reading of the text thus appears to be not orality, but linguistic difference, a supposition that is further

79

supported by the translation's peritext.[10] According to such a framework, strangeness in style is to be read as linguistic incompetence and/or variation, and while such an interpretation may in many cases be valid – Birahima's identity as someone who speaks *petit nègre* is after all foregrounded in the opening pages of the novel – it runs the same risk of "pigeonholing", rather than encouraging interrogation of each variation of style in its specificity. Furthermore, when coupled with a target-oriented translation approach, such as the one used in the German translation of *Allah n'est pas obligé*, it renders such stylistic variations highly vulnerable to standardization on the basis that they are not considered good style in the target language.

Implications of a translation-of-trauma reading for postcolonial translation approaches

The interpretative frameworks governing the English and German translations of *Allah n'est pas obligé* (the "orality matrix" and the "linguistic difference" matrix, respectively) can be linked to two strands of interpretation that have dominated critical reception of African literature from the mid-twentieth century to the present day. If there is a growing sense, both among postcolonial studies scholars and translation studies theorists, that such strands are no longer – or perhaps never have been – sufficient, this brief study of *Allah n'est pas obligé* across three languages may be seen as adding to that sense of unease, illustrating the way in which potential alternative readings run the risk of being shut down when translations are carried out according to the assumed relevance of a dominant paradigm. This article is thus in some senses an argument in favour of postcolonial translation approaches that are literary translation approaches, first and foremost, rather than "postcolonial", taking a literary approach as "the translation of style, because style is the expression of mind, and literature is a reflection of mind" (Boase-Beier 2006, 112).

Yet to argue in favour of such an approach neither presents any straightforward practical translation solutions nor represents a move away from the notion of the postcolonial altogether. Both of these points can be illustrated by returning to the passage in which Birahima presents Kik's funeral oration. What would a translation based on style look like for this passage? Would a close rendering, retaining all of the repetitive patterns, be likely to open up similar readings to those associated with the French passage? If, as I have argued above, the syntactic patterning can be construed as therapeutic storytelling, bringing the story into line with Malinke storytelling patterns (or, in other words, as a specifically African, orality-inflected, instance of trauma-telling), would that same reading be open to a target audience with very different storytelling norms? Or would the simple, repetitive syntax connote something rather different – a regression into childishness, perhaps, that might be taken as a sign that the event had not been successfully processed at all by the speaker? Alternatively, if Peter Vakunta (2010, 9) is correct in his assertion that repetition is viewed as "anathema" in Western literary tradition, then would its retention simply connote poor style – and indeed, poor translation – for many readers, as argued by the German publishers of *Allah n'est pas obligé*? The notion of the "postcolonial" is undoubtedly needed here in order to interrogate differences among reading publics and writing traditions, and to stress the plurality of interpretations that is a feature of any literary reading but that becomes particularly acute in relation to languages used in very different geographical and cultural spaces.

ORALITY AND TRANSLATION

When such issues are considered not only in the academic abstract, but also in the real spaces of publishing and bookselling, the relevance of the postcolonial perhaps becomes even more apparent. For translators and publishers must deal not simply with questions of variation in stylistically aware readings, but with the perceptions (real or assumed) of "Africa" and "African literature" that dominate the target cultures into which they are looking to insert their text. The back cover blurb of the German version of *Allah n'est pas obligé* offers an intriguing insight into the way such perceptions can shape a translation's paratexts, the short summary of the plot evoking centuries-old tropes of "Africa" whose actual relevance to Kourouma's novel are highly debatable:

> In Westafrika herrscht Krieg, und der zwölfjährige Waise Birahima hat nur eine Chance, in diesem Chaos zu überleben: Er muss Kindersoldat werden. An der Seite eines erfahrenen Fetischpriesters aus seinem Heimatdorf erlebt er dabei unvorstellbare Grausamkeiten, aber auch *Momente, die erfüllt sind von der Magie seiner Vorfahren und der Schönheit seines Landes.* Und es sind genau diese Augenblicke, die Birahima Kraft schenken, niemals aufzugeben. (Kourouma 2004, my emphasis)
> [There is war in West Africa, and the twelve-year-old orphan Birahima has only one way of surviving the chaos: he must become a child-soldier. With an experienced fetish priest from his native village as his companion, he experiences unimaginable atrocities, but also moments that are filled with the magic of his ancestors and the beauty of his land. And it is precisely these moments that give Birahima the strength to carry on.]

Just what these moments are that are filled with the magic of Birahima's ancestors or with the beauty of the African landscape would be hard to pinpoint for any reader, and their irrelevance makes the use of these tropes in the marketing of the book highly significant, implying that these are the themes that a German reader associates with Africa, and with African writing – or at the very least that are deemed by publishers to make such a book marketable. The shift in emphasis enacted through the back cover blurb – supported, it might be noted, by the cover image which depicts a clean, brightly clothed young boy staring out over a clean ocean – reveals a strong parallel with the paratextual strategies that Richard Watts posits as characteristic of US publishers' approaches to francophone literature:

> On the whole, the information contained in these paratexts is less precise than in their French counterparts. The works are subtly pushed towards other, broader literary-cultural categories, which suggests that publishers perceive resistance among the prospective readership of these texts to the particularly foreign and to foreign particularity. One way to diminish the text's foreignness ... is to confine it to a past that cannot interfere with a present. The other way is to place the text in categories previously assimilated by the readership that no longer connote radical alterity. (Watts 2005, 171)

In some senses, all of the dominant interpretative paradigms that emerge through the textual and paratextual translation strategies studied here serve to edge Kourouma's novel towards comfortable, previously assimilated categories, whether these be oral literary traditions, colonial linguistic heritages, or, to draw on Watts' (2005, 164) analysis of US-published literature once again, "a nebulous, subtly romanticized, and exotic 'before'". While translators and publishers must inevitably take target audience considerations into account to some degree, having easy

81

recourse to existing tropes in an age when Western media is growing ever more aware of the problematic, outdated nature of its images of Africa must surely become increasingly inappropriate. Similarly, while the complexity of translation decisions is not diminished by working with a wider set of source text interpretations generated by paying maximum attention to specific variations in style, it is only through such an approach that thorny questions around assertion of agency, processing of traumatic memory, negotiation of victim or perpetrator status, questioning of belief systems, and international responses and responsibilities, will be able to fully emerge.

Notes

1. Throughout the article, where the English translation is adequate for the purposes of the immediate discussion, I have cited it directly; where it is not, I have cited the French original and provided my own translation in square brackets.
2. Kourouma's own insistence on the testimonial nature of all of his novels, as well as his biographer's account of how Kourouma wrote *Allah n'est pas obligé* in response to the pleas of Djiboutian child-soldiers and researched it by listening to the stories of children involved in the Liberian and Sierra Leonean conflict, indicate that there is also strong potential for reading the novel as a fictionalized testimony based on an amalgamation of real-life testimonies, or even as Kourouma's own effort to engage in therapeutic storytelling in response to becoming a witness of trauma. See Ouédraogo (2000, 1338) and Jean-Michel Djian (2010, 160–161).
3. On the other hand, the excess of words that characterizes the narrative, and, more specifically, the repeated foregrounding of the need to define and explain (notably through the bracketed explanations developed apparently with the help of various dictionaries), could be linked to the aporetic current in the sense that this tends to promote the view that "testimony is never adequate … it can never bridge the gap between words and experience" (Tal 1996, 2).
4. Such Eurocentric formulations are summarized by Craps and Buelens (2008, 5): "Within trauma studies, it has become all but axiomatic that traumatic experiences can only be adequately represented through the use of experimental, (post)modernist textual strategies." For a cogent summary of Craps and Buelens' project and of the issues at stake more generally in an attempted move towards postcolonial trauma theory, see Visser (2011).
5. Herman is drawing here on Robert Lifton (1980).
6. See Kourouma (2000, 39, 137).
7. It should be noted, however, that there is some variance in the degree to which Birahima appears to "own" the three belief statements: while "Allah is not obliged to be fair about all the things he does here on earth" and "that's the way it is with tribal wars" appear to be his own formulations, "Allah never leaves empty a mouth he has created" is repeatedly attributed to other people, notably to Yacouba and, in adapted form, Marie-Béatrice.
8. Such beliefs are epitomized in Birahima's summary of the villagers' response to his mother's death: "They all said maman would go straight up to heaven to be with Allah because of all the hardships and sufferings she'd had down here on earth and because Allah didn't have any more hardships and sufferings left to give her" (Kourouma 2006, 25).
9. Gyasi (1999, 82) pursues a similar line of thinking to that put forward by Bandia and Irele, arguing, for example, that "African writers are creative translators in the sense that in their works, they convey concepts and values from a given linguistic, oral culture into a written form in an alien language".
10. The wording on the inner title page of the German translation runs as follows: "Aus dem afrikanischen Französisch von Sabine Herting" [translated from African French by Sabine Herting] (Kourouma 2004).

ORALITY AND TRANSLATION

References

Adejunmobi, Moradewun. 2000. "Disruptions of Orality in the Writings of Hampaté Bâ." *Research in African Literatures* 31 (3): 27–36.

Bandia, Paul. 2008. *Translation as Reparation: Writing and Translation in Postcolonial Africa.* Manchester: St Jerome.

Boase-Beier, Jean. 2006. *Stylistic Approaches to Translation.* Manchester: St Jerome.

Bracht, Edgar. 2005. Letter to Dr Hug, June 8, 2005. http://www.uebersetzungswissenschaft.de/hug-erw.htm.

Caruth, Cathy. 1996. *Unclaimed Experience: Trauma, Narrative, and History.* Baltimore: Johns Hopkins University Press.

Craps, Stef, and Gert Buelens. 2008. "Introduction: Postcolonial Trauma Novels." *Studies in the Novel* 40 (1–2): 1–12.

Djian, Jean-Michel. 2010. *Ahmadou Kourouma.* Paris: Seuil.

Eaglestone, Robert. 2008. "'You would not add to my suffering if you knew what I have seen': Holocaust Testimony and Contemporary African Trauma Literature." *Studies in the Novel* 40 (1–2): 72–85.

Finnegan, Ruth. 1977. *Oral Poetry: Its Nature, Significance, and Social Context.* Cambridge: Cambridge University Press.

Gyasi, Kwaku. 1999. "Writing as Translation: African Literature and the Challenges of Translation." *Research in African Literatures* 30 (2): 75–87.

Gyasi, Kwaku. 2006. *The Francophone African Text: Translation and the Postcolonial Experience.* New York: Peter Lang.

Herman, Judith Lewis. (1992) 2001. *Trauma and Recovery: From Domestic Abuse to Political Terror.* London: Pandora.

Horowitz, Mardi. 1986. *Stress Response Syndromes.* Northvale, NJ: Jason Aronson.

Hron, Madelaine. 2009. *Translating Pain: Immigrant Suffering in Literature and Culture.* Toronto: University of Toronto Press.

Irele, F. Abiola. 2001. *The African Imagination.* New York: Oxford University Press.

Kerszberg, Annik Doquire. 2002. "Kourouma 2000: humour obligé!" *Présence Francophone* 59: 110–125.

Kourouma, Ahmadou. 1997a. "Ecrire en français, penser dans sa langue maternelle." *Etudes françaises* 33 (1): 115–118.

Kourouma, Ahmadou. 1997b. "Traduire l'intraduisible." In *L'écrivain francophone à la croisée des langues: Entretiens,* edited by Lise Gauvin, 153–162. Paris: Karthala.

Kourouma, Ahmadou. 2000. *Allah n'est pas obligé.* Paris: Seuil.

Kourouma, Ahmadou. 2004. *Allah muss nicht gerecht sein.* Translated by Sabine Herting. Munich: Goldmann.

Kourouma, Ahmadou. 2006. *Allah is Not Obliged.* Translated by Frank Wynne. London: William Heinemann.

Lifton, Robert. 1980. "The Concept of the Survivor." In *Survivors, Victims, and Perpetrators: Essays on the Nazi Holocaust,* edited by J. E. Dimsdale, 113–126. New York: Hemisphere.

Ouédraogo, Jean. 2000. "An Interview with Ahmadou Kourouma." *Callaloo* 23 (4): 1338–1348.

Regal, Stephen, and Stephen Joseph. 2010. *Post-Traumatic Stress*. Oxford: Oxford University Press.

Steemers, Vivan. 2012. "The Effect of Translating 'Big Words': Anglophone Translation and Reception of Ahmadou Kourouma's Novel *Allah n'est pas obligé*." *Research in African Literatures* 43 (3): 36–53.

Tal, Kali. 1996. *Worlds of Hurt: Reading the Literatures of Trauma*. Cambridge: Cambridge University Press.

Tymoczko, Maria. 1999. *Translation in a Postcolonial Context: Early Irish Literature in English Translation*. Manchester: St Jerome.

Vakunta, Peter W. 2010. *Indigenization of Language in the African Francophone Novel: A New Literary Canon*. Francophone Cultures and Literatures, vol. 59. New York: Peter Lang.

Visser, Irene. 2011. "Trauma Theory and Postcolonial Literary Studies." *Journal of Postcolonial Writing* 47 (3): 270–282. doi:10.1080/17449855.2011.569378.

Watts, Richard. 2005. *Packaging Post/Coloniality: The Manufacture of Literary Identity in the Francophone World*. Lanham: Lexington Books.

Wynne, Frank. 2006. "Translator's Note." In *Allah is Not Obliged*, by Ahmadou Kourouma. London: William Heinemann.

Zabus, Chantal. 2007. *The African Palimpsest: Indigenization of Language in the West African Europhone Novel*. Amsterdam: Rodopi.

Translating orality, recreating otherness

Alexandra Assis Rosa

Department of English and University of Lisbon Centre for English Studies, School of Arts and Humanities, University of Lisbon, Portugal

> This article discusses the problem posed by linguistic variation for interlingual translation, in particular by the relation between language, context and identity in speech and orality, within the framework of descriptive translation studies. It starts by defining linguistic variation as a correlation of linguistic form, communicative meaning and sociocultural value. It examines the particular case of literary representation of varieties to suggest strategies and procedures for their translation. It ends with an analysis of selected examples of canonized British fiction and their translation into European Portuguese, and a discussion of causes and consequences of the patterning resulting from the translation of speech and orality in fiction.

This article aims to discuss the use of formal features predominantly associated with orality and speech (spoken discourse) to represent otherness and a marginalized identity in fiction and more specifically the problem such formally mimetic diction poses for interlingual translation – by associating language, identity and context. It first defines linguistic variation as a correlation of linguistic features and contextual, extralinguistic meaning. Second, it considers how spoken discourse is represented in fictional dialogue, as literary speech and orality. The third part examines the interlingual translation of such literary varieties, analyzing examples drawn from Charles Dickens' *Oliver Twist* and its European Portuguese translations published in the second half of the twentieth century.

Orality and linguistic variation

No language is homogenous. Oral and written discourse, dialects and accents vary and correlate with contextual information. Orality – defined as "the aesthetic representation of otherness, the assertion of marginalized identities through a variety of art forms" (Bandia 2011, n.p.) – is here considered as literary representation of spoken discourse to show (vs. tell) a character's marginality by giving him/her a specific voice (i.e. a formally mimetic characterizing diction).

According to Bell (1991, 185), linguistic features of an individual's discourse convey information about uses and users. Hatim and Mason (1990, 58) relate

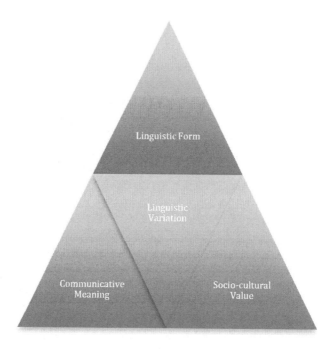

Figure 1. Language and context in linguistic variation (based on Rosa 2012, 80).

structure and texture to extralinguistic dimensions of meaning: communicative and pragmatic meaning and socio-semiotic value. This study of translation addresses linguistic varieties defined as (1) a patterning of sounds, grammatical structures, vocabulary, texture, structure (linguistic form) that may carry (2) contextual information on users and uses, in terms of time, space, sociocultural group, situation and individuality (communicative meaning), that is also associated with (3) a given social status and prestige within a linguistic community (sociocultural value; Rosa [2012, 80]).

A speaker's communicative competence – encompassing both linguistic competence and extra-linguistic knowledge of the experiential context in which a language is used (i.e. verbal and non-verbal codes) – offers awareness of the relation of a set of linguistic features with communicative meaning and sociocultural value.[1] Communicative meaning includes information on time (to identify a speaker's age), physical space (to identify a speaker's region) and social space (to identify a speaker's sociocultural group), as well as a specific communicative situation (to identify relations between speakers, the use of channels or the functions of interaction), and sometimes even a particular speaker's preferences (to identify a speaker's individuality). It is also the communicative competence developed within a given community's evaluative attitudes towards varieties that enables their association with various degrees of power, social status and prestige; that is, the sociocultural value of varieties, here equated with overt prestige (Labov 1972).

Taking the parameter of sociocultural value or prestige as focal point, varieties may be represented along an axis extending from maximum to minimum prestige (or even stigma, i.e. negative evaluation of a linguistic form), based on the speakers' evaluative attitudes towards language use. A standard variety (especially in its formal and written use) is associated with high sociocultural status and prestige and located at the extreme of maximum prestige; other varieties, because of their deviation from the standard, are identified as non-standard (Taavitsainen and Melchers 1999, 8) and located further along this axis, according to the speakers' attitudes.

Speech and orality

Oral and written discourse, speech and writing tend to differ linguistically, by exhibiting different patternings of textual-linguistic features. However, as linguistic varieties, rather than two watertight separate modes, oral and written discourse should be considered two extremes of a continuum that displays overlap.[2]

Some formal features are, however, expected to occur more frequently in (spontaneous oral) speech and consequently tend to be associated with spoken discourse: such as ejaculations and exclamations (clausal: "Aren't you clever?" and phrasal: "Goodness gracious!"), tags ("You failed, didn't you?"), fillers ("well", "um"), changes of topic ("By the way, are you coming?"), reformulations ("I gave you the book back ... well, both books actually"), false starts ("I was offered ... she offered me a lift."), stressing ("I really need that!"), hedging (i.e. word/s used to lessen the impact of an utterance, e.g. "kind of"), backchanneling (listeners' behavior during communication, e.g. "Seriously?"), forms of address (pronouns, verbs, titles and nouns used to address a specific speaker, e.g. "Aunt May, are you coming?"), frequent use of deictic forms ("here/there", "this/that"), lower lexical density (fewer lexical vs. grammatical words), higher dependence on context ("Give me that!"), and strong interpersonal component (vs. referential component) (see Amador-Moreno and McCafferty 2011, 3–4).

Regarding the contextual dimensions of meaning, communicatively, spoken and written discourse are mainly correlated with different (auditive or visual) channels; socio-semiotically, speech tends to lose in prestige to writing, because speakers' evaluative attitudes tend to consider speech as deviant or even incorrect (Leith 1997, 34).

However, Walter J. Ong offers a different view by means of "orality", defined as a specific way of "managing knowledge and verbalization in primary oral cultures (cultures with no knowledge at all of writing) and in cultures deeply affected by the use of writing" (1982, 1). He suggests that primary orality and primary oral cultures ("untouched by writing"; ibid., 9) are associated with a more frequent recourse to mnemonics, formulae and aggregative structures (rather than analytic), additive structures (such as long sentences with clauses coordinated by "and" instead of complex subordinate structures), redundancy, conservativeness, a special focus upon matters of immediate human activity, agonistically toned discourse, an emphasis upon interpersonal meaning, empathetic and participatory identification (instead of objective and distanced communication, focused on ideational meaning) and strongly situational and minimally abstract frames of reference (ibid., 31–57).

Orality has been operative in studying intercultural and interlingual relations in a postcolonial context, which is not the focus of this article. However, important here is the statement that "to varying degrees many cultures and subcultures, even in a high-technology ambiance, preserve much of the mindset of primary orality" (Ong

1982, 11). This may also have a bearing on the translation of some varieties interpretable as the distinctive voices of marginalized social groups whose characterizing diction also includes features of orality. As stated by Taivalkoski (2013, 2): "[v]oices represent identities and subject positions; they can be silenced, manipulated or cherished" by translation. Interestingly, such individuals and groups tend to lose visibility in translated texts due to translation strategies that manipulate or silence their singularity.

Speakers' attitudes tend to apply a binary opposition between the extremes of the currently most prestigious use of formal written standard language (the grapholect), and the less prestigious or even disparaged use of spoken language – encompassing oral standard, regional and social non-standard. These varieties are seldom or never used in writing, where they tend to be considered wrong or lacking.[3]

Literary varieties

Literary fictional varieties defined as "the representation of nonstandard speech in literature" (Taavitsainen and Melchers 1999, 13) cannot, however, be equated with authentic language use. They have been most influentially studied by Chatman (1978), Page (1988), Blake (1981) and Chapman (1994), who suggest that several filters contribute to their representation, such as linguistic stereotypes, or the organizing of authentic language use into categories defined by salience and deviation from the standard,[4] and especially a fictional repertoire of selected linguistic features previously used to represent literary varieties, which results from a culture-specific literary tradition. Further filters may also result from the repertoire of a given author, or the need for readability constraining the density of deviant features.

For our purposes, fictional discourse will be defined as characterizing vs. non-characterizing discourse; and group vs. individual characterizing discourse.[5] Characterizing discourse usually enables the distinction between narrator discourse (which tends to be standard and non-characterizing) and character discourse. It tends to concentrate in dialogue representation and may convey situation-related information (e.g. degree of formality, emotions) and speaker-related information (e.g. social group, profession, region or individuality). Characterizing discourse can offer information on a group (related to time, space, profession or age) or individual. It contributes to character profiling by generating a specific voice or formally mimetic characterizing diction.

Literary speech and orality

Linguistic features associated with speech and orality are also used to create a specific and verisimilar discursive profile. Among the features of such character diction are: simulation of non-linguistic signs (silences, sounds of laughter); graphic signals of paralinguistic signs (intonation, volume); forms of address; literary non-standard accents and dialects; and a predominance of phatic, expressive and conative functions (Jakobson 1960) revealed by the use of exclamations, questions, expletives, imperatives, repetitions, emphatic structures, and the use of the words "yes" and "no" (Chatman 1978, 202; Chapman 1994).

Additionally, fiction may also recreate the mindset of orality as a specific discursive profile associated with illiteracy, sociocultural marginality, and lack of power and skills by resorting to linguistic features such as those mentioned by Ong (1982), which tend to be stigmatized as are their users and contexts.

In a nutshell, literary varieties can be understood as a rather complex recreation of a correlation of linguistic features, information on speaker and situation, and prestige, which is filtered by norms of literary discourse representation. Translating formal features is not particularly difficult. Translating formal features correlated with information on speaker, situation and prestige, further filtered by a poetics of fiction and used to indirectly offer contextual information about a character, however, does pose problems.

Translating literary speech and orality

The first studies to focus on the negotiation of prestige to examine the translation of linguistic varieties were Brisset (1996; on theatre translation into "Québécois" in Canada), Cronin (1996; on fiction and theatre translation into Hiberno English and Irish Gaelic in Ireland), Dimitrova (1997; on the translation of Swedish fiction into English and Russian), Rosa (1999, 2001; on the subtitling of British English into European Portuguese), and Leppihalme (2000a, 2000b; on the translation of Finnish fiction into English and Swedish). Following Dimitrova (1997), Rosa (1999, 2003, 2012), and Leppihalme (2000a, 2000b), this article also addresses the translation of literary varieties by focusing on the parameter of prestige, represented as an axis, to identify translation strategies. The prestige of each variety depends on the language under consideration and is as variable as its speakers' evaluative attitudes. The organization of varieties along an axis of prestige will consequently depend on the axiomatic of values of a given linguistic community towards language use at a given moment in time.

Maximum prestige ---Minimum prestige

European Portuguese Standard – Oral Non-standard – Regional Non-standard –Social Non-standard

Figure 2. Sociocultural value of contemporary European Portuguese varieties.

Figure 2 represents contemporary varieties of European Portuguese along a prestige axis, simply identified as standard, oral, regional and social non-standard following evaluative attitudes of speakers. Maximum prestige is associated with the written, standard and formal use. Less prestigious varieties considered non-standard are speech, followed by regional and – the least prestigious – sociocultural non-standard. User attitudes towards language use consider European Portuguese oral varieties as distinct from the standard (Rosa 1999, 2003, 2012; Ramos Pinto 2009), even if for the descriptive linguist this is not the case.

This appears to be the case for English, too: "standard English is particularly associated with the written language. In fact, it can be said that the grammar of spoken language is stigmatised" (Taavitsainen and Melchers 1999, 5). Non-standard accents tend to be associated with provinciality or lower social status (Wells 1982, 34, quoted in Taavitsainen and Melchers 1999, 15; although regional accents have been rising in prestige); non-standard grammar and lexis have been associated with lower prestige (e.g. with rough, rustic, simple, uneducated or vulgar speakers) since the sixteenth century (Leith 1997, 42–43).

Translating literary varieties: Shifts, procedures, strategies

Following Rosa (2012), to understand, describe and explain the translation of literary varieties, this study also adopts the concepts of shifts, procedures and strategies, adapted to study the translation of literary varieties. According to Chesterman (2005, 24), translation strategy is defined in "its basic problem-solving sense as a plan that is implemented in a given context" and will be understood as a global strategy resulting from a patterning of micro-level procedures. Translation techniques/procedures are defined as "routine, micro-level, textual procedures". Their operation may be analyzed by a comparative textual analysis of source and target texts (STs and TTs) to identify dissimilarities or shifts, defined as "the result of a procedure ... observable as kinds of difference between target and source".

If an ST has features of literary varieties deviating from the standard (or grapholect), translators may choose among a range of translation procedures, namely the omission, addition, maintenance or change of such linguistic features and their associated contextual information. All translation procedures except for maintenance operate shifts that far from being merely formal also have consequences in terms of the above-mentioned contextual dimensions of meaning. A different patterning of formal features in the TT may consequently portray a different user, a different communicative situation and a different degree of prestige.

The patterning of shifts reveals three strategies: normalization, when ST less prestigious discourse is translated as standard; centralization, when ST less prestigious discourse is translated as more prestigious, though not normalized; and decentralization, when the opposite occurs and ST standard (written and formal use) is translated as less prestigious discourse.

Maximum prestige -- Minimum prestige

Portugal: European Portuguese standard – Oral Non-standard – Regional Non-standard – Social Non-standard

(1)

(2)

(3)

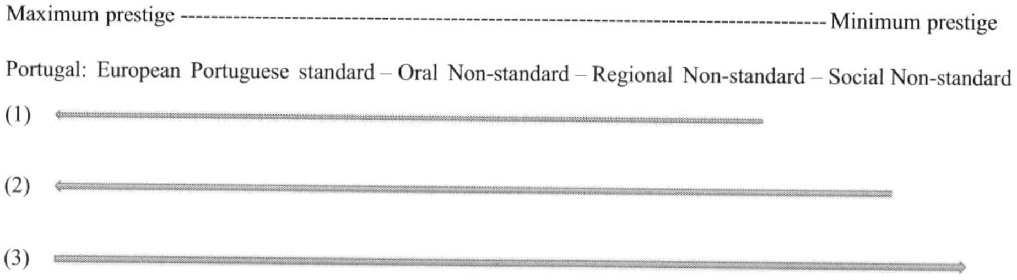

Figure 3. Translation strategies for literary varieties.

Interestingly, most translation shifts appear not to be motivated by formal differences between source and target languages (obligatory shifts) but are non-obligatory, constrained by the target context (Toury 1995, 57) and influenced by stylistic, ideological or cultural factors (Bakker, Koster, and van Leuven-Zwart

1998, 228). Accordingly, such shifts may contribute to identifying ideological, evaluative and intersubjective preferences for translation strategies, which appear to be strongly motivated by linguistic stereotypes whose profile also heavily depends upon prestige. In sociocultural contexts still strongly marked by the written standard's power and prestige, it comes as no surprise that normalization has proven to be the most pervasive strategy.[6] It has even been posited as a translation universal (formulated as the law of growing standardization by Toury [2012, 303]). Though less frequent, centralization occurs in translations attempting to recreate some type and degree of deviance (Dimitrova 1997; Rosa 1999, 2003). Decentralization strategies are rare, usually resulting from a very strong ideological and/or political motivation, such as the influence of nationalist movements or the aim of increased translator visibility (see Brissett 1996; Cronin 1996; Lane-Mercier 1997; Findlay 2000; Chapdelaine 2006).

As for the consequences, a normalization strategy that omits less prestigious discourse obliterates ST variation and creates a TT fully reduced to the prestige of the TL grapholect. ST characterizing discourse becomes non-characterizing in translation, both in relation to external authentic use and to the narrator's internal diction. Character and narrator diction thereby coincide and narrative functions associated with such ST distinctions are not replicated in the TT. All other translation procedures (i.e. maintenance, change or addition of less prestigious discursive traits) contribute to centralization or decentralization strategies, to some degree recreate literary variation in the target text, and maintain or increase the repertoire of characterizing discourse, even if the contextual meanings associated with TT discourse representation suffer shifts, as is often the case.

Analyzing the translation of literary speech and orality

Let us examine a selection of English-language marginal discursive profiles created by formally mimetic discourse, resorting to less prestigious oral, regional or socially non-standard literary varieties in order to consider the consequences that may result from translation shifts in the indirect characterization of literary characters in the novel.[7] Literary precedent to the use of literary varieties of English goes as far back as Chaucer, and many novelists make use of them to indirectly characterize traditionally minor socioculturally and morally marginal characters (Page 1988, 58, 86, 103–104; Chapman 1994, 18, 23, 59, 221). However, Charles Dickens' "commitment to the spoken language" (Page 1988, 168) makes him stand out among other English language novelists for his use of group and mostly individual characterizing discourse. Furthermore, Dickens is the most retranslated nineteenth-century canonized British author in Portugal, which also allows for the consideration of more retranslations. Dickens was initially translated into European Portuguese in the 1860s, first serialized in periodicals and later published in book form. Among the most retranslated texts are his 1843 first Christmas book, *A Christmas Carol: A Ghost Story of Christmas* (over 25 translations, 1863–2010), and his third novel, *Oliver Twist* (1837–39; 17 translations, 1876–1993). This article considers three characters appearing in the initial scenes of *Oliver Twist*: Mrs Thingummy (the nurse who helps Oliver's mother), Mrs Mann (the woman who takes care of Oliver until he turns nine) and Mr Bumble (the beadle who takes Oliver to the workhouse on his ninth birthday) to consider how their ST marginal diction is recreated in retranslations into European Portuguese (published 1952–93).

Mrs Thingummy, the nurse: "Lor bless her dear heart!"

As often happens with Dickensian characters, Mrs Thingummy is immediately defined in her social marginality and insignificance by both her name and her use of socially non-standard discourse (marked by a deviant grammar, lexis and spelling), as illustrated by (1):

> (1) Lor bless her dear heart, when she has lived as long as I have, sir, **and** had thirteen children of her own, **and** all on 'em dead except two, **and** them in the wurkus with me, she'll know better than to take on in that way, bless her dear heart! (Dickens [1837–39] 1999, 2, my emphasis)

In (1), Mrs Thingummy's discourse is represented using forms relatable to both speech and orality. The repeated formulaic exclamations that flank her sentences ("Lor bless her dear heart", or later "poor dear") are features of orality, associated in the first case with low sociocultural status and in the second with the oral expression of sympathy and affection. The deferential form "sir" used to address the doctor also signals his superior rank within both the communicative situation and the wider fictional social hierarchy (Chapman 1994, 79). The marked orality of the succession of additive clauses coordinated by "and" (in which she seems to lose track of the purpose of the initial subordinative "when") reaches a climax with "**and** all on 'em dead except two, **and** them in the wurkus". Her discourse becomes more markedly marginal here: spelling is deviant and slurred (probably also as a result of the alcohol ingested, as the narrator does not fail to mention), grammar becomes clearly deviant (marked by the choice of the preposition "on" for "of" in "all **on** 'em", or the oblique form of the pronoun instead of the subject form in "and **them** in the wurkus"). This is further strengthened by the immediacy of the aggregative formula later used to address Oliver's mother: "Think what it is to be a mother, there's a **dear young lamb** do" (Dickens [1837–39] 1999, 2, my emphasis). Interestingly, after this initial concentration of features of socioculturally marginal speech and a markedly speech-like and orality-like style, her subsequent discourse incoherently adopts standard grammar, lexis and spelling. Perhaps once the intended narrative effect had been attained, legibility determined that Mrs Thingummy's utterances should then be represented as standard.

In the European Portuguese translations, Mrs Thingummy adopts a much less characterizing diction, since the TTs exhibit fewer features of mainly spoken discourse only occasionally relatable to orality and sociocultural marginality:

TT Examples	Gloss[8]
(1a) **Que Deus a abençoe,** pobre mulher -disse a empregada, guardando à pressa no bolso uma garrafa cujo conteúdo acabava de provar, com evidente satisfação - Quando ela tiver vivido tanto como eu, senhor doutor, quando tiver treze filhos e perdido onze; visto que não tenho senão dois que	"**May God bless her**, poor woman," said the maid, quickly tucking inside her pocket a bottle, the contents of which she had just tasted, with evident satisfaction. "When she has lived as long as I have, Doctor, when she has had thirteen children and lost eleven; since I do not have but two, who are with

ORALITY AND TRANSLATION

estão comigo no albergue, <u>então</u> há-de pensar de outra maneira. (Dickens 1952, 18)

me in the workhouse, <u>then</u> she will think differently."

(1b) **-Valha-me Deus!** -exclamou por sua vez a enfermeira. -Ninguém morre por ter um filho, pobre mulher. Eu tive treze <u>e</u> ainda aqui estou. (Dickens 1972, 1)

"God help me!" exclaimed the nurse. "Nobody dies because of having a child, poor woman. I have had thirteen <u>and</u> I am still here."

(1c) **Que Deus a guarde!** <u>Quando</u> chegar à minha idade, <u>depois de</u> ter treze filhos como eu tive, <u>embora</u> Deus me tenha levado onze e deixado apenas dois, <u>que</u> vivem comigo aqui no albergue, pensará de outro modo, <u>em vez de</u> deixar-se abater assim pelo desgosto. (Dickens 1980, 6)

"May Good keep her! <u>When</u> she reaches my age, <u>after</u> having had thirteen children as I have, <u>although</u> God took eleven of them and left only two, <u>who</u> live with me in the workhouse, she will think otherwise, <u>instead of</u> letting grief bring her down."

(1d) **-Deus a abençoe, coitadinha,** <u>quando</u> tiver vivido tanto como eu, Sr. Doutor, <u>e</u> tiver tido treze filhos, todos eles mortos excepto dois, e todos eles no asilo comigo, <u>nessa altura</u> saberá que não deve falar assim, **valha-a Deus!** (Dickens 1981, 18)

"May God bless her, the poor thing, <u>when</u> she has lived as much as me, Doctor, <u>and</u> has had thirteen children, all of them dead but two and all of them in the workhouse with me, <u>by that time</u> she will know that she should not speak like this, **God help her!**

(1e) **-Ora, valha-a Deus!** -exclamou Sally. (Dickens 1993, 8)

"God help her!" exclaimed Sally.

Formulaic clausal exclamations marked by exclamation marks (and transcribed in bold above) are recreated in the TTs and may be interpreted as orality features also associated with low sociocultural status, but their aggregative formulaic nature is reduced (Lor bless **her dear heart**" becomes "God help/bless **her!**"; my emphasis) and their redundant though expressive and agonistic repetition, which corresponds to another feature of orality, is avoided in all TTs but one (the 1981 translation). The nurse's diction is dramatically transedited into standard European Portuguese by syntactical shifts, which transform the ST's rather long sentence into: (a) three smaller and mainly simple standard sentences (1968); (b) only one brief and simple standard exclamatory sentence (1993); (c) an only slightly less fluent but still standard sentence (1952: "when ... and ... and ... by that time"; 1980: "When ... after ... although ... and ... who ... instead of"); or (d) an elaborately clear, markedly written standard long sentence with a succession of impeccably subordinated clauses (1952: "When ... when ... since ... who ... then"). All these versions display a centralizing strategy and stand in marked opposition to the non-standard marginal voice of the ST's poor, probably illiterate, socioculturally marginalized, drunken workhouse nurse.

Mrs Mann, the baby farm operator: "My Heart alive!"

Mrs Mann's discursive nature is very strongly marked by the ingratiating hypocrisy with which she addresses Mr Bumble, upon whose goodwill she depends. This creates a very strong contrast to the agonistic harshness with which she addresses her maid, Susan, or refers to the children in her care, when she is sure nobody else is listening, as in the following aside:

(2) (Susan, take Oliver and **them** two brats upstairs, and wash 'em directly.) (Dickens [1837–39] 1999, 5, my emphasis)

This is said right after Mr Bumble kicks the locked entrance gate, which prevents him from entering. A further illustration of the orality of Mrs Mann's speech is provided when she flatteringly piles on several forms of address, marking a crescendo of deference with the clear interpersonal purpose of eliciting empathy and appeasing his anger:

> (3) "Goodness gracious! Is that **you, Mr. Bumble, sir**?" said Mrs. Mann, thrusting her head out of the window in well-affected ecstasies of joy. (Ibid., 5, my emphasis)

The following sentence, in turn, allows the reader to picture her accompanying the staccato of her syntax with an additional bow, after each repetition of a deferential form of address, and subservient invitation for Mr Bumble to enter her house, which consequently stress her lower status and especially, as she intends, his power:

> (4) Walk in, **sir**; walk in, pray, **Mr. Bumble**, do, **sir**. (Ibid., 6, my emphasis)

The discursive profile of Mrs Mann is markedly orality-like (through addition, redundancy, repetition and agonistic tone) and also socioculturally low status, marked by deviant grammar, lexis and spelling. A further example occurs when she mentions bolting the gate as one of her own good deeds, thus offering an excuse and begging for empathy from the still angry Mr Bumble:

> (5) That I should have forgotten that the gate was bolted on the inside, **on account of them dear children**! (Ibid., 6, my emphasis)

Here (as in example 2) the salience of the oblique personal pronoun "them" in place of the standard demonstrative determinant ("those") or even the possessive determinant ("my") is more than enough to signal her low status. The following line has a similar effect, with her status marked by the relative clause introduced by "as is" instead of the standard "who are", the southern English and dialectal "a-telling" and "a-coming", which are also accompanied by uses of an occasional non-standard "ain't" in other sentences:

> (6) "I'm sure Mr. Bumble, that I was only **a-telling** one or two of the dear children **as is so fond of you**, that it was you **a-coming**," replied Mrs. Mann with great humility. (Ibid., 6, my emphasis)

In the European Portuguese translations, the orality of this character's strongly agonistic (either empathetic, ingratiating and subservient or aggressive, harsh and authoritarian), repetitive, redundant, grammatically deviant and socioculturally non-standard discourse is normalized. The Portuguese Mrs Mann uses a literary, mostly written standard, which predominantly coincides with narrator diction. In the 1968 translation, her only spoken line is rendered in indirect discourse without any formally mimetic features. The normalization of her lines is signaled by the lack of any formally mimetic features deviating from standard grammar, lexis and spelling (which would be marked in bold as in the examples above). In her complex sentences in Portuguese, all instances of subordination are absolutely correct if not even formal (as in 1972: "so as to"; my emphasis):

ORALITY AND TRANSLATION

TT Examples	Gloss
(5+6a) E neste meio tempo libertaram-se as crianças -Esqueci-me totalmente de que a porta estava fechada por dentro, por causa das crianças. [...] -Oh, não, senhor Bumble! -respondeu muito humildemente a senhora Mann - Eu tinha ido dizer a um ou dois desses pequenitos queridos, que tanto o estimam, que o senhor Bumble vinha aí. (Dickens 1952, 22)	And in the meantime, the children had been set free. "I totally forgot that the gate had been locked inside, because of the children." [...] "Oh, no, Mr Bumble," replied Mrs Mann very humbly, "I had gone to tell one or two of those little darlings, who care for you so much, that you were coming."
(5+6b) A porta está fechada, senhor Bumble? Oh, não sabia! [...] -Fui à procura dos meninos a fim de avisá-los de que o senhor estava aqui. (Dickens 1972, 4)	"Is the door locked, Mr Bumble? Oh, I did not know. [...] I was looking for the children so as to let them know that you were here."
(5+6c) -Como me esqueci que a porta estava fechada por dentro por causa destes queridinhos! [...] -Desculpe, senhor Bumble, é que fui avisar três destas criancinhas, que tanto o amam, que o senhor tinha chegado. (Dickens 1980, 14–15)	"How I forgot that the door was locked inside because of these little darlings! [...] I am sorry, Mr Bumble, I went to warn three of these little children, who love you so much, that you had arrived."
(5+6d) - Imaginem, esquecer-me de que a porta estava trancada do lado de dentro, por causa dos queridos pequenos, coitadinhos. [...] -Garanto-lhe, Sr. Bumble, que estava apenas a dizer a um ou dois dos queridos pequenos que tanto o estimam que o senhor vinha aí -respondeu-lhe a Sra. Mann, cheia de humildade. (Dickens 1981, 21)	"Imagine, to forget that the door was locked inside because of the dear children, the poor little things." [...] "I assure you, Mr Bumble, that I was only telling one or two of the dear children, who care for you so much, that you were coming," answered Mrs Mann very humbly.

In these sentences, only the interjections (not always recreated) and the use of "no" and forms of address signal a residually speech-like characterizing diction. Mrs Mann is entirely translated as a literate, standard-speaking character, with only very occasional features of speech.

Mr Bumble, the superlative beadle: "I inwented it."

Mr Bumble, whose name suggests a fat-bellied bumblebee (very noisy but without any sting), is characterized by pompous diction and a presumptuously elaborate discourse, as expected of a character of his importance, namely a beadle. Nevertheless, his low sociocultural provenance is revealed by a strongly agonistic orality – with profuse irate exclamations – and social marginality, featured in both the deviant spelling representing his low-status pronunciation and the deviant dialect marked by mostly grammatical but also lexical shifts from the standard. One particular spelling shift immediately identifies him as a speaker of Cockney: the use of "w" instead of "v", already established by literary tradition (Page 1988, 65).

Further examples of deviant spelling marking an urban low-class accent abound, such as "ineddicated" (Dickens [1837–39] 1999, 28). However, "porochial", "aweer", "just a leetle drop" (ibid., 6) or "supernat'ral exertions" (ibid., 7) are examples of eye-dialect, since their use of non-standard deviant spelling (to mark ellipsis, and vowel or intonation changes) actually comes closer to representing speech that is actually standard speech. However, in the cases of eye-dialect the deviance from standard

ORALITY AND TRANSLATION

spelling has the effect upon average readers of saliently marking sociocultural low status, similarly to the other deviant spellings (Golding 1985, 9; Chapman 1994, 21).

The most ironically salient lexical deviation is his use of "fondlins" instead of "foundlings" (Dickens [1837–39] 1999, 7), when referring to the children in the baby farm; among the various grammatically deviant lines, sentences such as the following are worth quoting:

(8) The kind and blessed gentlemen **which is** so many parents to you, Oliver, when you have none of your own: are a going **to 'prentice** you. (Ibid., 19, my emphasis)

(9) – and all for a naughty orphan which **nobody can't** love. (Ibid., 19, my emphasis)

(10) "If **we was** to bind him to any other trade tomorrow, he'd run away **simultaneous**, your worship," replied Bumble. (Ibid., 21, my emphasis)

(11) "Juries," said Mr Bumble, grasping his cane tightly, as was his wont when working into a passion: "**juries is ineddicated**, vulgar, grovelling wretches." (Ibid., 28, my emphasis)

In some examples, Mr Bumble's agonistic nature is expressed by a higher number of non-standard instances, which are also used to express his anger. Among these are: non-standard number concord, and the non-standard choice of a relative pronoun for a human antecedent requiring the use of "who", instead of "which" (8); the clearly non-standard double negative and again non-standard concord of a relative pronoun with a human antecedent, since "which" is used instead of the standard "that" or "whom" (9); the non-standard lack of concord in number between a plural subject and a singular verb form, and the use of an adjective instead of an adverb (10); as well as examples of the above-mentioned deviant spelling (8, 9, 11).

When calm, Mr Bumble carefully chooses pompous vocabulary, which he involuntarily combines with serious grammatical mistakes. The density of such "slips of the tongue" increases in direct proportion to his anger, something that is ignored in the Portuguese translations. Perhaps his most salient grammatically deviant feature is a severe difficulty with superlatives; for example:

(12) "Well! Of *all* the **ungratefullest**, and **worst-disposed** boys as ever I see, Oliver, you are the –" (Dickens [1837–39] 1999, 29, my emphasis)

(13) "Well! of all the artful and designing orphans that ever I see, Oliver, you are one of **the most bare-facedest**." (Ibid., 22, my emphasis)

Let us consider the translations of only two sentences. The first is used to state bombastically that he invented Oliver's family name, where his Cockney accent is marked by deviant spelling:

(14) The beadle drew himself up with great pride, and said, "I **inwented** it." (Dickens [1837–39] 1999, 7, my emphasis)

The reason for this pride deserves further consideration. Mr Bumble is proud to have invented a system to provide orphans with a proper family name. This system is based on his knowledge of the alphabet, and significantly for him being literate is reason enough to be proud. But he is particularly proud because in addition he

ORALITY AND TRANSLATION

imposes the literate abstract categorization of alphabetical order upon the orphans by inventing family names for those who do not have one – even if this abstract system is useless to tell the orphans apart, since it is not based on distinguishing physical (such as red hair, height or girth) or psychological features (such as being shy, talkative or expressive).[9] This renders Mrs Mann's praise even more meaningful: "Why, you're quite a **literary character**, sir!" (ibid., 7, my emphasis). Mr Bumble is indeed a literary character, his discourse is strongly marked by features prominent in the literary tradition (such as those which distinguish him as a speaker of Cockney), but what she really means is that he is quite a "literate" character, and that his mastery of the alphabet is something to marvel at.

The sentence in example (14) is translated into European Portuguese without any features of deviant spelling, except for the 1981 translation, which changes the second vowel (using "invintei" instead of "inventei"), a change which is faintly evocative of a socioculturally marginal use.

TT Examples	Gloss
(14a) -Fui eu quem o inventou -disse ele. (Dickens 1952, 23)	"It was I who invented it," he said.
(14b) O apelido que ele tem foi inventado por mim. (Dickens 1968, 6)	"His surname was invented by me."
(14c) -Fui eu quem o inventou. (Dickens 1972, 5)	"It was I who invented it."
(14d) -Fui eu que o inventei. (Dickens 1980, 17)	"It was I who invented it."
(14e) O bedel endireitou-se, cheio de orgulho, e redarguiu-lhe: -Eu **invintei**-o. (Dickens 1981, 23)	The beadle drew himself up, full of pride, and replied to her: "I **inwented** it."
(15f) -Fui eu quem lhe pôs o nome -disse o senhor Bumble, com presunção. (Dickens 1993, 9)	"It was I who named him," said Mr Bumble presumptuously.

The second sentence chosen for analysis (13) exhibits the non-standard grammatically deviant superlatives that characterize Mr Bumble, who angrily exclaims that Oliver is "one of the most bare-facedest" orphans he knows. Again, it is only the 1981 translation that attempts to recreate this grammatical non-standard instance:

TT Example	Gloss
-Francamente, Oliver, de todos os órfãos manhosos e astutos que já conheci, tu és **o mais descaradíssimo!** (Dickens 1981, 34)	"Frankly, Oliver, of all the cunning and astute orphans I have ever know, you are **the most cheekiest!**"

With the sole exception of the 1981 version, all Portuguese translations normalize Mr Bumble's diction, which consequently corresponds in all TTs to standard Portuguese, pompously elaborate in vocabulary, as in the ST, but without the ironic counterpoint of socioculturally marginal dialect and pronunciation, which are indispensable to recreate this caricatured character. His orality remains marked in the Portuguese by redundancy, repetitions and formulaic renderings, as well as by his agonistic tone. But his socioculturally stigmatized discourse disappears and the reader is left with only the comments from the narrator, who often distances himself with ironic comments that alone stress Mr Bumble's sociocultural, moral and narrative marginality.

Final remarks

Discursive otherness represented by a formally mimetic, characterizing diction marked by linguistic features of speech and orality is used to indirectly characterize the three socioculturally (and morally) marginal characters of *Oliver Twist* selected for analysis. Their otherness is primarily for the purpose of comic effect and caricature and it both signals these characters' marginality and encourages the reader to judge them morally.

Such characterizing dictions undergo significant translation shifts resulting from the procedures of omission and change. Their discursive marginality and otherness is brought very close to the normative center of prestige occupied by the narrator's (usually standard and written style) voice. As a result, their marginal discursive profiles are erased by centralizing and normalizing strategies. Once translated, these characters speak more like the printed page. Characterizing discourse is rendered as almost non-characterizing discourse: ejaculations and exclamations are simplified or omitted; aggregative formulae are simplified, reduced or omitted; repetition and redundancy are cleaned up; coordinative additive syntax is transedited sometimes into the standard subordination of rather complex sentences; and vocabulary is normalized, grammar corrected and standard spelling used throughout (except for a very few instances). A less varied translated text results, which brings speech closer to writing, character diction closer to narratorial diction, and less prestigious or stigmatized discourse closer to the standard, written and most prestigious language use. Deviance is corrected, the aesthetic representation of otherness is obliterated, the assertion of marginalized identities silenced because orality is brought significantly closer to literacy.

Notes

1. Communicative competence corresponds to an awareness of linguistic routines, of the use of speech in social situations or of its use for the expression of personality in a linguistic community; it also includes attitudes, judgments and intuitions towards speech (Hymes 1972, 282–288).
2. Such hybridity is also stressed by Gambier and Lautenbacher (2010, 5). On further mode variation, see Hatim and Mason (1990, 49).
3. Orality appears systematically related to speakers' attitudes toward illiteracy, poverty, rural and non-western areas, and defined as a deficit or lack of skills needed to read, write and use the internet or mobile phones. However, Ong (1982, 11) also mentions the rising prestige of secondary orality or new orality.
4. Some formal features have an indexical function, leading speakers to evaluate other speakers; linguistic stereotypes include the most salient elements in a variety (Hickey 2000, 58, 65).
5. For a more thorough discussion, see Chatman (1978), Page (1988), Chapman (1994) and Rosa (2003).
6. See Gellerstam (1986, 91), Robyns (1992), Ben-Shahar (1994, 1998), Venuti (1995), Berman (1996, xviii), Dimitrova (1997, 63), Hatim and Mason (1997, 145), Bassnett and Lefevere (1998, 4) and Leppihalme (2000b, 253). House (1973, 167) and Lane-Mercier (1997, 43) even consider literary varieties untranslatable.
7. Analysis of the English examples is based on Hughes, Trudgill, and Watt (2012, 19–36), Melchers and Shaw (2011, 50–55), Gramley and Pätzold (2004, 227–249), and on Chatman

(1978), Page (1988), Blake (1981) and Chapman (1994); analysis of the Portuguese examples is based on the author's native command of standard European Portuguese. Both the analyses of English and Portuguese versions are based on Ong (1982).

8. Glosses have been back-translated by the author; both examples and glosses are marked for emphasis by the author (orality and speech features in bold; written standard underlined).
9. This creates a very strong contrast to the use of family names or orality in Charles Dickens, whereby his caricatured characters are made memorable.

References

Amador-Moreno, Carolina, and Kevin McCafferty. 2011. "Fictionalizing Orality: Introduction." *Sociolinguistic Studies* 5 (1): 1–13.

Bakker, Matthijs, Cees Koster, and Kitty M. van Leuven-Zwart. 1998. "Shifts of Translation." In *Encyclopedia of Translation Studies*, edited by Mona Baker, 226–231. London: Routledge.

Bandia, Paul. 2011. "Orality and Translation." In *Handbook of Translation Studies*, edited by Y. Gambier and L. van Doorslaer, n.p. Amsterdam: John Benjamins.

Bassnett, Susan, and André Lefevere. 1998. "Introduction: Where Are We in Translation Studies?" In *Constructing Cultures*, edited by Susan Bassnett, 1–11. Clevedon: Multilingual Matters.

Bell, Roger T. 1991. *Translation and Translating*. London: Longman.

Ben-Shahar, Rina. 1994. "Translating Literary Dialogue: A Problem and its Implications for Translation into Hebrew." *Target* 6 (2): 195–221.

Ben-Shahar, Rina. 1998. "The Language of Plays Translated into Hebrew from English and French: A Cultural Stylistic Study." *Meta* 43 (1): 54–67.

Berman, Antoine. 1996. Foreword to *A Sociocritique of Translation: Theatre and Alterity in Quebec, 1968–1988*. By Annie Brisset. Translated by Rosalind Gill and Roger Gannon, xii–xxii. Toronto: University of Toronto Press.

Blake, N. F. 1981. *Non-Standard Language in English Literature*. London: André Deutsch.

Brisset, Annie. 1996. *A Sociocritique of Translation: Theatre and Alterity in Quebec, 1968–1988*. Translated by Rosalind Gill and Roger Gannon. Toronto: University of Toronto Press.

Chapdelaine, Annick. 2006. "Retraduire le Hamlet de Faulkner: la réflexion à l'oeuvre, la réflexion par l'oeuvre." *TTR* 20 (2): 121–209.

Chapman, Raymond. 1994. *Forms of Speech in Victorian Fiction*. London: Routledge.

Chatman, Seymour. 1978. *Story and Discourse: Narrative Structure in Fiction and Film*. Ithaca, NY: Cornell University Press.

Chesterman, Andrew. 2005. "Problems with Strategies." In *New Trends in Translation Studies in Honour of Kinga Klaudy*, edited by K. Károly and Ágota Fóris, 17–28. Budapest: Akadémiai Kiadó.

Cronin, Michael. 1996. *Translating Ireland: Translation, Languages and Identity*. Cork: Cork University Press.

Dickens, Charles. [1837–39] 1999. *Oliver Twist*. Edited by Kathleen Tillotson. Introduction and notes by Stephen Gill. Oxford: Oxford University Press.

Dickens, Charles. [1843] 1988. *Christmas Books Including 'A Christmas Carol'*. Edited with an introduction by Ruth Glancy. Oxford: Oxford University Press.

Dickens, Charles. 1952. *A Estranha História de Oliver Twist*. Translated by Mário Domingues. Lisboa: Romano Torres.

Dickens, Charles. 1968. *Oliver Twist. A história de uma criança a quem a vida martiriza*. Condensation by Raul Correia. Lisboa: Agência Portuguesa de Revistas.

Dickens, Charles. 1972. *Oliver Twist*. Adapted by J. M. Carbonell. Translated by Pereira da Silva. Amadora: Bertrand.

Dickens, Charles. 1980. *Oliver Twist*. Revised translation by R. Correia. Lisboa: Amigos do Livro.

Dickens, Charles. 1981. *Oliver Twist*. Translated by Fernanda Pinto Rodrigues. Mem-Martins: Europa-América.

Dickens, Charles. 1993. *Oliver Twist*. Portuguese version by M. Mendonça Soares. Lisboa: Verbo.

Dimitrova, Brigitta Englund. 1997. "Translation of Dialect in Fictional Prose: Vilhelm Moberg in Russian and English as a Case in Point." In *Norm, Variation and Change in Language: Proceedings of the Centenary Meeting of the Nyfilologiska Sällskapet Nedre Manilla 22–23 March 1996*, 49–65. Stockholm: Almquist & Wiksell International.

Findlay, Bill. 2000. "Translating Standard into Dialect: Missing the Target?" In *Moving Target: Theatre Translation and Cultural Relocation*, edited by Carole-Anne Upton, 35–46. Manchester: St Jerome.

Gambier, Yves, and Olli Philippe Lautenbacher. 2010. "Oralité et écrit en traduction." In "Oralité et écrit en traduction", edited by Yves Gambier and Olli Philippe Lautenbacher, special issue, *Glottopol*, no. 15: 5–17.

Gellerstam, Martin. 1986. "Translationese in Swedish Novels Translated from English." In *Translation Studies in Scandinavia: Proceedings from the Scandinavian Symposium on Translation Theory*, edited by Lars Wollier and Hans Lindquist, 88–95. Lund: CWK Gleerup.

Golding, Robert. 1985. *Idiolects in Dickens*. London: Macmillan.

Gramley, S., and K. M. Pätzold. 2004. *A Survey of Modern English*. 2nd ed. London: Routledge.

Hatim, Basil, and Ian Mason. 1990. *Discourse and the Translator*. London: Longman.

Hatim, Basil, and Ian Mason. 1997. *The Translator as Communicator*. London: Longman.

Hickey, Raymond. 2000. "Salience, Stigma and Standard." In *The Development of Standard English, 1300–1800: Theories Descriptions, Conflicts*, edited by Laura Wright, 57–72. Cambridge: Cambridge University Press.

House, Juliane. 1973. "Of the Limits of Translatability." *Babel* 4 (3): 166–167.

Hughes, Arthur, Peter Trudgill, and Dominic Watt. 2012. "Dialect Variation." In *English Accents and Dialects: An Introduction to Social and Regional Varieties of English in the British Isles*, 5th ed., 19–36. London: Routledge.

Hymes, D. H. 1972. "On Communicative Competence." In *Sociolinguistics: Selected Readings*, edited by J. B. Pride and J. Holmes, 269–293. Harmondsworth: Penguin.

Jakobson, Roman. 1960. "Comments." In *Style in Language*, edited by T. A. Sebeok, 278–279. Cambridge, MA: MIT Press.

Labov, William. 1972. *Sociolinguistic Patterns*. Philadelphia: University of Pennsylvania Press.

Lane-Mercier, Gillian. 1997. "Translating the Untranslatable: The Translator's Aesthetic, Ideological and Political Responsibility." *Target* 9 (1): 43–68.

Leith, Dick. 1997. *A Social History of English*. 2nd ed. London: Routledge.

Leppihalme, Ritva. 2000a. "Päätalo Idioms and Catchphrases in Translation." In *Erikoiskielet ja käännösteoria/LSP and Theory of Translation. VAKKI-symposium XX, Vaasa 11.- 13.2.2000* Vol. 27, edited by Päivi Jauhola, Outi Järvi, and Detlef Wilske, 224–234. Vaasa: University of Vaasa.

Leppihalme, Ritva. 2000b. "The Two Faces of Standardization: On the Translation of Regionalisms in Literary Dialogue." *Translator* 6 (2): 247–269.

Melchers, Gunnel, and Philip Shaw. 2011. *World Englishes*. 2nd ed. London: Routledge.

Ong, Walter J. 1982. *Orality and Literacy: The Technologizing of the Word*. London: Methuen.

Page, Norman. 1988. *Speech in the English Novel*. 2nd ed. London: Macmillan.

Ramos Pinto, Sara. 2009. "Traduzir no vazio: a problemática da variação linguística nas traduções de Pygmalion, de G. B. Shaw e de My Fair Lady, de Alan Jay Lerner" [Translating into a Void: The Problem of Linguistic Variation in Portuguese Translations of Bernard Shaw's *Pygmalion* and Alan Jay Lerner's *My Fair Lady*]. PhD diss., University of Lisbon.

Robyns, Clem. 1992. "Towards a Socisemiotics of Translation." *Romanistische Zeitschrift für Literaturgeschichte – Cahiers d'Histoire des Littératures Romanes* 1 (2): 211–226.

Rosa, Alexandra Assis. 1999. "The Centre and the Edges: Linguistic Variation and Subtitling Pygmalion into Portuguese." In *Translation and the (Re)Location of Meaning. Selected Papers of the CETRA Research Seminars in Translation Studies 1994–1996*, edited by Jeroen Vandaele, 317–338. Leuven: Cetra.

Rosa, Alexandra Assis. 2001. "Features of Oral and Written Communication in Subtitling." In *(Multi)Media Translation: Concepts, Practices and Research*, edited by Yves Gambier and Henrik Gottlieb, 213–221. Amsterdam: John Benjamins.

Rosa, Alexandra Assis. 2003. "Tradução, Poder e Ideologia. Retórica Interpessoal no Diálogo Narrativo Dickensiano em Português (1950–1999)." [Translation, Power and Ideology. Interpersonal Rhetoric in Dickensian Fictional Dialogue Translated into Portuguese 1950–1999]. PhD diss., University of Lisbon.

Rosa, Alexandra Assis. 2012. "Translating Place: Language Variation in Translation." In "The Place of Translation," guest-edited by Rui Carvalho Homem and Teresa Caneda, special issue, *Word and Text: A Journal of Literary Studies and Linguistics* 2 (2): 75–97.

Taavitsainen, Irma, and Gunnel Melchers. 1999. "Writing in Nonstandard English: Introduction." In *Writing in Nonstandard English*, edited by Irma Taavitsainen, Gunnel Melchers, and Päivi Pahta, 1–26. Amsterdam: John Benjamins.

Taivalkoski-Shilov, Kristiina. 2013. "Voice in the Field of Translation Studies." In *La traduction des voix intra-textuelles/Intratextual Voices in Translation*, edited by Kristiina Taivalkoski-Shilov and Myriam Suchet, 1–9. Québec: Vita Traductiva, Éditions Québecoises de l'œuvre.

Toury, Gideon. 1995. *Descriptive Translation Studies and Beyond*. Amsterdam: John Benjamins.

Toury, Gideon. 2012. *Descriptive Translation Studies and Beyond*. 2nd ed. Amsterdam: John Benjamins.

Venuti, Lawrence. 1995. *The Translator's Invisibility*. London: Routledge.

Wells, J. C. 1982. *Accents of English 2: The British Isles*. Cambridge: Cambridge University Press.

Translating orality in the postcolonial Arabic novel: A study of two cases of translation into English and French

Mustapha Ettobi

Arabic Translation Service, Department of General Assembly and Conference Management, United Nations, New York, USA

> This article explores the translation of orality in two postcolonial Arabic novels, namely Najīb Mahfūz's *Awlād Hāratinā* and Muhammad Shukrī's *al-Khubz al-Hāfī*, into English and French. It is argued that assimilation and non-assimilation of cultural aspects of foreign texts can have both positive and negative effects depending on the case examined. Specific examples are analyzed to show the various factors that can influence the way orality is translated as well as the hybridity of the methods used by the translators. This article further illustrates the complexity of evaluating assimilation and non-assimilation as they have an impact on linguistic, semantic, aesthetic, discursive, and cultural levels. It also sheds light on the translator's role by analyzing the effects of his/her interpretation and choices and the patterns detected in his/her work.

In translation studies, there has been a broad consensus on the emergence of a "cultural turn", with the discipline shifting away from a focus on the linguistic and textual aspects of translation. Mary Snell-Hornby, for example, "exhorts linguists to abandon their 'scientific' attitude and to move from 'text' as a putative 'translation unit,' to culture – a momentous step that would go far beyond the move from the word as a 'unit' to the text" (Bassnett and Lefevere 1995, 4). Translation has been placed within a larger context in which various factors – social, political, economic, historical, etc. – are recognized and examined, with power and ideology being granted particular significance. It is therefore helpful to use some of the theories that explore various cultural issues in translation to examine the rendition of oral aspects of literary texts, and orality in general, as part and parcel of the source culture. The objective is to assess the importance given to assimilation or non-assimilation and to highlight the translator's role and ideology. I intend to show the intrinsically hybrid nature of any method used to translate literary texts, including their orality, as there are various considerations, tendencies and repercussions which can be paradoxical if not contradictory. I also argue that the value of each method cannot be determined beforehand, by assuming that the adoption of an assimilating or a non-assimilating method, for example, will lead to a successful translation. Any assessment of a given method should be based on an examination of its actual results in a specific case.

Culture, assimilation/non-assimilation and orality

In this article, culture means the way(s) in which a community lives, communicates, sees and imagines itself and the world around it, represents and reflects on its existence and environment, produces cultural products (books, movies, songs, paintings, etc.) about its experience, presents itself to others and defines itself in relation to them. Culture reflects a world view that stems from the community's beliefs, values, customs and traditions. This world view is homogenous only insofar as it serves to set boundaries between one culture and another and strengthen identity as well as real or perceived uniqueness (since each culture encompasses subcultures with various competing world views). In this sense, orality can be a determining factor in asserting difference between cultures, even those which use the same language. For example, Egyptian *'āmmiyya* contains words from Turkish, French and English, the result of colonization by the Ottoman and British empires and France, whereas Moroccan *dārija* includes French and Spanish words (as a result of colonization by France and Spain) as well as Amazigh languages. Such different borrowings serve partly to explain some of the differences between these two variations of spoken Arabic and their respective cultures.

Assimilation refers to the substitution of components of the target culture and language for elements of the source culture and language with a view to enhancing intelligibility and readability, among other goals. Non-assimilation, on the other hand, is the preservation and promotion of the difference of the foreign culture and language, sometimes at the expense of comprehensibility and fluency. The use of these terms is intended to stress the difference of my view on the effects and value of assimilating or not assimilating a foreign text's cultural elements. Attribution of a predetermined value to maintaining or eradicating these elements can be misleading and may hinder an appreciation of the full impact of assimilation and non-assimilation in a translation.

Antoine Berman, who focused on the cultural dimension of translation, maintains that Western translation is "ethnocentrique" and recommends a non-assimilating approach that respects "la traduction de la lettre" (i.e. attending to the letter of the text; 1999, 25). Such translation allows one to "recognize and receive the Other as Other" (ibid., 74; my translation). Like Berman, Lawrence Venuti asserts that Western translation is "ethnocentric" (1998, 11) and favors the preservation of cultural difference. He calls this approach "foreignization" (which is opposed to "domestication"): "foreignizing translation signifies the difference of the foreign text, yet only by disrupting the codes that prevail in the target language" (1995, 20). As he points out: "A translation project can deviate from domestic norms to signal the foreignness of the foreign text and create a readership that is more open to linguistic and cultural differences – yet without resorting to stylistic experiments that are so estranging as to be self-defeating" (1998, 87). He seems to relate "foreignization" more to challenging the "norms" and "codes" of the target culture than to the preservation of the foreign aspects of the source culture. Noteworthy here is Venuti's view of language which gives insight into how he sees "foreignization" and the means to achieve it, especially by challenging domestic linguistic norms and "standard dialect": "I prefer to translate foreign texts that …, in translation, can be useful in minoritizing the standard dialect and dominant cultural forms in American English" (ibid., 10). He sees translation as a way to reduce, inter alia, the difference between "minor" and "major" dialects within the target culture.

While the methods advocated by these theorists encourage the retention of cultural difference, they may not be applicable in all cases, and assimilation may in fact be a better choice in certain situations for reasons related to ideology, discourse and readability. Moreover, Venuti's theory, even if it recognizes the potential unfavorable effects of translation on relations among cultures and people, tends to focus more on the dynamics and struggle within the target culture: "What I am advocating is not an indiscriminate valorization of every foreign culture or a metaphysical concept of foreignness as an essential value; indeed, the foreign text is privileged in a foreignizing translation only insofar as it enables a disruption of target-language cultural codes" (1995, 41–42).

Although assimilation leads to suppressing cultural components of texts, this impact cannot be fully appreciated simply by stating a general rule and applying it to a text regardless of its nature and the various factors that come into play when it is translated. Analyzing a translation on this basis may be neither adequate nor fair when exploring patterns in a translation and their relation to the translator's particular perspective – as revealed through discursive choices as well as aesthetic preferences that may entail the use of assimilation and non-assimilation, the mitigation or omission of certain aspects and the intensification of others to suit the translator's and/or reader's taste. Indeed, a consideration of the translator's ideology may be crucial to assessing the translation techniques used. As André Lefevere points out, "ideology dictates the basic strategy the translator is going to use and therefore also dictates solutions concerned with both the 'universe of discourse' expressed in the original ... and the language the original itself is expressed in" (1992, 41).

Yet the relevance of studying the rendition of a literary text's oral aspects into other languages arises from not only developments in translation studies (the "cultural turn"), but also the inherent importance of orality in translation. Here, orality means the use of everyday spoken language in a literary text, whether as part of the narration, in dialogue or simply quotations of oral material such as songs, proverbs and sayings.

Orality poses problems and challenges for the translator on various levels, including the linguistic, conceptual and aesthetic. Translating a given text's oral aspects requires consideration of how they represent, imitate or allude to ways in which people converse daily in a different society/culture and what strategies to use to reflect their presence in the original. The issue is more complex than it may appear, since differences between languages and cultures vary, thus creating more possibilities or difficulties in some cases than in others. Moreover, relations among languages/cultures are unequal. When translating literary texts from ex-colonized countries or regions, it is important to preserve their indigenous cultural aspects, in recognition of their existence and value, and avoid the creation or perpetuation of bias. This means, inter alia, preventing colonial or neocolonial discourses from being (re)generated in the translation. As Paul Bandia notes:

> A conscientious translator['s] ... task becomes even more complicated when he is working between two languages of divergent sociocultural backgrounds and the issue takes another twist when the translation is between the languages of the "colonizer" and

the "colonized." The translator must then be particularly careful about how he handles the material of the source language in his desire to be faithful to the target language and culture. Although this is true of any translation, what sets it apart is the fact that the translator should strive to avoid exacerbating tensions created by past historical events (colonialism), by ensuring that no "negative stereotyping" due to ignorance of the source culture occurs in the translation. (1993, 56–57)

Bandia's main focus is the translation of African (literary) works, as he argues for the specificity of postcolonial translation and the translator's delicate role in a situation where power and its impact on mutual perceptions are major factors. His idea can be applied to the translation of Arabic literary texts from North Africa into the languages of the former European colonizers (especially English, French and Spanish). Such cases illustrate the importance of taking into consideration *geo-culture*, a term used here to indicate the existence of a network of cultures and subcultures as well as the (power) relations between them at a given time. As Edward Said maintains in *Culture and Imperialism*: "Just as none of us is outside or beyond geography, none is completely free from the struggle over geography" (1993, 7). Said also specifies the importance of culture in that "struggle": "It is not only about soldiers and cannons but also about ideas, about forms, about images and imaginings" (ibid.). Translating postcolonial literary texts into the languages of ex-colonial cultures renders more visible relations of hegemony and subordination, autonomy and dependence, alliance and antagonism, and so on, placing an additional burden on the translator: that of not reproducing the 'inequality' between the languages and cultures of the ex-colonized and colonizers, and not reiterating the "stereotypes", "images" and "imaginings" that may create tensions or justify occupation.

In this article, the term "postcolonial" refers to the shift of indigenous literature from focusing more on colonialism and the struggle for independence to depicting the postcolonial reality and addressing local issues such as the individual's well-being, social justice, or the status of women and minorities. It also refers to the evolution of indigenous literature after decolonization, with formal experimentation being used to reflect a new reality. Orality can be a way of strengthening the authenticity of Arabic literary texts, as the oral material borrowed is an integral part of local traditions, and may also be aimed at vividly depicting contemporary life in the Arab world. I would now like to explore the oral aspects of two postcolonial Arabic novels, Najīb Mahfūz's *Awlād Hāratinā* (translated variously as *Children of Gebelawi, Children of the Alley* and *Les fils de la médina*; see below for more details) and Muhammad Shukrī's *al-Khubz al-Hāfī* (translated as *For Bread Alone* and *Le pain nu*; see below).

Orality in the selected novels

The appropriateness of using spoken Arabic dialect in literary writing is an issue that goes back to the colonial period (El Kaladi 2003, 201). The issue was whether to "write in classical Arabic, the vernacular, or the colonizer's language" (ibid.). After decolonization, it became a more urgent matter, especially for authors writing in the former colonizers' languages (especially French), who were pressed to use their national languages (Memmi 1985, 13). Among those who attempted to switch to

ORALITY AND TRANSLATION

Arabic were the Algerian writers Rachid Boudjédra and Kateb Yacine, the latter having tried to encourage writing drama in the colloquial (ibid.).

Yet the debate for most writers in the Arab world became focused on the use of the colloquial in literature – Shukrī, Iliās al-Khūrī and others have come out in favor of this, while writers such as Taha Husayn have come down against it. Figuring prominently in the latter camp is Mahfūz, the Egyptian writer and 1988 Nobel laureate, who believed that "[t]he colloquial is one of the diseases from which the people are suffering, and of which they are bound to rid themselves as they progress" (Allen 1995, 36). Still, he did use it in some of his writings, including *Awlād Hāratinā*. This may be explained by the nature of the text: a tale that the narrator writes down to save it from falling into oblivion. This dimension that Mahfūz establishes on the narrative level brings a true intertextuality to his novel; that is, by integrating the traditional storytelling mode in his otherwise modern text. Such intertextuality is common to other texts, whether by Mahfūz or other writers who use traditional oral narratives, such as *al-hikāya* [the tale, e.g. the *Arabian Nights*], which are largely considered as authentic elements of the contemporary Arabic narrative.[1]

In *Awlād Hāratinā*, the narrator tells the story of a *hāra* [neighborhood] where the inhabitants strive to re-establish the order, social justice and respect for human beings that they had enjoyed under the patriarch al-Jabalāwī. While his successors in the management of the *waqf* [unsalable estate] – Adham, Jabal, Rifā'a and Qāsim – succeed in fulfilling people's wishes, the outcome is ephemeral, and injustice and oppression by the rulers and *futuwwas* (those in charge of the security and protection of the *hāra*) return. The last struggle is led by 'Arafa, who fails, and his disciple Hanash promises to change the order of things. Somekh (1973, 152) notes the predominance of orality in the novel, especially in the form of dialogue, which "betrays, more than ever before, the patterns and syntax of the original spoken idiom" (ibid.). Moreover, "words from the *'āmmiyya* now permeate the written language of the author with an unprecedented frequency" (153).

In Shukrī's autobiographical novel, his use of the *dārija* aptly reflects the life of the poor and illiterate people depicted, imparting strong realism. Standard Arabic would tend to leave out much of the raw, graphic and shocking details. Moreover, the use of the *dārija* is linguistically and symbolically subversive, ridding the standard language of its respectability and forcing it to adapt to the social, psychological and political aspects described in his story. Shukrī recounts his difficult childhood and coming of age. Born to a poor Riffian family in Nador in northern Morocco, he moves with his parents to Tangier and then to Tetouan, larger and more promising cities, to escape famine. He describes his suffering from hunger, his father's cruelty and his family's miserable living conditions. Growing up, he is initiated into a life of drugs, debauchery and crime, but his decision to go to school for the first time at the age of 20 will bring about a significant change.

A major difference between these two texts lies in the divergent linguistic combinations chosen by the authors. Mahfūz uses standard Arabic and an Egyptian dialect that all Egyptians can understand. As for Shukrī, he combines standard Arabic with the dialect of northern Morocco and includes words and expressions from Riffian (an Amazigh language spoken in the Rif region), French and Spanish. Thus, his text represents a mostly colonial context in Morocco in general, and Tangier in particular. Rendering the linguistic heterogeneity is important for both artistic and historical reasons.

ORALITY AND TRANSLATION

In terms of reception, both novels faced tremendous challenges. *Awlād Hāratinā* was condemned by the religious circles in Egypt while being serialized in the local daily *Al-Ahrām* in 1959. After this publication, it was banned by a decree issued by al-Azhar (Jayyusi 2005, 25), the highest Egyptian religious authority, primarily owing to "Mahfouz's apparent disregard for the Islamic belief that the prophets are infallible, and, because of the divine message entrusted to them by God, should not be the subject of criticism by mere men" (Moosa 1994, 274). The novel was first published in book form by Dār al-Adāb in Lebanon in 1962 but would not be published in Egypt until 2006, by Dār al-Shurūq. Shukrī's text was published in 1982, only to be banned a year later because of complaints by some Moroccan committees of students' parents (Barrāda and Shukrī 2000, 69); the criticism focused on its sexual content. That ban was lifted in 2000, but the novel was also banned in 1998 in Egypt, on grounds of "immorality", when Samia Mehrez tried to teach it in an Arabic literature course at the American University in Cairo.

Translation analysis

Mahfūz's allegorical novel was first rendered into English by Philip Stewart in 1981 and published by Heinemann as *Children of Gebelawi*. Retranslated in 1994 by Peter Theroux as *Children of the Alley*, published by Doubleday, it was also translated into French by Jean-Patrick Guillaume in 1995, as *Les fils de la médina*, published by Sinbad. Shukrī's autobiographical novel was first rendered into English in 1973 by Paul Bowles, as *For Bread Alone*, published by Peter Owen. A French translation by Tahar Ben Jelloun, entitled *Le pain nu*, was published by François Maspero in 1980. The following analysis will examine how each of the translators deals with cultural difference, focusing on their rendition of the texts' oral aspects. The effects of assimilation and non-assimilation will be discussed and some patterns revealed.

The first case

Idioms and expressions

The first example concerns the translation of "على العين والرأس" in Mahfūz's text (1986, 13); this is an expression used in Egyptian culture to indicate obeisance or acceptance "with pleasure". In the novel, it shows Ridwān's total acceptance of his father al-Jabalāwī's decision to entrust the management of the estate to Adham rather than to Idrīs. Stewart translates it as "[a]nything you say" (Mahfūz 1981, 7), which suppresses the cultural aspect of the expression and constitutes a perfect example of assimilation to the target culture, or "traduction ethnocentrique". Similarly, Theroux translates it as "I will obey" (Mahfūz 1996, 11), keeping the general meaning without conveying the absolute obeisance implied. Both renditions can be described as "domesticating" since they use fluent English. As for Guillaume, he maintains the original image: "Sur ma tête et mon œil" [on my head and eye] (Mahfūz 2000, 14), but rationalizes the expression for Western readers by placing "head" before "eye". Although this choice retains cultural difference and may be described as "foreignizing", one is left to wonder how readers will understand it without any explanation. Guillaume's choice imparts strangeness and exoticism to the text for those readers who are unfamiliar with the expression's cultural significance; that is, the fact that Egyptians refer to the eyes and head as valuable

107

ORALITY AND TRANSLATION

organs that they are willing to use/sacrifice to comply with another person's desire. The implicit understanding of the source-text reader is not shared by the target-text reader. Noteworthy here is the fact that the exoticizing aspect of the French translation is betrayed through the use of the word *médina* despite the fact that this notion is specific to the Maghreb and alien to Egyptian culture; Salama-Carr argues that this "questionable" title is indeed an "exotisation" (2001, 281).

In another example, Mahfūz uses the *'āmmiyya* in the description of Narjis, al-Jabalāwī's servant, when the patriarch expels her from the "Big House" after discovering that she has been impregnated by his son Idrīs. The narrator says: "غادرت نرجس البيت وهي تصوت وتلطم خديها" (1986, 25), literally: "Narjis left the house wailing and slapping herself on the cheeks". The verb "صوّت" is not used in its standard Arabic sense ("to vote" or "to cry out"); here, it means "to wail", constituting a borrowing from the spoken dialect. Guillaume renders the sentence as "la malheureuse sortit donc, se lamentant et se frappant le visage" (Mahfūz 2000, 41). In so doing, he more or less retains its cultural aspect, but over-dramatizes and explicitates Narjis' suffering, inserting "la malheureuse" [the unhappy one] and saying that she "beats herself on the face", conveying utter despair. What she actually does is "slap herself on the cheeks", a typical Egyptian gesture to express dismay at a catastrophe or a disaster. Similarly, Stewart maintains the image, judging it intelligible – "Narjis left the house, wailing and beating her cheeks" (Mahfūz 1981, 14) – but his translation refers more accurately to the specific part of the face. The same applies to Theroux's translation: "Nargis left the mansion wailing and smiting her cheeks" (Mahfūz 1996, 21), but his choice of verb exaggerates Narjis' behavior, indicating more force and pain. Far from an isolated example, the choice reflects a general tendency throughout Theroux's translation to intensify violence. Thus, the translators deem this image intelligible and opt for non-assimilation, but lose the oral aspect represented by the verb "صوت".

In another example, the *hāra*'s estate manager insults Jabal, who demands a share of the income for his people, Āl Hamdān: "يا حارة حشاشين يا أولاد الكلب" (Mahfūz 1986, 186). Stewart renders this as: "Alley of hashish addicts! Sons of bitches!" (Mahfūz 1981, 120). Although keeping the meaning of the statement and its rawness intact, he assimilates it by using the word "bitches" instead of "dog". This is another example of "domestication", but one that helps maintain the text's oral aspect. It creates, to borrow Muhawi's term used in discussing the translation of Palestinian folktales into English, an "echo" of the original (2004, 75). However, the term "bitches" has a greater feminine connotation, thus affecting the image of women in Stewart's translation. Theroux renders the insult more accurately as "[y]ou alley of hashish addicts, you sons of dogs" (Mahfūz 1996, 151). As for Guillaume, he chooses to significantly change the wording and even the meaning: "Quartier de fumeurs de haschich et d'enfants de putains" (Mahfūz 2000, 186). Although the low register of the term "putains" is relatively appropriate for rendering the *futuwwa*'s harsh colloquial statement, the word gives a negative image of women, a tendency noted in the French translation. Here, it should be said that the use of words such as "bitches" and "putains" in translation does not necessarily mean that the translator wants to give a certain image of women, but when it is repeated for no apparent reason or forms a pattern with similar choices regarding the same subject (women), then it becomes a tendency and possibly part of a discourse implanted in the text.

ORALITY AND TRANSLATION

Guillaume's approach can be further illustrated by another example in which the narrator relays the insult "صباح القطران يا ابن القديمة" (Mahfūz 1986, 276), uttered by an angry *futuwwa* named Batīkha in response to Rifāʻaʼs polite morning greeting. This is translated as "tes carottes sont cuites, fils de pute!" (Mahfūz 2000, 269), assimilating the statement to French culture by using the familiar expression "your carrots are cooked", meaning that everything has been decided; nothing can be changed. Guillaume also augments the *futuwwa*'s threat, increasing the violence and tension: literally, the speaker wishes Rifāʻa a "morning of tar" (which means simply a very bad morning). He then uses the phrase "fils de pute" [son of a bitch] to render "son of the old one", despite the fact that in Egyptian culture this refers to an "old shoe" (الجزمة القديمة), not necessarily a prostitute. The choice confirms this translator's tendency to further aggravate the situation of women and rewrite scenes to make them more intense. Stewart translates the segment by "[a] black morning to you son of an old baggage" (Mahfūz 1981, 198), assimilating the image, with the insertion of a reference to women as prostitutes. Theroux translates the statement as follows: "A bad morning to you and your mother" (Mahfūz 1996, 225), paraphrasing a part of the meaning ("bad morning") and changing the insult. This is a good example of rewriting the text to enhance violence and making events more "interesting", but it has a significant effect on the image of women who are repeatedly made the object of men's hateful insults.

Critics such as Abboushi-Dallal (1998) have maintained that certain Arabic literary works are chosen for translation because they "confirm" the stereotype of the oppressed Arab woman, and we see here the text being assimilated to a discourse that describes Arab women as being disrespected. This cannot help but reinforce stereotypes of violence and mistreatment of women in the Arab world and promote a biased representation of Arab culture. They implant the kind of discourse criticized by Said:

> Underlying all the different units of Orientalist discourse – by which I mean simply the vocabulary employed whenever the Orient is spoken or written about – is a set of representative figures, or tropes. These figures are to the actual Orient ... as stylized costumes are to characters in a play. (1978, 71)

In Theroux's book *Sandstorms: Days and Nights in Arabia*, which is about the years he spent in various Arab countries, he refers to the stereotypes used to describe the Arab world (as part of the Middle East), which was seen, according to him, as "wild-eyed, fanatical and violent" (1990, 35). He also makes reference to Said's criticism of orientalism (especially with regard to sexuality; 37). However his own translation choices intensify the violence of Mahfūz's *hāra*.

The above examples show that various techniques are used in the translations to render cultural aspects, including orality. These techniques combine assimilation and non-assimilation. They take into account the similarities and differences between languages and cultures in terms of subject matter and oral communication, but also show the translator's preferences and indicate the influence of the (Western) target-culture discourses on certain of his choices.

Songs

Of interest as well is the translation of songs, which Stewart and Theroux tend to render, whereas Guillaume often omits them entirely or merely refers to them.

109

ORALITY AND TRANSLATION

There is an example from Mahfūz's text in which Yāsamina, Rifā'a's future wife, sings: "آه من جماله يامه" (1986, 212). Stewart renders this as follows: "Jasmine was singing: 'Oh mother, what a handsome son'" (Mahfūz 1981, 145). One notes the assimilation of the character's name, the explicitation of its meaning and an improvement of the image given of this woman in his text by revealing the beauty of her name. The transliteration of the Arabic name is far less evocative. This choice partly contradicts some of the renditions seen above, yet it is a part of this translator's general approach, which is often the opposite of Guillaume's and occasionally Theroux's as well. The latter renders the segment by "[he] heard Yasamina's voice singing, 'Mama, what a pretty boy!'" (Mahfūz 1996, 182) – the word for mother here assimilates the statement to the target culture and imparts informality to it. This "domestication" could be viewed as having a positive effect since it enhances the preservation of orality. As for Guillaume, he opts to summarize the scene: "Elle chantait une chanson d'amour" [she was singing a love song] (Mahfūz 2000, 220). This is a clear deviation from his usual preservation of the cultural aspects of the novel, especially given that he elsewhere uses a translator's note and footnotes to explain foreign concepts. This omission of the lyrical content is a kind of "hypertextuality" (for Berman [1999, 29], the term refers to the formal transformation of the original) that should be interpreted not only on the level of assimilation/non-assimilation, *domestication/foreignization*, but also in the light of the translator's other choices and overall perspective. In fact, similar omissions occur elsewhere in Guillaume's version (Mahfūz 2000, e.g. the songs on pages 181, 227 and 264), depriving the novel of an important aspect of its orality: popular songs that enhance its relation to Egyptian culture and provide a realistic, romantic or comic touch.

One of the few songs that Guillaume does translate is that sung by a group of children who mock Rifā'a: "يارفاعة ياوش القملة / مين قلك تعمل دي العملة؟" (Mahfūz 1986, 257). Stewart renders this as: "Rifaa you louse-face rat! / Who told you to do like that?" (Mahfūz 1981, 166). He adds the word "rat" apparently to introduce rhyme, thus reflecting the original Arabic rhyme (*qamla/'amla*), although with different phonetic choices. This could be considered a *travail sur la lettre*, since it reproduces some of the rhythmic properties of the text, but the meaning has been partially changed. He also aggravates the insult. Theroux in turn translates the Arabic lines as follows: "Rifaa, Rifaa, you little louse, / Who told you to do what you did?" (Mahfūz 1996, 210); thus he, too, intensifies the negative comparison. Needless to say, the term "louse" refers to the extreme poverty and inhumane living conditions in the *hāra* and forms part of the text's social criticism. However, instead of reflecting a need to create rhyme, it once again merely intensifies verbal violence. For his part, Guillaume renders the text as follows:

> Rifaa face de rat
> Tu auras des cornes!
> Rifaa face de rat
> Des cornes tu auras!
> (Mahfūz 2000, 251)

He omits the comparison to "a louse" and replaces it with a "rat", which rhymes with *auras* (another *travail sur la lettre*). Moreover, this translator adds an image that reflects his creativity: in French, the expression *avoir des cornes* [to be a cuckold] belongs firmly to the colloquial. It is thus a perfect case of assimilation or "domestication". Guillaume also rewrites the scene by having the children utter these harsh words on the wedding day of Rifāʿa and Yāsamina, whom everybody knows is a woman of ill repute. Attributing such words to children is an over-translation and over-sexualization of their imagination. It implicitly strengthens the biased discourse inserted to describe the Arab world in the story, and indirectly affects women's image. Neither in this version can the *travail sur la lettre* be sufficient to evaluate positively the translator's overall decision. One has to see the tendencies and patterns as well as the discourse inserted to describe certain aspects of the society referred to (such as violence and sexuality).

No doubt, one can brush aside these changes as insignificant words spoken by a group of children. But it is hard not to see here a striking dichotomy between the retention/alteration of certain images and the suppression of Arabic (love) songs. Guillaume is driven by a desire to increase the violence and strangeness of the text that may promote a stereotypical perception of Arab culture in terms of violence, the "bad" situation of women and possibly an obsession with sexuality. Non-assimilation, if not seen within a broader discursive context (the Foucauldian "universe of discourse" mentioned by Lefevere [1992, 41], but which I use here to describe the target-culture discourses), will be misleading. It creates the impression of preserving cultural difference by inserting footnotes and keeping some foreign elements as in Guillaume's version, while omitting certain aspects of this culture's image and inserting others in a way that reflects the translator's perspective and ideology. As for Theroux, his version increases the violence in this text even if it does not aim directly at exoticism. He too has a perception of the culture involved as violent or prone to violence. His approach produces more negative images of Arab culture than positive ones, even if of course the latter should not be a translation aim per se. Stewart is relatively less inclined to reproduce stereotypes, although as we have seen certain of his assimilating choices increase tension and conflict and affect the portrayal of women.

The second case

In analyzing the translations of Shukrī's autobiographical novel, the ambivalent nature of non-assimilation will be discussed, along with some positive aspects of assimilation, especially in terms of enhancing a text's artistic properties.

Multilingualism

Bowles reflects the multilingualism of Shukrī's work by preserving the languages and dialects used or referred to. For example, the narrator describes a scene in which, as a child, he is suddenly hit hard by a policeman in the street following a theft he was not involved in: "قفزت في الهواء صارخا بالريفية 'أيمانو! أيمانو!(أماه! أماه!)" (Shukrī 2001, 13). Bowles renders the first part accurately, and retains the phonetic aspect in the second part: "I leapt into the air, crying out in Riffian: Ay mainou! Ay mainou!" (Shukrī 1973, 12). He specifies that the language used is Riffian but does not explain the meaning (i.e. Mother! Mother!), thus choosing non-assimilation or "foreignization" and the preservation of the sound of the foreign language. The glossary he provides (151) does not include the phrases transliterated from Riffian. Ben Jelloun renders

ORALITY AND TRANSLATION

the same sentence as: "je bondis en l'air, criant en riffain: 'Mère! Mère!' " (Shukrī 1980, 16), retaining the linguistic origin of the expression, but excluding its transliteration, and explicitating the meaning.

Bowles often preserves the foreignness of the text, keeping the distance between the two (Moroccan/American) cultures. One finds over 60 instances in which words or phrases are transliterated mostly from the *dārija* into English, of which Bowles explains only about a third. He retains Spanish words and expressions used by Shukrī like "*macho!*" (Shukrī 1973, 70) and "*eres fuerte*" (34) and inserts others such as "*limonada*" (54) and "*Hasta la vista!*" (70). He also includes some Spanish dialogue. For example, when the narrator meets a Spanish man and gets into his car, he asks him: "إلى أين نحن ذاهبان؟" [where are we going?] (Shukrī 2001, 112). The narrator specifies that he spoke in Spanish, but does not actually use the language; Bowles renders this question as "*[a]donde vamos?*" (Shukrī 1973, 69). As for Ben Jelloun, he opts for reported speech: "Je lui demandai en espagnol où nous allions" [I asked him in Spanish where we were going] (Shukrī 1980, 82). Bowles' renditions are hard to categorize as they are produced not in English but a third language (Spanish) suggested by the colonial context of the story. This might be described as historicist non-assimilation, reproducing the story as it would probably have occurred. While collaboration between Bowles and Shukrī might be the source of this Spanish influence, these notions could have been clearly conveyed in English. Such choice could also be considered as an assimilation to a dominant language/culture in the story, that of the ex-colonizer (Spain). In this case, "foreignization" is certainly not "minoritizing", although it could be seen as such given the dominance of English over Spanish.

Moreover, Bowles includes the Spanish names of places and institutions such as Zoco Chico and *jefatura*; he also uses French words and expressions such as "*allez!*" [come on!] (Shukrī 1973, 45) and "*bravo!*" (134). Thus, he reconstitutes a richer multilingual context in the text which betrays his nostalgia for the colonial atmosphere of the international Tangier. In an interview, he has said that "Tangier is not part of Morocco. It's international. I have lived here for many years. I came in 1931, went through all the thirties and the forties, part of the fifties, living in an international city.... Naturally I wish it were international again, of course" (Elghandor 1994, 16). His stance on the issue of colonialism could not be more clear.

Sayings

In another example, the narrator, faced with the disdain of other children for being Riffian, uses a saying that summarizes how certain social groups are unjustly seen: "الريفي خداع والجبلي نية" (Shukrī 2001, 16–17). Its colloquial nature is revealed by the term "نية," meaning "intention" in standard Arabic. Here, however, it describes a person who believes everything that people tell him/her and can thus be easily deceived. Both published translations render the general meaning and omit the cultural specificity of the term. Bowles translates this as: "The treacherous Riffian and the gullible Djibli" (Shukrī 1973, 14). Once again, he uses a word that readers may not know, *djibli* or "mountain man". The French translation, for its part, is clear and accurate: "[L]'on considère le Riffain comme un traître et le montagnard comme un pauvre type, un naïf" [The Riffian is considered as treacherous, and the mountain-dweller as dumb and naive] (Shukrī 1980, 19).

ORALITY AND TRANSLATION

In fact, including extra-textual information in the translation so as to explain the notion "نية" would unnecessarily divert the reader's attention from the story and affect the text's readability. Non-assimilation should not be an absolute rule, but ought to be considered in the light of other factors that determine the translation method, including the artistic dimension and thematic relevance of the explanation given. Denys Johnson-Davies, a prominent translator of Arabic literature, rightly states that numerous notes "will leave one with a treatise on the 'manners and customs of modern Egyptians' rather than a piece of fiction which demands readability and continuity" (quoted in Ghazoul 1983, 85; the allusion here is to the Orientalist Edward Lane's *Account of The Manners and Customs of the Modern Egyptians*). Including too many notes in the text does risk transforming it into an anthropological or ethnographic study.

Bowles' preservation of cultural difference is sometimes so extreme that it tends toward unintelligibility. In fact, he transliterates a whole proverb mentioned by the narrator, "الداخل إلى وهران زربان (مستعجل) / والخارج منها هربان (هارب)" [one enters Oran hurriedly and leaves it fleeing] (Shukrī 2001, 72), as "*Ed dakhel en Oueheran zerbanne, / Ou el harej menha harbanne*" (Shukrī 1973, 47). The only aspect that may be interesting, given the translation's semantic opacity to readers who do not know Arabic, is the phonetic representation of the rhyme. Non-assimilation reaches a high level, but has the effect of mystifying the source culture. Maier arrived at a similar conclusion about Bowles' translation of "The Half Brothers" by al-'Arbī al-Ayāshī, a Moroccan storyteller: "Bowles does not translate or explain a number of Moroccan terms and references, thus giving the narrative an exotic quality" (1991, 17). In the original, Shukrī explains in standard Arabic the meaning of the words that some readers may not know. This *intralinguistic* translation shows the author's awareness of the possible impact of his use of the *dārija* on the reception of his work. Unlike Bowles, Ben Jelloun retains the meaning of the sentence: "On entre à Oran pressé et on la quitte en s'enfuyant" (Shukrī 1980, 57). This choice is not unexpected, given this translator's interest in proverbs as part of the oral tradition, which, as already mentioned, he uses in his own writings in French. Regardless, the rhyme is lost, and the French belongs to a higher register than the Arabic.

Songs

With regard to translating songs, comparing the original and its translations shows that Bowles renders them whereas Ben Jelloun sometimes omits them. For example, the narrator mentions one by Syrian singer Farīd al-Atrash, entitled "امتى تعود ياحبيب الروح؟" (Shukrī 2001, 156). Bowles renders this as "[w]hen will you return, love of my soul?" (Shukrī 1973, 96). He keeps the Arabic text's meaning and orality, yet without a trace of the Egyptian *'āmmiyya*. Ben Jelloun, too, renders the text in fluent French: "Quand reviendras-tu mon âme?" (Shukrī 1980, 105). He slightly shifts the meaning, as it is literally about "love of my soul" and not "my soul", thus adding to and intensifying the song's beauty and romantic quality. This could be considered an attempt at aesthetically improving the text, another tendency detected in his translation.

In a different example, however, Ben Jelloun omits the title of a song by the Egyptian singer Umm Kulthūm. The narrator says that Bushrā, an acquaintance of his, "قامت ووضعت في الحاكي أسطوانة 'أكذب نفسي؛ لأم كلثوم" (Shukrī 2001, 145). Bowles

113

translates the sentence as follows: "[S]he got up, went to the phonograph and put on a record. *Oukkeddibou Nafsi* it was, with Om Kaltoum singing" (Shukrī 1973, 89). His translation is accurate, although the transliteration eclipses once more the meaning of the song's title, namely "I tell myself I am wrong." One can see the opacity created in this text, which is not conducive to learning about the source culture. Ben Jelloun, on the other hand, renders it as "[Bouchra] se leva et mit un disque d'Oum Kalthoum. C'était une belle chanson d'amour" (Shukrī 1980, 100). He comments on the song, describing it as a "beautiful love song". His choice is relatively similar to decisions made by Guillaume in the previous case, but Ben Jelloun focuses instead on the "beauty" of the song of the Egyptian diva. Here, too, the aesthetic effect is apparently deemed more important than accuracy. Such assimilation can be considered part of this francophone writer's attitude toward women and interest in their situation. The fact that some of his own novels are mainly about women's status (*La nuit sacrée* and *L'enfant de sable*) in a traditional Moroccan society explains such decisions in translation: "I go toward woman because, in our society, she is the victim of a not-so-nice situation. So I serve as her witness" (Ben Jelloun, quoted in Spear 1993, 41). This is not to say that all his decisions are aimed at achieving this goal, since social criticism is also conveyed through the depiction of the plight of certain women (e.g. the narrator's mother), but he does sometimes create a better image of them.[2] This example confirms that the use of intensification and reduction of the text's content and assimilation and non-assimilation of its foreign cultural aspects relates more to the translator's specific interpretation and not necessarily to a general method chosen, regardless of his/her specific stance on the various issues raised by the literary work (here women's situation) and the effects desired.

Conclusion

The above analyses of various examples from the English and French translations of Mahfūz's and Shukrī's novels show the diverse techniques used to render their oral aspects. These techniques encompass omission, total assimilation (by using words, expressions and/or different registers from the target languages/cultures), paraphrasing of the meaning in plain English or French, complete non-assimilation through transliteration, and translation into a third language (Spanish). All these choices indicate the presence of various linguistic, aesthetic, cultural and ideological considerations and constraints, and each translator uses a variety of techniques to render different interpretations.

These analyses also demonstrate that assimilation and non-assimilation can have positive and negative effects on a text's themes as well as its form. Preserving cultural difference can promote exoticism even if it stresses foreignness, and assimilation can enhance the readability of the text and create an "echo" of the orality of the original, even though it eliminates cultural specificity. Therefore, the value and impact of these techniques cannot be adequately assessed unless all of the effects of assimilation and non-assimilation are considered in a specific case and in relation to the translator's viewpoint and the discourses (e.g. the orientalist discourse) used in the target culture to describe various components of the source culture. Further, the aesthetic considerations that influence the selection of certain ways of translating orality or cultural aspects in general should be highlighted and examined. If critics,

ORALITY AND TRANSLATION

analysts and theorists focus merely on the cultural issues of translation, the aesthetic properties of literary texts, a crucial component thereof, may not be appropriately considered.[3]

Notes

1. This aspect is not limited to Arabic-language literary writings but likely also applies to literary works by Arab authors writing in European languages. Ben Jelloun has used Arabic oral tradition in his writing, especially through establishing an intertextuality with the *Arabian Nights* in novels such as *La prière de l'absent*. Critic Samia Mehrez has written as follows about his novel *La nuit sacrée*: "As in *L'Enfant de sable*, the readers find themselves confronting a text that injects the French with the language of an Other, namely that of an Arabic oral tradition of storytelling that still exists, not just in Morocco, but all over the Arab world" (1992, 128). Ben Jelloun also, in *Moha le fou, Moha le sage*, for example, makes use of Moroccan proverbs.

2. Another example of the improvement of women's image in Ben Jelloun's translation is his omission of the narrator's comparison of a girl's scarfed hair to cabbage: "شعرها ملفوف في المنديل الأبيض الملطخ بالحنة. ملفوف مثل رأس الملفوف" (Shukrī 2001, 18–19). Bowles renders it by "[t]he white cloth around her head, stained with henna, was like the outer leaves of a cabbage" (Shukrī 1973, 15). Ben Jelloun, on the other hand, translates the description as follows: "Ses cheveux étaient couverts par un fichu blanc taché de henné" [her hair was covered by a white scarf stained with henna] (Shukrī 1980, 20).

3. The views expressed herein are those of the author and do not necessarily reflect the views of the United Nations.

References

Abboushi-Dallal, Jenine. 1998. "The Perils of Occidentalism: How Arab Novelists Are Driven to Write for Western Readers." *The Times Literary Supplement*, April 24.

Allen, Roger. 1995. *The Arabic Novel. An Historical and Critical Introduction*. New York: Syracuse University Press.

Bandia, Paul F. 1993. "Translation as Culture Transfer: Evidence from African Creative Writing." *TTR* 6 (2): 55–78.

Barrāda, Muhammad, and Muhammad Shukrī. 2000. *Wardun wa Ramād: Rasā'il* [Roses and Ashes: Letters]. Morocco: Publications of the Ministry of Cultural Affairs.

Bassnett, Susan, and Andre Lefevere. 1995. "Introduction: Proust's Grandmother and the Thousand and One Nights: The 'Cultural Turn' in Translation Studies." In *Translation, History and Culture*, edited by S. Bassnett and A. Lefevere, 1–13. London: Cassell.

Ben Jelloun, Tahar. 1978. *Moha le fou, Moha le sage*. Paris: Seuil.

Ben Jelloun, Tahar. 1981. *La prière de l'absent*. Paris: Seuil.

Berman, Antoine. 1999. *La traduction et la lettre ou l'auberge du lointain*. Paris: Seuil.

Elghandor, Abdelhak. 1994. "Atavism and Civilization: An Interview with Paul Bowles." *ARIEL* 25 (2): 7–30.

El Kaladi, Ahmed. 2003. "Discours rapporté et traduction: le cas de l'arabe". In *Traductologie, linguistique et traduction*, edited by Michel Ballard and Ahmed El Kaladi, 201–212. Arras: Artois Presses Université.

Ghazoul, Ferial. 1983. "On Translating Arabic Literature: An Interview with Denys Johnson-Davies." *Alif* 3 (Spring): 80–93.

Jayyusi, Salma Khadra, ed. 2005. *Modern Arabic Fiction: An Anthology*. New York: Columbia University Press.

Johnson-Davies, Denys. 2006. *Memories in Translation: A Life between the Lines of Arabic Literature*. Cairo: American University in Cairo Press.

Lefevere, André. 1992. *Translation, Rewriting and Literary Fame*. London: Routledge.

Mahfūz, Najīb. 1981. *Children of Gebelawi*. Translated by Philip Stewart. London: Heinemann.

Mahfūz, Najīb. 1986. *Awlād Hāratinā*. Beyrouth: Dar al-Ādāb.

Mahfūz, Najīb. 1996. *Children of the Alley*. Translated by Peter Theroux. New York: Anchor Books.

Mahfūz, Najīb. 2000. *Les fils de la médina*. Translated by Jean-Patrick Guillaume. Paris: Sinbad/Actes Sud.

Maier, John. 1991. "Two Moroccan Storytellers in Paul Bowles' *Five Eyes*: Larbi Layashi and Ahmed Yacoubi." *Postmodern Culture* 1 (3). https://muse.jhu.edu/journals/postmodern_culture/v001/1.3maier.html

Mehrez, Samia. 1992. "Translation and the Postcolonial Experience: The Francophone North African Text." In *Rethinking Translation. Discourse, Subjectivity, Ideology*, edited by Lawrence Venuti, 120–138. London: Routledge.

Memmi, Albert, ed. 1985. *Écrivains francophones du Maghreb: Anthologie*. Paris: Seghers.

Moosa, Matti. 1994. *The Early Novels of Naguib Mahfouz: Images of Modern Egypt*. Gainesville: University Press of Florida.

Muhawi, Ibrahim. 2004. "On Translating Oral Style in Palestinian Folktales." In *Cultural Encounters in Translation from Arabic*, edited by Said Faiq, 75–90. Clevedon: Multilingual Matters.

Said, Edward. 1978. *Orientalism*. New York: Pantheon.

Said, Edward. 1993. *Culture and Imperialism*. New York: Vintage Books.

Salama-Carr, Myriam. 2001. "L'Oralité dans les traductions anglaises et françaises de Naguib Mahfouz." In *Oralité et traduction*, edited by Michel Ballard, 279–290. Arras: Artois Presses Université.

Shukrī, Muhammad. 1973. *For Bread Alone*. Translated by Paul Bowles. London: Peter Owen.

Shukrī, Muhammad. 1980. *Le pain nu*. Translated by Tahar Ben Jelloun. Paris: François Maspero.

Shukrī, Muhammad. 2001. *Al-Khubz al-Hāfī*. Casablanca: Matba'at al-Najāh al-Jadīda.

Somekh, Sasson. 1973. *The Changing Rhythm: A Study of Najīb Mahfūz's Novels*. Leiden: E. J. Brill.

Spear, Thomas. 1993. "Politics and Literature: An Interview with Tahar Ben Jelloun." *Yale French Studies* 83 (2): 30–43.

Theroux, Peter. 1990. *Sandstorms: Days and Nights in Arabia*. New York: Norton.

Venuti, Lawrence. 1995. *The Translator's Invisibility: A History of Translation*. London: Routledge.

Venuti, Lawrence. 1998. *The Scandals of Translation: Towards an Ethics of Difference*. London: Routledge.

Index

Abboushi-Dallal, J. 109
Achebe, C. 56
acrostics 27
Adam, A.K.M. 35
Adejunmobi, M. 78
Aeschines 5, 7, 12
Africa 52, 53, 58–9, 105; Cameroon 38, 54;
    Central African Republic 37; diaspora 63;
    European languages in 55, 56–7, 58–9,
    60, 62–3; Horn of Africa: reviewing
    directionality in writing and translation *see*
    separate entry; linguistic counter-penetration
    63; Sesotho *see* Bible translation: orality of
    Old Testament and orality of Sesotho;
    translation studies and 54–5; *see also*
    Kourouma: study of repetition in *Allah n'est*
    pas obligé
Ahmed, H. 53
Albucius 7
Allen, R. 106
alterity and similarity in translating orality of
    Old Testament in oral cultures 32–47;
    Biblical Performance Criticism (BPC) and
    translation 33, 35–8; media history of the
    Bible 34–5; oral performance and alterity
    38–9; performance translation of Psalm 24 in
    Sesotho 39–46
Amador-Moreno, C. 87
American University of Cairo 107
Amharic language 53–4, 57, 60, 61, 62–3
anadiplosis 70–2, 74–6
anthropology 18, 21, 22, 23, 24, 25, 29, 113
anti-idealism 20
Arabic 53, 60; translating orality in
    postcolonial Arabic novel 102–15
al-'Arbī al-Ayāshī 113
Arén, G. 61
Askani, H. 18
Atangana Nama, C. 52, 59, 64
audio cassettes with Bible stories 24
Avanzini, A. 53

Bâ, Amadou Hampaté 78
Bahrey 62
Bakker, M. 90
Bandia, P.F. 33, 34, 37, 55–6, 57, 58–9, 68, 78,
    85, 104–5
Bantu language: Sesotho *see* Bible translation:
    orality of Old Testament and orality of
    Sesotho
Barrāda, M. 107
Bassnett, S. 102
Bausi, A. 53
Bell, R.T. 85
Ben Jelloun, T. 107, 111–12, 113, 114
Berlin, A. 45
Berman, A. 103, 110
Besnier, N. 24, 25
Biber, D. 24, 25, 34
Bible: Genesis 25:26 21; Habakkuk 38;
    Leviticus 1:2 21; Mark 15:21 23; Psalms *see*
    separate entry; Romans 24
Bible translation: Horn of Africa 53, 61
Bible translation: orality of Old Testament and
    orality of Sesotho 32–47; Biblical
    Performance Criticism (BPC) and translation
    33, 35–8; media history of the Bible 34–5;
    oral performance and alterity 38–9;
    performance translation of Psalm 24 in
    Sesotho 39–46
Bible translation: perspectives on orality
    17–29; first perspective: *Gesprochenheit* or
    'spokenness' 18–21, 28, 29; second
    perspective: Universalist dichotomies 18,
    21–4, 28–9; third perspective: local oral–
    written interfaces 18, 24–8, 29
biblical commentaries (*andemta*) 54
big data 24
Blake, N.F. 88
Boase-Beier, J. 78, 80
Botswana 33
Botterweck, J. 19
Boudjédra, R. 106

INDEX

Bowles, P. 107, 111, 112, 113–14
Bracht, E. 79
Bratcher, R.G. 46
Brisset, A. 89, 91
Brodzki, B. 51, 52
Brown, R. 24
Buber, M. 18–21, 28–9, 36
Buddhism 26

Calvus, Licinius 9, 11, 12
Cameroon 38; University of Buea 54
Canada 89
Carr, D.M. 18, 22, 24, 25, 26, 27, 29, 32, 36
Caruth, C. 69
Casalis, E. 33
Cato the Elder 6, 7
Catullus 8–9, 11
Central African Republic 37
Cerulli, E. 54, 58, 60
Chafe, W.L. 22, 34
chanting 27
Chapdelaine, A. 91
Chapman, R. 88, 91, 92, 96
Chatman, S. 88
Chaucer 91
Chelati Dirar, U. 60
Chesterman, A. 90
Chouraqi, A. 21
Cicero 4, 5, 7, 8, 10–13
colonialism 52, 55–7, 58, 60, 61, 63, 103, 104–5, 112
Cowley, R. 54
Craigie, P.C. 46
Craps, S. 69
Crassus 8
Crenshaw, J.L. 45
Cronin, M. 4, 89, 91
Crummey, D. 60
Culley, R.C. 32
culture 102; assimilation/non-assimilation and orality 103–5, 114; orality in selected novels 105–15
Cumming, W. 26–7

Dahood, M. 46
de Almeida, Manoel 62
de Vries, L. 18, 19, 20, 21, 22, 23, 25, 26, 27, 28, 29, 36, 37, 38
Demosthenes 5, 7, 12
Di Giovanni, E. 52
Dickens, C. 85, 91–8
Dimitrova, B.E. 89, 91
directionality *see* Horn of Africa: reviewing directionality in writing and translation
Drewes, A.J. 60
DVDs with Bible stories 24

Egypt 52, 62, 103, 107–11, 113
El Kaladi, A. 105
electronic-aided orality 35
Elghandor, A. 112
Ellenberger, D.-F. 33
English: Hiberno 89; language in Africa 56–7; translating literary speech and orality 89–90, 91–8; translating orality in postcolonial Arabic novel 105, 107, 108, 109, 110, 111, 112–14; version of *Allah n'est pas obligé* 74, 75–6, 77–8, 80
Eritrea *see* Horn of Africa: reviewing directionality in writing and translation
ethics 39
Ethiopia *see* Horn of Africa: reviewing directionality in writing and translation
ethnography/ethnographers 55, 57, 113
Evans, N. 26
existential ontology 20

Findlay, B. 91
Finland 89
Finnegan, R. 32, 35, 36–7, 38, 70
First World War 19
Foley, W.A. 24, 25, 26, 35
Fowler, R.M. 34
Fox, E. 20, 21
Franklin, K.J. 24
French language: study of repetition in Kourouma's *Allah n'est pas obligé* 67–82; translating orality in postcolonial Arabic novel 105, 107–12, 113, 114; US publishers' approaches to francophone literature 81

Gallus, Cornelius 8
Gbaya language 37
Gebremedhin, E. 62
Ge'ez language 53–4, 57, 58, 59–60, 61–2
geoculture 105
German version of *Allah n'est pas obligé* 74–7, 78–80, 81
Ghazoul, F. 113
Golding, R. 96
Goody, J. 1, 22, 36
Gordon, E.P. 18, 20
Gori, A. 53, 60
Greek and Greeks 4–6; Cicero, oral translation and its marks on his work 10–13; Greeks, their help in translation, and their elision in Roman texts 8–9; Horn of Africa 53, 61–2; oral–written interfaces 27; role of Greek and Greeks in Roman elite culture 6–8; why the Romans elide Greek help in translation 10
Guillaume, J.-P. 107–9, 110–11, 114
Guinea-Bissau 38
Gunkel, H. 32, 35
Gusarova, E. 62

INDEX

Gutenberg, J. 27, 34
Gyasi, K. 68, 78

Hannibal 7
Harries, P. 33
Hatim, B. 85–6
Havelock, E.A. 35
Hegel, G.W.F. 18, 19
Heidegger, M. 18, 19–20
Herder, J.G. 19
Herman, J. 69–70, 71, 72, 73
Hiberno English 89
Holmes, J. 51
Homer 23
Horace 7
Horn of Africa: reviewing directionality in
    writing and translation 51–64; closer look at
    few texts 61–3; directionality 58–9; Horn of
    Africa: directionality revisited 59–61;
    translation studies and Africa 54–5; why
    Horn of Africa 52–4; writing as translation
    55–7, 59; writing as translation in the Horn
    57–8
Horowitz, M. 72
Horsfall, N. 8
Hron, M. 68
Husayn, T. 106

ideology 102, 104, 114
ideophones 37, 68, 77, 78
Indonesia: Makassarese of Sulawesi 26–7
Inggs, J. 52
Ireland 89
Irele, F.A. 78
Islam 53, 60, 73, 107
Israel, ancient 35, 36, 40, 46–7
Italian 60, 61

Jakobson, R. 68, 88
Jayyusi, S.K. 107
Jesuit missionaries 53, 59–60, 62
Johnson-Davies, D. 113
Jousse, M. 35, 36, 37, 38

Kalkman, G. 24
Karlik, J. 38
Kerszberg, A.D. 71–2
al-Khūrī, I. 106
Kolmodin, J. 62–3
Kourouma: study of repetition in *Allah n'est
    pas obligé* 67–82; contextualizing
    interlingual translation practice 77–80; from
    inter-semiotic to interlingual translation
    74–7; implications of translation-of-trauma
    reading for postcolonial translation
    approaches 80–2; repetition as development
    of new schemata 72–4; repetition as

therapeutic storytelling 70–1; trauma theory
    69–70
Kracauer, S. 28

Labov, W. 86
Lane, E. 113
Lane-Mercier, G. 91
Latin 53, 58, 59; Roman translation and orality
    4–13
Laye, Camara 71
Lebanon 107
Lefevere, A. 104, 111
Lefevre, R. 58
Leith, D. 87, 90
Leonessa, M. da 57
Leppihalme, R. 89
Lesotho 33
Lévi-Strauss, C. 22
Levinas, E. 38–9
Lévy-Brühl, L. 22
linguistic variation and interlingual translation
    85–98; literary fictional varieties 88–9;
    orality and linguistic variation 85–8; speech
    and orality 87–8; translating literary speech
    and orality 89–98
literacy rates 27, 33
literary translation: linguistic variation and
    interlingual translation 85–98; repetition in
    Kourouma's *Allah n'est pas obligé* 67–82;
    translating orality in postcolonial Arabic
    novel 102–15
literate versus oral cultures 21–6, 35, 36
Littau, K. 27, 34
Livy 7
local oral–written interfaces: Bible translation
    18, 24–8, 29, 36, 38
logic and writing 26, 29
Lord, A. 1, 23, 36
Loubser, J.A. 36
Loyola, Ignatius 58
Lucian 10
Lucilius, Gaius 7
Ludolph, H. 57

McElduff, S. 8, 11
MacMullen, R. 6
Macrobius 8
Mahfūz, N. 105, 106–11, 114
Maier, J. 113
Makutoane, T.J. 32, 33
Malinowski, B. 55
Manjaku language 38
Maranhão, T. 28
marginal identities silenced *see* linguistic
    variation and interlingual translation
Mathews, J. 37–8
Maxey, J.A. 33, 35, 38

119

INDEX

Mazrui, A. 63
Mehrez, S. 107
Memmi, A. 105
memorization 34, 37; ancient oral–written
  interfaces 26–7
Millard, A. 32
Miller, C.L. 45
Miller, R.D. 35
Miller-Naudé, C.L. 40
missionaries: Bible translators 23–4, 28–9, 33,
  53, 55, 60–1; Horn of Africa 53, 55, 60–1, 62
modernism 34, 70
Molon 7
Moosa, M. 107
Morag, S. 32
Moreno, M.M. 61
Morocco 103, 111–14
Muhawi, I. 108
music 27, 77; songs 109–11, 113–14

Naarden Bible 21
Nandwa, J. 36
Nässelqvist, D. 37
nationalism 91
Naudé, J.A. 32, 35
Negash, G. 62, 63
Neo-Romantic constructions of orality 18
Netherlands 27–8, 36
Nida, E.A. 33
Niditch, S. 32
Nissinen, M. 32
Norrick, N.R. 37
Noss, P.A. 32, 37
Nukalaelae 25

Octavius, Gnaeus 7
Okpewho, I. 36, 38
Olson, D. 22–3
Ong, W. 1, 18, 21, 23, 24, 34, 36, 37, 38, 87, 89
oral versus literate cultures 21–6, 35, 36
oral–written interfaces: Bible translation 18,
  24–8, 29, 36, 38
orientalism 57, 58, 62, 109, 114
otherness, recreating *see* linguistic variation
  and interlingual translation
Ouédraogo, J. 67
Oussoren, P. 21

Paez, Pero 62
Page, N. 88, 91, 95
pain *see* trauma theory, orality and interlingual
  translation
Papua New Guinea 23, 25, 36, 37, 38
parallelism 27, 37, 68, 70–1, 74–5
Parry, M. 23, 36
Parthenius 8, 10
Paul III, Pope 58

Paullus, Aemilius 7
Pauper Bible 34–5
Peacock, H.F. 45
Pennec, H. 60, 62
performance translation 39, 46–7; of psalm 24
  into Sesotho 33, 39–46; translation for
  performance 35, 36–8
Physiologos 61–2
Pictor, Fabius 7
pilgrimage and Ethiopian Christianity 57–8
Plato 7, 10–11
Pliny the Younger 9, 10
Plutarch 6, 7
Polak, F.H. 32
Polybius 7
Polynesian language of Nukalaelae 25
Portugal/Portuguese 53, 59–60, 62; translation
  of literary speech and orality 85, 89, 91–8
postcolonialism 52, 54, 56–7, 63, 87–8, 104–5;
  implications of translation-as-trauma reading
  for postcolonial translation approaches 69,
  80–2; translating orality in postcolonial
  Arabic novel 102–15
postmodernism 34, 70
pre-colonialism: Africa 57, 58–9, 61–2, 63
prestige and sociocultural value *see* linguistic
  variation and interlingual translation
printing: Ethiopian version of New Testament
  58; invention of 27, 34
Protestants 28, 60–1
Psalms 19, 32; (6:5) 19; (24) 33, 39–46; (60:7)
  19

Quirke, S. 52

Ramos Pinto, S. 89
Redford, D.B. 34
Regal, S. 72
Reichert, K. 19
Renck, G. 23
repetition in Ahmadou Kourouma's *Allah n'est
  pas obligé* 67–82; contextualizing
  interlingual translation practice 77–80; from
  inter-semiotic to interlingual translation
  74–7; implications of translation-of-trauma
  reading for postcolonial translation
  approaches 80–2; repetition as development
  of new schemata 72–4; repetition as
  therapeutic storytelling 70–1; trauma theory
  69–70
Rhoads, D. 33, 35, 36
Rodriquez, R. 17, 24
Roman translation and orality 4–13; Attic Greek
  7–8; Cicero, oral translation and its marks on
  his work 10–13; dictionaries 8; Greek and
  Greeks in Roman elite culture, role of 6–8;
  Greeks, their help in translation, and their

INDEX

elision in Roman texts 8–9; orality and literary translation in Cicero and other authors 5–6; orality in Roman culture 5; why the Romans elide Greek help in translation 10
Romanticism 18, 19, 20–1, 28, 36
Rosa, A.A. 86, 89, 90, 91
Rosenthal, E. 33
Rosenzweig, F. 18–21, 28–9, 36
Russian language 89

Sabourin, L. 40
Said, E. 105, 109
Salama-Carr, M. 108
Sallustius 10
Sappho 8, 9
Schleiermacher, F. 19
Schmidt, G.G. 18
Schmied, J. 56
Schocken Bible 32
Schravesande, H. 20
Scipio Africanus the Elder 6–7
Scribner, S. 24, 26
Sesotho *see* Bible translation: orality of Old Testament and orality of Sesotho
sexuality 107, 109, 111
Shukrī, M. 105, 106–7, 111, 112, 113–14
similarity and alterity in translating orality of Old Testament in oral cultures 32–47
singing 27, 43; translating orality in postcolonial Arabic novel: songs 109–11, 113–14
slavery 7, 8, 9, 10
Small, J.P. 8, 10
Smit, A.P. 33
Snell-Hornby, M. 102
sociocultural value *see* linguistic variation and interlingual translation
Somekh, S. 106
South Africa 54
Southern Africa: Sesotho *see* Bible translation: orality of Old Testament and orality of Sesotho
Spanish language 105, 112, 114
Spear, T. 114
stereotypes 29, 105, 109, 111; linguistic 88, 91
Stewart, P. 107, 108, 109, 110, 111
Sturge, K. 32
Sturrock, J. 55
Swedish Evangelical Mission (Evangeliska-Fosterlands Stiftelsen) 60–1
Swedish language 89
symbolism, Christian 62

Taavitsainen, I. 87, 88, 89
Taivalkoski-Shilov, K. 88
Tamrat, T. 60

Tedlock, D. 37
Tesfatsion Malhaso, Abba 58
therapeutic storytelling 69–70, 74, 80; repetition as 70–2
Theroux, Peter 107, 108, 109, 110, 111
Thucydides 7
Tibet 26
Tigre language 57, 61
Tigrinya language 57, 60, 61, 62–3
Toury, G. 90, 91
trauma theory, orality and interlingual translation 67–82; contextualizing interlingual translation practice 7780; from inter-semiotic to interlingual translation 74–7; implications of translation-as-trauma reading for postcolonial translation approaches 80–2; repetition as development of new schemata 72–4; repetition as therapeutic storytelling 70–2; trauma theory 69–70
Tymoczko, M. 68

Ugaritic language 46
US publishers' approaches to francophone literature 81

Vakunta, P. 67, 68, 80
Valerius Maximus 6
van der Louw, T. 19, 20, 28
van Enk, G.J. 25
variation *see* linguistic variation and interlingual translation
Venuti, L. 103–4
Virgil 8
visibility, translator 91
Visser, I. 69
Voigt, R. 57

wa Thiong'o, N. 56–7
Wallace-Hadrill, A. 7
Walton, J.H. 34
Watts, R. 81
Weiser, A. 40
Wells, J.C. 89
Wendland, E. 29, 37
women 108–9, 110, 111, 114
writing as translation 55–7, 59, 68, 78; in the Horn of Africa 57–8
Wundt, W. 35
Wynne, F. 77, 78

Yacine, K. 106

Zabus, C. 67
Zimmerman, N. 38, 39